Approaches to Teaching
Coetzee's *Disgrace*
and Other Works

Approaches to Teaching
World Literature

For a complete listing of titles,
see the last pages of this book

Approaches to Teaching Coetzee's *Disgrace* and Other Works

Edited by

Laura Wright,
Jane Poyner,
and
Elleke Boehmer

The Modern Language Association of America
New York   2014

MLA and the MODERN LANGUAGE ASSOCIATION are trademarks
owned by the Modern Language Association of America.
For information about obtaining permission to reprint material from
MLA book publications, send your request by mail (see address below)
or e-mail (permissions@mla.org).

Library of Congress Cataloging-in-Publication Data
Approaches to Teaching Coetzee's Disgrace and Other Works / edited by Laura Wright,
Jane Poyner and Elleke Boehmer.
    pages cm. — (Approaches to Teaching World Literature ; 130)
Includes bibliographical references and index.
ISBN 978-1-60329-138-5 (hardcover : alk. paper) —
ISBN 978-1-60329-139-2 (pbk. : alk. paper) —
ISBN 978-1-60329-177-4 (EPUB) —
ISBN 978-1-60329-178-1 (Kindle)
1. Coetzee, J. M., 1940– Disgrace. 2. Coetzee, J. M., 1940—Study and teaching.
I. Wright, Laura, 1970– editor of compilation.   II. Poyner, Jane, editor of compilation.
III. Boehmer, Elleke, 1961– editor of compilation.
PR9369.3.C58Z526 2014
823'.914 — dc23   2014000030

Approaches to Teaching World Literature 130
ISSN 1059-1133

Cover illustration of the paperback and electronic editions:
Bone Girl, a smoke-and-charcoal drawing on paper by Diane Victor, 2011.
The photograph of the drawing was taken by Carla Crafford.

Published by The Modern Language Association of America
26 Broadway, New York, NY 10004-1789
www.mla.org

CONTENTS

ACKNOWLEDGMENTS

We would like to thank our families and friends for their support, and we specifically acknowledge the help of Brian Gastle and Annette Debo, both of whom recently published volumes in this MLA series, Approaches to Teaching World Literature, and provided us with models for the introduction; of Joseph Telegen, who worked as a research assistant on this project; and of Andrew van der Vlies and David Attwell, who read and provided us with feedback for part 1, "Materials."

—*LW, JP,* and *EB*

Part One

MATERIALS

Despite the critical acclaim greeting the entire oeuvre of the South African writer J. M. Coetzee, acclaim that began with his first novel, *Dusklands*, in 1974, it was only with his most controversial novel, *Disgrace*, published in 1999, that he received the global recognition his fiction deserves. In this novel, in which a disgraced, sexually predatory university professor struggles with his sense of place in the so-called new South Africa, Coetzee negotiates some of the weighty political and ethical questions that have preoccupied his writing and that have engaged and tantalized teachers and students of his fiction: questions about colonial history and accountability, about power and powerlessness, about representation and alterity, about sympathy and forgiveness. Coupled with the formal complexity and metatextual problems the novels pose, they have provided fertile ground for instructors and students to explore Coetzee's oeuvre. Indeed, it is the way in which Coetzee addresses the big questions of human (and animal) experience through his highly allusive yet deceptively spare prose that makes his writing so appealing yet difficult to teach and study. The "Materials" part of this volume therefore identifies secondary materials, including multimedia and Internet resources, that will help instructors guide their students through the contextual and formal complexities of Coetzee's fiction.

The sheer volume of good literary criticism of Coetzee is a testament to the quality of his fiction. Since the publication of *Disgrace*, critical attention to his writing has burgeoned: an *MLA International Bibliography* search reveals that ten single-authored books on Coetzee have appeared since then. This body of scholarship, however, can be bewildering for the student and overwhelming for the busy professor. The definitive criticism outlined below should help them overcome this problem. Suggested teaching resources should also illuminate the contexts and allusions of the fiction with which students are likely to struggle. Coetzee is known to be a difficult writer, but students supported by such criticism and resources will find his novels richly rewarding.

The editors of this volume were guided by the responses to a questionnaire circulated among university teachers across the globe but particularly in South Africa, the United States, and the United Kingdom. Thus the volume draws on up-to-date and varied pedagogical experiences. A section on editions is not included, because there are no variations in Coetzee's texts other than *In the Heart of the Country* (1977), which appeared in the United States as *From the Heart of the Country* and which, in the South African edition published one year later, contained dialogue in Afrikaans. Much of the contents of *Elizabeth Costello* has appeared in very different forms elsewhere. The first five lessons of this book, in which Costello delivers public lectures, including two on animals, are revised versions Coetzee delivered previously as lectures and that appeared later in journals or academic publications (the original version of "The Problem of Evil" was presented as a reading). Some adjustments to the earlier versions were needed to bring them together as a coherent whole, though Coetzee seems to overlook a few of these differences (Attridge, *J. M. Coetzee* 194n4). The postscript is also a republished version. But a word of caution: these versions should not be treated as different editions of what was to become *Elizabeth Costello* but as distinct texts, since, as critics like Michael Bell have argued (173–74), there is a significant shift in genre from lecture or journal article to a novel.

Contexts and Criticism

Disgrace

It is not surprising that race and gender and their confluence are the most frequently taught themes of *Disgrace*: for undergraduate students, these aspects of the novel are the easiest to grasp. The essays by David Attwell ("Race") and Peter D. McDonald in the 2002 *Interventions* special issue on *Disgrace* are good starting points for teachers wishing to approach the text from this perspective. They discuss the reception of *Disgrace* in South Africa, centering on the racism the novel is seen to encode. The controversy the novel sparked stems from the portrayal, at a time when the nation was preoccupied with discourses of reconciliation and forgiveness, of the gang rape of David Lurie's daughter, Lucy, by three intruders to her homestead on the Eastern Cape, who, we are led to believe, are black. (Racial markers in the novel are only suggested.) Attwell explores "how the novel actually manages racial discourse" and wonders whether Coetzee, a writer who consistently resists racialized discourse, provocatively invites accusations of racism (332). In a later article on "the social life of fiction," Attwell reflects on the difficulties of teaching *Disgrace* in the South African classroom—on why in South Africa "the space between reportage and fiction is so frequently and dramatically closed down" ("J. M. Coetzee" 167). Critics like Attwell argue that focus on the race theme, taken as expressing the legacy of apartheid, risks diminishing the other, more complexly rendered aspects of what is widely regarded as one of the most important English-language novels of the twentieth century.

A gender approach to teaching *Disgrace* typically centers on the juxtaposed stories of Lucy's rape and Lurie's deplorable treatment of women. Lucy Graham's "Reading the Unspeakable: Rape in *Disgrace*" and Meg Samuelson's *Remembering the Nation, Dismembering Women?* contextualize feminist debates in a time when the incidence of rape in South Africa is catastrophic. Drawing together race and gender, both essays point to the reemergence of the racist discourse of black peril during this period and to how Coetzee obliquely engages with it. See also Andrew van der Vlies's *J. M. Coetzee's* Disgrace: *A Reader's Guide*, which presents a succinct and accessible summary of the gender issue.

Several respondents to our questionnaire have taught *Disgrace* as a novel of the new South Africa, though this analysis is viewed by some as reductive. Essays by Jacqueline Rose, Elleke Boehmer ("Sorry"), and Rosemary Jolly ("Going") are among those that trace links, through different theoretical perspectives, between Lurie's "trial" by the University Disciplinary Committee and the processes of the Truth and Reconciliation Commission. Derek Attridge's essay on *Disgrace* ("Age") in his frequently recommended monograph *J. M. Coetzee and the Ethics of Reading* delivers a compelling rejoinder by contending that *Disgrace* is not so much about the new South Africa or Lurie's journey to self-forgiveness as about the West's increasing cultural hegemony in South Africa.

Land is a contentious issue in any of the former settler colonies, when in postcolonial times addressing questions of land possession and redistribution becomes imperative. In South Africa, the land question was compounded by apartheid. What Dutch and British colonialism began, apartheid saw to its radical conclusion: the segregation and restriction of property rights to the land for black Africans and so-called coloreds. From *Dusklands* to *Disgrace*, Coetzee's writing has provided one of the most sustained critiques of the land question in South African literature. Teachers wishing to address the problem of land in *Disgrace* will find illuminating articles that analyze the novel's antipastoral impulse by critics like Rita Barnard, James Graham, and Graham Huggan and Helen Tiffin. As Coetzee himself argued in his 1988 *White Writing: On the Culture of Letters in South Africa*, the pastoral emerges at moments of crisis in nationalist discourse when the assumed rights of the colonizers to the land come under threat. *Disgrace* depicts such a moment: Lurie has an increasing sense of being "out of place" in postapartheid South Africa (4). His alienation is heightened by the fact that Lucy's presumably black neighbor Petrus, on marriage to Lucy, will acquire rights to her land, thus symbolically dispossessing Lurie. Huggan and Tiffin's *Postcolonial Ecocriticism* includes a short section on what they read as the deconstructive strategies Coetzee employs in his reworkings of the colonial pastoral in *Disgrace* and *Life & Times of Michael K* (to these antipastoral novels might be added the second of the two stories in *Dusklands*, "The Narrative of Jacobus Coetzee"; *In the Heart of the Country*; and the fictionalized memoir *Boyhood*). Barnard's essays "J. M. Coetzee's *Disgrace* and the South African Pastoral" and "J. M. Coetzee's Country Ways" link the outmoded nature of the South African pastoral, realized in the stories of Lucy, who refuses to call her homestead a farm, and of Petrus, with a failure of translation, both linguistic and cultural, in the picture of the new South Africa Coetzee paints. (Barnard's earlier "Dream Topographies" considers how black peoples in *In the Heart of the Country* and *Life & Times of Michael K* are occluded from the myths of the pastoral.) James Graham, in *Land and Nationalism,* argues that in *Disgrace* Coetzee critiques the postapartheid idea that land might be a site of reconciliation rather than conflict. Historicizing the novel, Graham draws contrasts with the 1998 ANC government's "White Paper on South African Land Policy" (137).

Critical attention has increasingly focused on the ethical concerns of Coetzee's novels, particularly since the publication, shortly after *Disgrace*, of *The Lives of Animals* — a text often read as a companion piece to the novel in its treatment of animal rights debates. The question of the other and its representation is a popular approach to teaching *Disgrace*. Otherness in the novel is taken to signify the otherness of race, of gender, of language and narrative form, but perhaps most strikingly of nonhuman animal experience. Lucy Graham's "'Yes, I Am Giving Him Up': Sacrificial Responsibility and Likeness with Dogs in J. M. Coetzee's Recent Fiction" and the essays by Boehmer and Jolly mentioned above link the animal theme and the issue of rape in a familiar critical move that has also become popular in the classroom. Graham argues that Coetzee's world is one absent of grace, "where the only possibility for ethical action may be through non-violent 'felt contact' with fellow creatures" (4). Both Boehmer and Jolly read *The Lives of Animals* in conjunction with the novel to suggest that animal rescue in *Disgrace* is a form of redemption. Laura Wright argues that the opera in *Disgrace* is the space in which Lurie struggles to work through the trauma of his daughter's rape and that in so doing attempts to "embody" or perform the other (*Writing* 99) — here, black people, women, and animals. Adopting a different critical approach to alterity, Attridge ("Age") and Michael Holland draw attention to the otherness of Coetzee's literary language. The novelist John Banville, in an early review of the novel, is baffled by the Romantics theme and the opera narrative, which sit oddly, he believes, in the larger narrative. Yet, as critics have recognized, the otherness the operatta supplies is necessary for sympathetic identification.

Other Works

That Coetzee's first two novels, *Dusklands* and *In the Heart of the Country*, rarely find their way into university syllabi may be accounted for, as Dominic Head writes of *Dusklands*, by the "obliquity of the book[s'] method" (*J. M. Coetzee* 29). Nonetheless, these two texts allow us to trace the development of Coetzee's self-questioning white writer[1] and of his historical consciousness. His singular engagement with history draws, by his own admission, on poststructuralist theory. In his frequently cited address, "The Novel Today," given at a Cape Town book festival in 1987 and later published in the little South African journal *Upstream*, he favors a novel that "operates in terms of its own procedures and issues in its own conclusions, not one that operates in terms of the procedures of history and eventuates in conclusions that are checkable by history" (3). The novel is a genre that, if through experimentation it rivals rather than supplements history, has the capacity to demythologize history. Teachers wishing to explore the question of history in Coetzee's works might turn to essays by Attwell (e.g., "J. M. Coetzee and South Africa") and Stephen Watson ("Colonialism"). In what remains one of the best books on Coetzee, *J. M. Coetzee: South Africa and the Politics of Writing*, Attwell defines Coetzee's narrative mode as "situational metafiction," by which he means a mode of historicizing narrative that comments on its own procedures and in this way demythologizes history (3). History is revealed to be a discursive construct that, as Michel Foucault has taught us, is closely bound up with questions of power. Watson finds that Coetzee not only joins a tradition of South African writers representing the colonial venture (e.g., Olive Schreiner, William Plomer) but also makes significant departures in the artifice of novel construction—not least in the break with liberal realism, displaying a "seeming disregard for all historical veracity" ("Colonialism" [*Research*] 372). Watson argues that in Coetzee's first four novels, "colonialism is treated from both an external and an internal point of view." By this, Watson means that the novels map a "historical reality" (370) while giving us access to the colonizer's psyche, which is a product of that reality. Coetzee appears to be an exemplar of the South African writer engrossed by history, yet "in his conflation of historical moments, in his metaphysical preoccupations, his modernist leanings, he cannot help striking one as the most ahistorical of writers at the same time" (377). Taking a very different approach to the representation of history in Coetzee, Sam Durrant draws on psychoanalysis and poststructuralism to explore how history is memorialized in the works of Coetzee, Wilson Harris, and Toni Morrison through the act of bearing witness (*Postcolonial Narrative*).

Alterity and the silent or silenced other are most often the focus of classes on *Life & Times of Michael K* and *Foe*, embodied in the figures of Michael K and Friday, respectively. It is the adumbration of the other as silent and apparently unresistant that has sparked most controversy about these works. Nadine Gordimer's influential review, "The Idea of Gardening," gives a fairly damning critique of the passivity of Michael K in the face of the tyranny of the apartheid state and of history. She accuses Coetzee of failing to acknowledge the reality of black resistance to apartheid and argues that the "organicism" Georg Lukács identifies "as the integral relation between private and social destiny" in the writer is in Coetzee's novel skewed in favor of the private, threatening "the work's unity of art and life" (6). Benita Parry similarly argues that Coetzee, in the endeavor to present silence as emancipatory, unwittingly "re-enact[s] the received disposal of narrative authority" ("Speech" 150). Gayatri Spivak takes a more celebratory view—surprising in the light of her famous essay "Can the Subaltern Speak?" She argues that Friday is the "guardian of the margin" and, as the "unemphatic agent of withholding," is not simply a victim but an agent too ("Theory" 172). Because environmental concerns have become increasingly important in an age of resource depletion and land degradation, some teachers report employing an ecocritical approach to *Life & Times of Michael K* embedded in the ethics of alterity. Essays by Head ("'(Im)possibility'") and Derek Wright supplement such an approach.

The theme of the body of the other is commonly taught in postcolonial, feminist, and ethics-related courses. *Life & Times of Michael K*, *Foe*, and *Waiting for the Barbarians* are popular choices for teachers adopting this approach. Teachers will find the following criticism particularly helpful: Boehmer's "Transfiguring: Colonial Body into Postcolonial Narrative," which analyzes *Foe* through the lens of what Elaine Scarry has called "the body in pain"; Ato Quayson's *Aesthetic*

Nervousness: Disability and the Crisis of Representation, which, in its analysis of *Life & Times* and *Slow Man*, assumes that Coetzee's two protagonists are autistic; Laura Wright's "Minor Literature and 'The Skeleton of Sense'"; Brian May's "J. M. Coetzee and the Question of the Body," on *Waiting for the Barbarians*; and Barbara Eckstein's "The Body, the Word, and the State." Marcus Wood draws connections between the colonizer's gaze and the enslaved body in *Foe* in his book *Blind Memory: Visual Representations of Slavery in England and America, 1780–1865*.

In the shadow of President George W. Bush's "war on terror" and the abuse of prisoners in the notorious Abu Ghraib, the scenes of torture in *Waiting for the Barbarians* are ever more germane and accordingly have renewed interest in the novel. Early discussion of the depiction of torture in the novel, by Jennifer Wenzel ("Keys") and Jolly (the final chapter of her *Colonization*), can be usefully supplemented by Robert Spencer's hard-hitting "J. M. Coetzee and Colonial Violence," which draws parallels between Abu Ghraib and the torture scenes the novel so graphically depicts.

Coetzee has aroused the ire of some critics, particularly in South Africa, because of his apparent refusal to engage politically with the apartheid and post-apartheid contexts of his works. An elusive South African critic known only as Z. N. lambasted *Life & Times of Michael K* for the "absence of any meaningful relationship between Michael K and anybody else": "[I]n fact we are dealing not with a human spirit but an amoeba, from whose life we can draw neither example nor warning because it is too far removed from the norm, unnatural, almost inhuman" (qtd. in Attwell, *J. M. Coetzee* 92). Yet as Coetzee himself has said, "a contest of interpretations" between ethics and politics is "played out again and again" in his fiction (*Doubling* 338). The ethics/politics dialectic is drawn in *Age of Iron*, a novel that marks a shift toward a more realist mode. Mrs. Curren, its protagonist, claims to have scripted the story in the tumultuous years 1986–89, when apartheid oppression was at its most virulent yet when its architecture was visibly crumbling under the weight of protest and revolt. Attridge's reading of the novel provides an accessible introduction to the topic ("Trusting"). Jane Poyner argues that Curren is a failed intellectual who abhors the violence both of the apartheid regime and the revolutionaries—troublingly portrayed as black in the novel—but her ethical concerns, ultimately, are rendered ineffectual in the "age of iron" (*J. M. Coetzee and the Paradox* 111–27).

The ethics of animal rights in *The Lives of Animals* and *Elizabeth Costello* are generating keen interest among teachers and students of Coetzee, and considerable research is now available on the topic. Elizabeth Costello would certainly sympathize with the posthumanist turn in animal studies. Louis Tremaine charts the development of the animal narrative in Coetzee's oeuvre, reading against the prevailing tendency in the earlier criticism to understand his animals as signs for something else (605). Tremaine's reading, reflecting this broader posthumanist turn, resonates with Elizabeth Costello's desire for literature that engages with animals as animals rather than as metaphors for human experience. See also the section "Humans, Animals, and Morality" in *J. M. Coetzee and Ethics*, coedited by Anton Leist and the animal rights philosopher Peter Singer.

The Lives of Animals and *Elizabeth Costello* also pose interesting problems about the nature of genre and the relation between reality and fiction. Stephen Mulhall delves into the "ancient quarrel" between philosophy and literature staged in the two works (1–18). Other criticism in this context that teachers might find useful is by Laura Wright (*Writing*, ch. 5; "Feminist-Vegetarian Defense"; and "Minor Literature"), Bell, and Lucy Graham ("Textual Transvestism"). They point up the way Coetzee, through the lectures, performs his so-called alter ego and the effects that performance generates. Bell contends that the disjuncture between Costello and Coetzee is evident in Costello's tendency "to override the internal niceties of irony in a literary work and go directly for its existential premises" (175). Wright and Graham adopt a feminist perspective by suggesting that it is through what Judith Butler calls "excitable speech" (qtd. in Wright, "Feminist-Vegetarian Defense" 196) or "hystericized narrative" (Graham, "Textual Transvestism" 230), which necessarily undercuts the patriarchal site of authorship, that Costello makes her interventions. Wright explores the tensions generated by the juxtaposition of different modes of discourse: the lecture and the polemic. Graham argues that the Costello lectures should be read in the context of female voices in Coetzee's oeuvre, which all self-reflexively question "discourses of authority and origin" (219).

Form

Coetzee's novels often find their way into literature survey courses, in part because his literary experimentation complicates debates about form. Many critics have reflected on how to systematize the fiction: should it be labeled modernist, postmodernist, or, with works like *Age of Iron* or *Disgrace*, realist? The problem of systematization is closely bound to the contexts of the works. Some critics find Coetzee's high textuality problematic in the context of apartheid South Africa. The prevailing opinion among early reviewers and critics was that the works, since they draw heavily on poststructuralist theory, are postmodernist, but Neil Lazarus argues that Coetzee's fiction is modernist, not postmodernist, because the novels represent reality, rationalism, and an ethical-humanist critique of the status quo ("Modernism" 148). Attridge agrees: as a "late modernist" Coetzee "does not merely employ but extends and revitalizes modernist practices, and in so doing develops a mode of writing that allows the attentive reader to live through the pressures and possibilities, and also the limits, of political engagement" (*J. M. Coetzee* 6). Head defines the fiction somewhat differently, as "ethically oriented postmodernism," but all agree on its ethical weight (*J. M. Coetzee* 19).

Allegory provides instructors with fruitful points of entry into Coetzee's novels, including the recurring theme of self-diminishing allegory, or the allegory that calls into question the very nature of allegory. Essays on this subject are At-tridge's "Against Allegory" and Gordimer's "The Idea of Gardening." Abdul R. JanMohamed condemns *Waiting for the Barbarians* as "imaginary" colonialist literature that presents a universal and thus obscure allegory of colonial power that skirts the atrocities of the apartheid (73).

Intertextuality

A lack of familiarity with Coetzee's intertexts can impede understanding of the complexities of his writing. Allusion to the Romantics in *Disgrace* is a case in point. Knowledge of its Romantic intertexts, as one survey respondent put it, is "imperative for an understanding of the ethical ambition of the novel." A num-ber of essays on *Disgrace* have treated the Romantic narrative in some detail. Michael Marais fleshes out the Romantic allusions in terms of a failure of im-agination, which makes Lurie unable to resolve his writing project—the Byron operetta—with his place in the new South Africa ("J. M. Coetzee's *Disgrace*"). Pieter Vermeulen suggests that Lurie, a Wordsworth scholar, cannot harmonize the "imagination" and the "onslaughts of reality" (Coetzee, *Disgrace* 22; Vermeu-len 49) either in life or in his reading in class of *The Prelude*. Gerald Gaylard argues that Lurie misguidedly "decontextualise[s]" Romanticism, with the result that it is "ahistorical and lacking in agency" (320; see also Pechey).

Insights into Coetzee's use of intertexts in other works are provided by Attwell, who elucidates the remote intertexts of *Dusklands* (*J. M. Coetzee* 40–48); Pa-tricia Merivale, who summarizes the Franz Kafka connection in *Life & Times*; Paola Splendore, who discusses the intertextual resonances in *Foe*; Sheila Rob-erts, who provides useful background material on Dante's *Inferno* in *Age of Iron*; and Bell, who discusses Elizabeth Costello's philosophical musings and misinterpretations in *The Lives of Animals*.

Intertextuality in *Foe*—a novel in part about how texts enter the canon—and Susan Barton's challenge to the canon's authority through the figure of Foe, the author, provide students with ground on which to explore the politics of in-tertextuality and canonization. Several critics engage with the text from this perspective, including Attridge ("Oppressive Silence") and Steven Connor (see also Parry, "Speech"; Spivak, "Theory").

Further Resources

Historical Background to South Africa

Although only six of the novels in Coetzee's oeuvre are set, or partially set, in South Africa, most teachers agree that his readers should have some grasp of South African history, particularly of apartheid and colonialism. One survey respondent suggested, however, that too much focus on South African history when teaching *Waiting for the Barbarians* detracts from the novel's universal critique of empire. (Universalism is, of course, the accusation leveled at Coetzee by his harsher critics.) Another commented that local history did not fit in the rubric of the course offered.

Recommended general histories of the colonial and apartheid era are William Beinart's *Twentieth-Century South Africa* and Leonard Thompson's survey *A History of South Africa*. Revised editions of both texts appeared in 2001 to include analyses of the heady years of political transition to democracy. Robert Ross's illustrated *A Concise History of South Africa* provides a list of suggested further readings. One survey respondent cited Allister Spark's *Tomorrow Is Another Country* as providing informative political background. Another recommended Nigel Worden's *The Making of Modern South Africa*, which closes with the elections of 1999 and Nelson Mandela's retirement, as a solid introduction to recent, revisionist South African historiography from the 1990s on that links racial oppression with the rise of capitalism. Chapters 2 and 9–12 of Coetzee's *Giving Offense: Essays on Censorship* provide perspectives on censorship under apartheid that reflect his interest in not censorship's political but psychological, ethical, and aesthetic effects. Coetzee comments on this interest in *Doubling the Point* (299).

The question of land that underpins *Disgrace*, *Life & Times of Michael K*, and *Foe* can be explored in the classroom through histories of South African land dispossession and, after apartheid, of the land reform program. Coetzee's own writing about land and the *plaasroman* ("farm novel") in *White Writing* provides valuable insights into the South African land question. Scholarship that recontextualizes the land debate in the present era includes Cherryl Walker's authoritative work on contemporary land reform, *Landmarked*, and her two essays, "The Limits to Land Reform: Rethinking the 'Land Question'" and "Relocating Restitution," and Marlene Winberg and Paul Weinberg's illustrated volume *Back to the Land*.

Teachers wishing to pursue the analogy of Lurie's hearing in *Disgrace* to the Truth and Reconciliation Commission of South Africa (TRC) can point students to the seven volumes of its final report, which are widely available in university libraries and free to access online (www.justice.gov.za/trc/report/index .htm). The report was originally in five volumes; a sixth reported on the amnesty hearings, and a seventh presented the victims' findings. Copious articles, books, and films have documented the workings and afterlife of the TRC. Many are mentioned by survey respondents as beneficial teaching aids to both *Disgrace* and *Age of Iron*. The first two chapters of *No Future without Forgiveness*, by Reverend Desmond Tutu, the TRC chairperson, are recommended. Mahmood Mamdani is one of the best known and respected critics of the TRC. His "The Truth according to the TRC," drawing a distinction between institutional truth and individual (moral) truth, supplements readings of *Disgrace* that explore the politics and ethics of the TRC's constitution (see also his "Amnesty"). Richard Wilson also makes an important contribution to this debate. (See also Alexander;

Parry, *Postcolonial Studies* 179–94; Posel; Nuttall and Coetzee; Holiday.) For rejoinders to these mostly negative critiques, see Mark Sanders's *Ambiguities of Witnessing* and the South African journalist and poet Antjie Krog's autobiographical account of the TRC hearings, *Country of My Skull*. Krog's book is useful for acquainting students with the processes of the TRC as well as the ethical issues involved in lyricizing the suffering of others.

Biographical Resources

Most teachers concur that biographical knowledge of Coetzee is unnecessary to teach his work, a sentiment that reflects Coetzee's aversion to exposing his private life to public scrutiny. Some of our survey respondents did find biographical information useful but, as one respondent put it, "not essential." Biographical resources on Coetzee are relatively scarce, because in interviews the author is reluctant to disclose personal information. John Kannemeyer's biography, *J. M. Coetzee: A Life in Writing*, translated by Michiel Heyns, has appeared also in Afrikaans. Teachers might refer to "Coetzee's Life" in Head's *Cambridge Introduction to J. M. Coetzee*, in which Head points out that much can be gleaned about the early years of this very private man from the two memoirs, *Boyhood* and *Youth* (the part-autobiographical, part-fictional *Summertime* [2009] had not yet been released at the time of publication of Head's book). Head rightly adds a word of caution: these memoirs are fictionalized accounts and should be treated accordingly. (See also the introductory chapters to Attwell, *J. M. Coetzee*; Head, *J. M. Coetzee*; L. Wright, *Writing*; and see Attridge, *J. M. Coetzee*, ch. 6.) Biographical information can be pieced together from the interviews given by Coetzee, though in recent years these have become infrequent. The ones conducted by Attwell in Coetzee's essay collection *Doubling the Point*, referred to by Attwell ("Life" 28) and by Barnard ("Imagining" 11) as "intellectual autobiography," provide little information about Coetzee's private life. Coetzee is more forthright on his political and cultural opinions in the earlier interviews, but characteristically we do not learn much about him personally.

Supplemental Student Reading

Many survey respondents said that they preferred not to overwhelm their students with additional reading, but for the theoretical approach most commonly employed to teach Coetzee, postcolonialism, the following background material is recommended: Boehmer's *Colonial and Postcolonial Literature*; Patrick Williams and Laura Chrisman's anthology of abridged essays, *Colonial Discourse and Post-colonial Theory*; and edited volumes by Bill Ashcroft, Gareth Griffiths, and Helen Tiffin (*Postcolonial Studies Reader*) and by Lazarus (*Cambridge Companion*)—the Lazarus volume includes essays on subalternity (e.g., Gopal) and intertextuality (Marx). John McLeod's *Beginning Postcolonialism* is designed as an introductory guide, presenting accessible synopses of key debates in the field together with useful lists of further reading.

Survey respondents found invaluable the work of theorists who have been co-opted into the field of postcolonial studies: Frantz Fanon, Albert Memmi, and Edward Said. Fanon's *The Wretched of the Earth* is cited in the survey as useful for discussing torture (see "On Violence"), resistance and the problems it engenders (see "The Pitfalls of National Consciousness"), and history (the subaltern's history from below). For a discussion of race that is grounded in an early form of colonial discourse analysis, see Fanon's *Black Skin, White Masks*. Memmi's *The Colonizer and the Colonized* sheds light on issues of intellectual authority and white guilt. Coetzee represents, in Memmi's words, the colonizer who refuses. Said's *Orientalism*, credited as being foundational in the field, will help students make sense of Coetzee's critique in the early works, particularly *Dusklands*, *In the Heart of the Country*, *Waiting for the Barbarians*, and *Foe*, of the binarism of enlightenment thinking.

The issue of the writer's commitment colors any postcolonial text, but in South Africa it accrues local cultural and political specificities. Gordimer's essay collection *The Essential Gesture: Writing, Politics, and Places*, edited by Stephen Clingman, is an important polemic in South African studies about that commitment. Albie Sachs's provocative if jocular "Preparing Ourselves for Freedom," first delivered as a speech to an ANC gathering, will provide students with an engaging introduction to the topic. A broader discussion of the issue of literary commitment can be explored through Roland Barthes's *The Pleasure of the Text* and *Writing Degree Zero*. Barthes provides teachers with counterarguments to the traditional Marxist approach popularized in South Africa during the apartheid years. Further background reading for the cultural context of Coetzee's novels can be found in Michael Chapman's *Southern African Literatures* and Attridge and Attwell's *Cambridge History of South African Literature*. These are the only volumes to address South African literature comprehensively, in its eleven official languages, and *Cambridge History* is the first that is multiauthored.

On the politics of form, Kwame Anthony Appiah argues that postcolonial fiction's appeal to the universal cannot be termed postmodern: he prefers the term "postrealist," which acknowledges a break in what he calls "second stage" postcolonial texts with postcolonial nationalism (349). For a divergent perspective, see Linda Hutcheon, who makes a case for postmodernism's subversive strategies that have the potential to delegitimize systems of power (see also During). *The Legacies of Modernism*, edited by David James, contains a part titled "Modernism's Global Afterlives," in which Coetzee's *Diary of a Bad Year* is discussed, and the editor's introduction situates experimental contemporary literature in a late-modernist paradigm inflected by postcolonial debates. Attridge's *The Singularity of Literature* supplements his *J. M. Coetzee and the Ethics of Reading* by advocating a critical mode that resists the worldly reading of texts popular in postcolonial studies in favor of a more formalist approach that, first and foremost, is attentive to the text as a work of literature.

Teachers have turned to *Boyhood* not only for clues about Coetzee's life but also for insights into the pastoral or *plaasroman* genre to which his writing both contributes and lays bare. Students requiring additional material on the land question and the South African pastoral might also turn to Coetzee's reflections on the subject, the nonfictional study *White Writing* and his 1987 "Jerusalem Prize Acceptance Speech" (collected in *Doubling the Point*), in which, in what might be taken as a veiled criticism of Israeli policy toward Palestine, he identifies the pastoral impulse in Afrikaner nationalist ideology that occludes the racially marginalized. (See also Jennifer Wenzel's penetrating analysis of *Boyhood* and *White Writing* ["Pastoral Promise"].)

Renewed interest in *Waiting for the Barbarians* followed the United States–led invasion of Iraq in 2003 and the uncovering of subsequent incidents of human rights abuse by allied forces. Students wishing to pursue reading the novel from this perspective can be directed to "Into the Dark Chamber," in which Coetzee delves into the moral conundrum of representing man's inhumanity to man, and to Alfred McCoy's *A Question of Torture*, a study of CIA torture tactics practiced at Abu Ghraib (see also Danner). Works in trauma theory that teachers may find useful for discussion of torture and the consequences of colonial violence are Shoshana Felman and Dori Laub's *Testimony* and Dominick LaCapra's *Writing History, Writing Trauma*. Both volumes focus on the Jewish Holocaust but might be applied to the South African context.

For literary and philosophical essays on confession in its voluntary forms that supplement the historical study of the TRC, survey respondents most frequently introduce students to Coetzee's formative essay "Confession and Double Thoughts," in which the problem of truth in confession is explored. Jacques Derrida's "On Forgiveness" provides a surprisingly accessible ethical discussion of the shortcomings of the TRC and the thorny concept of forgiveness in the sphere of politics.

Coetzee's fiction has received wide critical attention from feminist and gender scholars, in part because of his endeavor to narrate from a female point of view. Situating itself at the intersection of postcolonial and gender studies, Anne McClintock's *Imperial Leather: Race, Gender, and Sexuality in the Colonial Context* will help contextualize the gendering of the colonial other (see also Boehmer, *Stories*). Judith Butler's *Gender Trouble* and *Bodies That Matter* elucidate the question of gender performativity, especially relevant to the teaching of *The Lives of Animals* and the other Costello lectures.

In interviews, Coetzee has conceded that his writing has been influenced by poststructuralist thinking. His essay "The Novel Today" raises important questions about history as discourse and about the discourse of the novel, which in its antirealist form he regards as a worthy opponent to history. Written in engaging prose, it provides an introduction to the concept of discourse for undergraduate students.

A poststructuralist notion of the gendered or racialized body proves a popular topic for teachers. Scarry's pathbreaking *The Body in Pain* is an important text in any discussion of the representation of the suffering body in Coetzee's work.

Her argument that pain brings "certainty" (4) to the otherwise subjected body resonates with Coetzee's often quoted remark that "[t]he body with its pain becomes a counter to the endless trials of doubt. . . . [I]t is not that one *grants* the authority of the suffering body: the suffering *takes* this authority: that is its power" (*Doubling* 248). Any discerning reader of Coetzee's fiction will recognize the influence of Foucault on his writing. Foucault's work on power and discourse has proved a valuable resource for teachers, especially on the question of the subjected body (see his *Discipline and Punish*, *Madness and Civilization*, and *The History of Sexuality*). Foucault's "What Is Enlightenment?" and *The Order of Things* provide critical insights into enlightenment thinking, particularly useful for Coetzee's earlier novels, like *Dusklands*, *Waiting for the Barbarians*, and *Foe*.

Teachers frequently comment on the need to supplement students' reading not only with studies of Coetzee's intertexts but also with background material on the problems intertextuality raises. Because Coetzee is engaged with works firmly situated in the Western literary tradition, this intertextuality often links to the notion of writing back to the canon. To discuss the politics of the canon, several teachers report turning to Ashcroft, Griffiths, and Tiffin's early postcolonial study *The Empire Writes Back*. Alternatively, teachers might wish to refer students to John Marx's more recent "Postcolonial Literature and the Western Literary Canon."

For background material on the Romantics that supports the teaching of *Disgrace*, see Aidan Day, Stephen Copley and John Whale, and Marilyn Butler. The Norton Critical Editions of Wordsworth's *The Prelude* and *Wordsworth's Poetry and Prose* (Halmi) include criticism and interpretation suitable for undergraduate students. Teachers might direct students of *Foe* to Ian Watt's *The Rise of the Novel* for its analysis of the realism of Defoe's text. Peter Hulme's *Colonial Encounters* contains a rich postcolonialist study of *Robinson Crusoe* and the politics of realist form. Students may find it helpful, when reading *Life & Times of Michael K* or *Waiting for the Barbarians*, to have access to Kafka's short stories "The Burrow" and "The Penal Colony," respectively, and, for *Life & Times*, the parables "A Hunger Artist" and "The Hunger Strike." Kafka's "Before the Law" is an intertext in more than one Coetzee novel (e.g., "Lesson 8: At the Gate," in *Elizabeth Costello*). For critical studies of Kafka, see Harold Bloom and *Kafka's Selected Stories*, a Norton Critical Edition. Constantine Cavafy's poem "Waiting for the Barbarians" (1904), from which Coetzee borrowed the title for his novel, is readily available through poetry Internet sites such as *Poetry Foundation*.

Multimedia, Internet, and Other Resources

Other resources recommended by survey respondents fall into three categories: Coetzee's life and works, apartheid, and the new South Africa—including the TRC. In the light of renewed interest in Coetzee's portrayal of torture in *Waiting for the Barbarians* and with the publication of *Diary of a Bad Year*, many respondents have provided students with documents and photographic images from Abu Ghraib. Teachers should, of course, consider carefully the implications and impact of using such material in the classroom.

On Coetzee's life and literary heritage, see the documentary *J. M. Coetzee: Passages*, directed by Henion Han. Contributors to this hour-long documentary include well-known Coetzee scholars, like Attwell and Barnard, and South African writers, like Lionel Abrahams. Coetzee makes an appearance, speaking briefly about his childhood in Cape Town and reading from his early novels. The South African novelist and poet Christopher Hope scripted and narrates a half-hour BBC4 documentary on Coetzee, *Profile: Coetzee: Stranger at the Gate*. Both are available in United States and South African university libraries. BBC4 also adapted Coetzee's *The Lives of Animals*, which was warmly received by Coetzee scholars, though Coetzee was unhappy about the script (Kannemeyer, *J. M. Coetzee: A Life* 670n71). Steven Jacobs's film *Disgrace*, starring John Malkovich and filmed in part at the University of Cape Town, was well received by critics, who considered it faithful to the novel. Coetzee required editorial approval of Jacobs's film following the poor reception of *Dust*, the film adaptation of *In the Heart of the Country*, but scholars have noted the problematic loss of David Lurie's focalization. Van der Vlies examines this adaptation in some detail in his reader's guide (86–91).

For materials on apartheid, the series made by the United Kingdom–based company Granada Television and broadcast by the PBS *Frontline* series in the United States (*Frontline*) and *Aluka*, a digital database of resources from and about Africa and available through participating not-for-profit higher education institutions, are recommended by our survey respondents. The "Struggles for Freedom in Southern Africa" collection on the *Aluka* site, for instance, contains an extensive archive of periodicals, local newspapers, correspondence and personal papers, oral testimonies, speeches, and biographies. See also the South African Film and Video Project, a collaborative undertaking between Michigan State University and partners in South Africa.

Jillian Edelstein's photographic narrative *Truth and Lies* offers a visual account of the TRC hearings. Frances Reid and Deborah Hoffmann's documentary *Long Night's Journey into Day* and Ian Gabriel's drama *Forgiveness* are two films about the TRC. The South African Government Information and dedicated Truth and Reconciliation Web sites give access to the seven volumes of the Truth and Reconciliation Commission final report. Teachers also use ANC and governmental resources, especially those relating to the constitution, and the Web site *Polity*.

NOTE

[1] I borrow from Coetzee's definition of *white writing*: "[W]hite writing is white only insofar as it is generated by the concerns of people no longer European, not yet African" (*White Writing* 11).

Part Two

APPROACHES

Introduction: Teaching with/out Authority

Laura Wright

> One does not, of course, "like" Coetzee. Oily smooth,
> prickly, repellent, the prose presses, probes, and lets
> drop the conditions it touches.
> —Regina Janes, "Writing without Authority"

Since J. M. Coetzee won the Nobel Prize for Literature in 2003, his work has received increased international attention—both in terms of the critical scholarship it has generated and in terms of the pedagogical richness it affords instructors and students of literature. In particular, the text that preceded Coetzee's receipt of the Nobel Prize, his 1999 Booker Prize–winning novel *Disgrace*, has established and maintained a place at the forefront of Coetzee studies, generating wide critical attention and finding its way into an increasing variety of undergraduate literature classes, including, for example, courses with specific foci on the novel, postcolonial and world literature, postmodern fiction, animal rights and ecocriticism, and ethics, as well as more general and introductory literature survey courses. There are many reasons for *Disgrace*'s popularity, not the least of which is the novel's arresting depiction of interpersonal relationships in the new South Africa, a country trying to come to terms—historically, politically, socially, economically, culturally, and ethically—with the legacy of apartheid, the National Party's government-sanctioned policy of racial segregation that was officially abolished in 1994, only five years prior to the publication of Coetzee's novel. *Disgrace*'s popularity and success have also lead to increased readerly and pedagogical interest—both in South Africa and abroad—in his larger body of work, novels and essays spanning the period from the 1970s to the present, written in and about a variety of contexts and locales, from, for example, the 1760s of South Africa to the 1960s of America depicted in *Dusklands* (1974) to the ahistorical Empire of *Waiting for the Barbarians* (1980) to Australia in 2005–06, the setting of *Diary of a Bad Year* (2007).

We take Stephen Clingman's question, which he raises in an essay included herein, as the guiding concern of our volume: What does one need to know contextually in order to teach Coetzee? The essays that compose this volume attempt to answer that question, as they engage with various pedagogical challenges that arise in the teaching of Coetzee's work. The primary issues raised and addressed in these essays include the role of silence and nonparticipation in Coetzee's work, particularly as these entities represent a connection between the political and the personal—that is, silence as personal choice and (often unwitting) act of political resistance; the meaning of authorship and questions of authority; the act of voicing various "others," and the purpose of literature, particularly in terms of how Coetzee's works complicate notions of ownership, politics, and genre; the role of power as it is shaped by variables of race and gender; and the role and importance of South African historical and social contexts in terms of referentiality. In their dialogic nature, Coetzee's works call into question conceptions of a master narrative of history and a monolithic version of the "truth." For this and other related reasons, teaching Coetzee's works is fraught with a kind of inherent ambiguity that underscores the importance of careful and sustained examination of the relationship between situating and understanding his texts.

The title of this introduction pays playful homage to Fiona Probyn's 2002 essay "J. M. Coetzee: Writing with/out Authority," in which Probyn argues that "Coetzee's adoption of the feminine narrative voice [in *In the Heart of the Country*, *Age of Iron*, and *Foe*] constitutes *both* a strategic evasion of a lack of an adequate vantage point from which to speak *and* a strategic encoding of that lack of authority in the figure of the white woman." In this essay, Probyn explicates the ways that Coetzee writes in the middle voice (as noted by such critics as Teresa Dovey and Brian Macaskill), the narrative position between the active and passive, thereby occupying a space, in the case of his white female narrators, of self-negation: white women are, on the one hand, agents of colonization and, on the other, subjected citizens. Writing from such a vantage point, then, Coetzee—via the personae of Afrikaner frontierswoman Magda in *In the Heart of the Country* (1977), would-be novelist Susan Barton in *Foe* (1986), and Mrs. Curren, the former classics professor in *Age of Iron* (1990)—consistently critiques the very concepts of historical, literary, and academic authority. While this narrative position is perhaps most easily discernible in his novels narrated by white women, Coetzee's authorial refusal to occupy a space of monologic authority is also a refusal to engage in the production of a master narrative of South African—or any other—history. This stance is pervasive throughout his oeuvre, from the contradictory accounts of a trek into the South African interior offered by Jacobus Coetzee in *Dusklands* to the third-person narrated *autre*biographies *Boyhood* (1997), *Youth* (2002), and *Summertime* (2009) to the free indirect discourse and dialogic questioning so prevalent in *Disgrace*. Because in Coetzee's writing the "truth" (personal, historical, political) is always illusive and relative and because authority is never easily accessible or, for that matter, trustworthy, we, as teachers of Coetzee's works, must perhaps learn to teach with/out authority, to, instead, engage dialogically with our students as we seek to parse and interrogate Coetzee's fictional truths. The essays included in this collection are aware of this reality, the decentralizing and often uncomfortable position Coetzee's work asks its teachers to engage. In the service of this endeavor, this introduction seeks to illuminate some of the issues that provide pedagogical challenges with regard to teaching Coetzee's fiction, particularly the pervasive tendency to treat Coetzee's fiction as allegory; international reception of his work; and genre considerations in terms of classification of that work as *autre*biographical, postmodern, and postcolonial.

Questions of Categorization: *Allegory, Postmodernism, and* Autrebiography

One of the most common terms used to describe much of Coetzee's fiction prior to the publication of *Disgrace*, a novel set in "this place, at this time" (112)—South Africa in the period immediately following the end of apartheid—is "allegory." The reasons for the popularity of this classification stem from the easily understood desire to situate a body of work that has, at best, tangential correspondence to the time period and location from which it emerged. Derek Attridge notes that this factor, coupled with "the scrupulous avoidance of any sense of an authorial presence . . . encourage[d] the reader to look for meanings beyond the literal" ("Against Allegory" 63) in many of Coetzee's earlier novels. And the tendency to read Coetzee via an allegorical lens also stems from the often explicit assumption that any artist living in South Africa during the apartheid era was in some sense ethically required to engage with—essentially to denounce through one's art—the oppressive politics of that regime.[1] That Coetzee's work often does not directly engage with South African politics has placed it at odds with an ethical imperative dependent upon active engagement and denunciation of racial oppression. Michael Marais notes of this dilemma, "in this climate, Coetzee's writing was found wanting," and he goes on to note the hostility with which Coetzee's 1986 publication of *Foe* was met: "[W]hile the country was burning, quite literally in many places, the logic went, here was one of our most prominent authors writing of a somewhat pedestrian eighteenth-century English novelist" ("Death" 83).

At issue, then, is how one, as a teacher of Coetzee's "allegorical" novels, engages with the complexities inherent in any allegorical reading of Coetzee's fiction. Tony Morphet notes of Coetzee's early work, "to all readers, but perhaps especially to South Africans, the work was challenging, strange, and difficult" (14) in its often experimental forms and avoidance of the more discernible South African realism depicted in works by such writers as Nadine Gordimer. In an interview with David Attwell in *Doubling the Point*, Coetzee refers to realism as "illusionism" and notes that "anti-illusionism—displaying the tricks you are using instead of hiding them—is the common ploy of postmodernism" (27), and critics like Marni Gauthier have sought to explicate the links between postmodernism and postcolonialism, to determine how postmodernism functions within the postcolonial novel. She notes that the "pith of the intersection between the postmodern and the postcolonial is their mutual concern with historiography, or the investigation of how events and people are represented, and who does the representing" (55). Given that Coetzee's take on the so-called real world is necessarily informed by his "awareness of the postmodern crisis of representation [that] has problematized forever the relationship between text and world" (Harvey 20), his anti-illusionist treatment of South African historiography constitutes a conscious act of postcolonial game playing,[2] at work to achieve a specific end, the generation of a mode of writing that might follow postmodernism. Coetzee notes in the aforementioned interview with Attwell that anti-illusionism characterizes the postmodern moment, but that moment, despite the fact that we still seem to find ourselves within it, is a phase. Coetzee says to Attwell, "[T]he question is, what next?" (*Doubling* 27).

Allegorical readings of such works as the ahistorical *Waiting for the Barbarians* and the aforementioned metafictional *Foe* allow for readers to engage with an implicit critique of the South African apartheid condition, even as these and others of Coetzee's fictions do not explicitly address this political circumstance. As Attridge notes, one reason for the ubiquitous allegorical treatment of Coetzee's pre-*Disgrace* fictions is "the widespread assumption that any responsible and principled South African writer, especially during the apartheid years, will have had as a primary concern the historical situation of the country and the suffering of the majority of its people" ("Against Allegory" 64). Furthermore, in his famous 1986 essay "Third-World Literature in the Era of Multinational Capitalism" (published the same year as *Foe*), Fredric Jameson asserts that "all third-world texts are necessarily . . . allegorical, and in a very specific way: they are to be read as what I will call national allegories, even when, or perhaps I should say, particularly when their forms develop out of predominantly western machineries of representation, such as the novel" (69).

Jameson's often contested assertion provides a way of conceptualizing *all* "third-world" literature as engaging in allegorical representation, and Coetzee's work—particularly the three novels published in the period between 1980 and 1986, *Waiting for the Barbarians*, *Life & Times of Michael K*, and *Foe*—historically have been read in this manner. In the case of *Waiting for the Barbarians*, the novel's lack of specific setting and time period, its nameless characters, and its deconstruction of the concepts of "barbarians" and "Empire," reading allegorically seems incredibly logical. The events chronicled in the novel, the work's examination of torture and confession, could easily constitute an allegory for the machinations of apartheid; or, to make the narrative more contemporary, one could map the rhetoric underlying the United States' so-called war on terror onto the ahistorical Empire's preemptive strike on the illusive barbarians. Yet as a seemingly direct commentary on the problems engendered by any allegorical reading of the novel, when he is questioned by Colonel Joll about the unknown text written on wooden slips the Magistrate collects during archaeological exploration, the Magistrate pretends to know their meaning. He says, "[T]hey form an allegory. They can be read in many orders. Further, each slip can be read in many ways" (112). A problem arises when we assume that Coetzee's works are allegories and only allegories or, more broadly, when we assume that allegorically is the only way to comprehend postcolonial works that do not directly engage with the oppressive regimes under which they were produced.

And a reductive danger comes from agreeing in entirety with Jameson's claim above, as to do so is to deny "Third World" texts and artists the ability to represent anything other than the oppressive regimes that violate human rights in the so-called "Third World." *Life & Times of Michael K*, another of Coetzee's works often delineated as allegorical, deals with this very problem. Michael's singular goal is to be "out of all the camps at the same time" (182), but despite his best efforts to operate "outside" of categorizations that are essentially limiting, he is consistently placed within one camp or another, continually renamed and reinterpreted, with the medical officer going so far as to categorize him as allegorical: "[Y]our stay in the camp was an allegory . . . of how scandalously, how outrageously a meaning can take up residence in a system without becoming a term in it" (166). In both this instance and the Magistrate's aforementioned "reading" of the wooden slips as allegory in *Waiting for the Barbarians*, the limits of allegorical readings are made manifest, and Coetzee seemingly speaks back to an audience that would render his work merely allegorical. Both the Magistrate and the medical officer invoke allegory when they are unable to understand the text before them, whether that text is a set of wooden slips inscribed in an unknown language or the body of the other, in this case, Michael K, a man who refuses to participate in a war he does not understand and alternately refuses to provide a narrative of his reasons for this nonparticipation.

Acts of nonparticipation and game playing also factor into discussions of Coetzee's three autobiographical works—or works of autobiographical fiction, or works of *autre*biography, depending on the critic—*Boyhood*, *Youth*, and *Summertime*. Inga Clendinnen refers to *Summertime*, the final installment about a biographer researching the late John Coetzee, as "a Federer game we are watching, all touch, balance and fluency, and its shapes need time to settle in the mind." Katha Pollitt asks of the same work, "[T]he book is obviously a novel, so why should the reader assume it accurately depicts the writer's life? Or does he assume that we know his biography as well as he does and are in on the game all along?" *Boyhood* and *Youth* are narrated in the third person, as are the opening and closing sections of *Summertime*; the rest of the book is written as a series of interviews between an English researcher named Mr. Vincent and several people who knew the late John Coetzee. While the first two volumes correspond to factual elements of Coetzee's life as a child in South Africa and later as a computer programmer in England, the events described in *Summertime* are clearly contrafactual: Coetzee is neither dead nor did he live with his father in South Africa during the period of 1972–75. Given that autobiographical writing is by its very nature confessional writing, and given Coetzee's discomfort with confession as a mode of supposed truth telling—as he notes in *Doubling the Point*, confession engenders "problems regarding truthfulness, problems whose common factor seems to be a regression to infinity of self-awareness and self-doubt" (274)—it is unsurprising that he would create works that problematize our more traditional understanding of autobiographical writing, confessional narrative, and personal acts of truth telling. In the service of such subversion, Coetzee has termed the act of writing in the third-person present tense as "*au-tre*biography" in an interview with Attwell (*Doubling* 394), and he notes that "all writing is story telling, all writing is autobiography" (391).[3]

Of *Boyhood*, Attridge asks, "is [I]s confession *possible* in the third person and in the present tense?" ("J. M. Coetzee's *Boyhood*" 80), and he concludes that what this mode of writing reveals is a kind of testimony with regard to what it was like to grow up in South Africa in the 1950s, just as the government began to institutionalize apartheid. But he also notes that the work reveals "the truth of confession, without transgression, repentance, or absolution, and the truth, or a truth, *about* confession, about confession and writing, confession *as* writing, writing as confession" (91). And perhaps *Youth* follows suit in its rendering of its protagonist John's time spent in London during the 1960s, an experience that corresponds with Coetzee's lived reality; indeed, both volumes are clearly linked in that "youth" follows "boyhood," and the works are subtitled "Scenes from Provincial Life" and "Scenes from Provincial Life II," respectively. But even though *Summertime* is the third volume in this series, it diverges from its *autre*biographical predecessors in conceit, declaring itself "fiction" on the title page, and further complicates how one might have previously read — and taught — the preceding volumes. And *Summertime*'s clearly fictional status, apparent in the work's engagement with a posthumous biography of John Coetzee, forces us to consider the nature of "truth" in the previous two volumes of the series. This deceased John Coetzee is the author of such works as *Disgrace* and *Dusklands*; he is in many ways the J. M. Coetzee who wrote him. In *Summertime*, Coetzee at once playfully engages with Roland Barthes's death of the author even as the work fully embraces the fictive nature of autobiography and biography. In the game that Coetzee plays, it is the next move in his quest for that which "comes next" after the postmodern moment in literary history.

Reception in South Africa and Abroad

According to Clive Barnett, "fiction by South African writers has . . . been constituted from the outside in, shaped by the international audiences upon which it depended as the consequence of its own marginalization" (288–89). Obviously, allegorical readings have contributed to Coetzee's popularity outside of South Africa, because "any significance beyond South Africa is ascribed not to the realm of politics but to the realm of morality." Therefore, the "universal qualities" that can be uncovered via allegorical readings "lie in this move beyond politics, a move that is taken to be the proper task of literature" (292). Non–South African audiences, particularly those in the United Kingdom and the United States, have perhaps expected South African literature to provide them with the historical reality of life in that country — as Coetzee is well aware. The writer from South Africa is necessarily constructed, in nonscholarly literary reviews and scholarly literary criticism, as South African and/or postcolonial first and foremost and as a writer secondarily. In an early interview with Morphet, Coetzee expresses his awareness of the "insidious pressures faced by South African writers to simplify and explain for a foreign audience" the so-called reality of South Africa. Further, he acknowledges the power of the "ideological superstructure constituted by publishing, reviewing and criticism that is forcing on [him] the fate of being a 'South African novelist'" despite his stated lack of engagement with "the kind of realism that takes pride in copying the 'real' world" of South Africa ("Two Interviews" 460, 455). When Coetzee's works fail to depict, via a realistic lens, the oppressive politics of his country of origin, allegorical readings, as discussed in the section above, allow audiences both within and outside South Africa to ascribe South African historical meaning to them. According to Barnett, from the 1940s through to the 1990s,

> [l]iterary writing by white South Africans was inserted into a moralised frame through which apartheid was constructed as an international issue. . . . The work of white writers such as Alan Paton, Nadine Gordimer, André Brink, Breyten Breytenbach and J. M. Coetzee came to hold a central place in defining an international canon of respectable, morally robust and liberal oppositional literature. Writing by white South African authors was grafted into particular circuits of international literary evaluation shaped by liberal humanist values. (288)

Expectations about what South African literature should represent, then, have shaped the reception of Coetzee's and other South African writers' works that have received international attention. More often than not, Coetzee's works that can be read as allegorical have been well received in the West, while Western literary reviews have been more dismissive of works that have been more difficult to read via an allegorical lens, like, for example, the metafictive *The Master of Petersburg*.[4]

However, as Agata Krzychyłkiewicz notes in "The Reception of J. M. Coetzee in Russia," Coetzee's scholarly attention to nineteenth-century Russian writers like Ivan Turgenev, Fyodor Dostoevsky, and Lev Tolstoy, as well as his fictional rendering of Dostoevsky in *The Master of Petersburg* (1994), has afforded him an increasing following in that country since his work appeared there in 1989. But she notes further that

> [m]any Russian commentators readily acknowledge Coetzee's profound understanding of Dostoevsky but . . . except the few remarks made so far, Coetzee's impressive erudition with respect to Russian literature as well as affinity with the Russian literary oeuvre, whether intended or not, remains largely unrecognized. It is only to be hoped that the rapidly growing interest in J. M. Coetzee's literary output will produce, in Russia, a more studious assessment of his writing. (345)

Indeed, since Krzychyłkiewicz published her article in 2005, there has been increased critical attention to reading Coetzee's and other South African authors' works in the context of their relevance to and engagement with

Eastern Europe. Monica Popescu's *South African Literature beyond the Cold War* (2010), for example, posits that "postcolonial studies can be best understood as an (uneven) layering of a Marxist component and a colonial discourse analysis that have been shaped by the Cold War context" (105). While Popescu's study examines South African literature in a broad sense, she devotes a chapter of her study to Coetzee, and she asserts that postcolonial discourse provides Eastern Europe with "critical tools for discussing relations of power between the center (Moscow) and the periphery . . . as well as issues of migration, dislocation, hybridized communities, and hegemonic discourses" (136). Popescu reads the influence of Eastern European literature, political ideology, and landscape as these entities permeated and influenced South African imagination and literary production both before and after the fall of apartheid and during and after the Cold War, and her study works to remap such categories as postcolonial and postmodern, European and African, Western and non-Western.

Within South Africa and abroad, the publication of *Disgrace* in 1999 and Coetzee's then unprecedented second Booker Prize win for that novel garnered him a broader readership—both popular and academic—than had any of his previous works. Michael Gorra's *New York Times* book review lauded the novel as a "brief but oddly expansive novel" about a "range of concerns that Coetzee has woven seamlessly together." *Disgrace*, narrated in the third person present tense, was and remains Coetzee's only novel to deal explicitly with South Africa's then (and now) postapartheid present-tense moment, and in addition to inspiring Coetzee's most positive reviews, the novel also incited harsh criticism, particularly in South Africa. In "Reading Coetzee in South Africa," Morphet claims that all of Coetzee's writing has "confounded readers everywhere, but it has implicated South African readers in particular ways"; with the publication of *Disgrace* in 1999, however, Coetzee's South African reception shifted from confounded to outright hostile. According to Morphet, as a result of the novel's focus on the rape of a white woman by three black men, "feminist indignation filled the popular press, and the political establishment branded the work with scandal and racism" (15). The African National Congress's submission in 1999 to the Human Rights Commission in South Africa makes the following assertions about *Disgrace*:

> In the novel, J. M. Coetzee represents as brutally as he can the white people's perception of the post-apartheid black man. . . . It is suggested that in these circumstances, it might be better that our white compatriots should emigrate because to be in post-apartheid South Africa is to be in "their territory," as a consequence of which the whites will lose their cards, their weapons, their property, their rights, their dignity. The white women will have to sleep with the barbaric black men.
>
> (qtd. in Jolly, "Going" 149)

In her *New York Times* essay on Coetzee's move to Australia in 2002—a move many have speculated was prompted by *Disgrace*'s hostile reception in South

Africa—Rachel Donadio discusses the reactions of Coetzee's fellow South African writers to *Disgrace*: according to Nadine Gordimer, "there is not one black person who is a real human being. . . . I find it difficult to believe, indeed more than difficult, having lived here all my life and being part of everything that has happened here, that the black family protects the rapist because he's one of them" (qtd. in Donadio). In this same piece, Donadio quotes another South African author, Chris van Wyk: "I believe *Disgrace* was a racist book. . . . The white characters are fleshed out, the black evildoers are not." As a writer often criticized for creating works that have tended to avoid direct engagement with the South African political milieu, Coetzee's explicit engagement with the postapartheid world of the "new" South Africa enraged both his fellow South Africans and his government. And according to Donadio, tensions escalated after Coetzee won the Nobel Prize in Literature in 2003: "[N]o sooner had the ANC congratulated this 'son of the soil' than an opposition party said the ANC owed Coetzee an apology for its earlier denunciation of *Disgrace*. The ANC stood by its criticism." After his move to Australia in 2002 and his acceptance of Australian citizenship in 2006, Coetzee, ever evasive and resistant to being defined simply in relation to his status as a "son of the South African soil," has written fiction situated in Australia and featuring Australian characters, particularly the novelist and Coetzeean alter ego, Elizabeth Costello.[5] As Sue Kossew notes, "Australia has begun to embrace Coetzee as an 'Australian writer'" ("Literary Migration" 114), honoring him with a special citizenship ceremony during Adelaide Writers' Week and posting a speech he gave at the ceremony on the Australian government's Web site. But in these works—*Elizabeth Costello* (2003), *Slow Man* (2005), and *Diary of a Bad Year* (2007)—Australia and Australians, as Melinda Harvey notes, are vaguely rendered, and "Coetzee's Australia becomes a kind of 'non-place' because it is an 'every-where' as he writes it" (20–21). It will indeed be telling to see if Australia affords Coetzee his seemingly long desired goal of existing, like Michael K, out of the camps, of being a writer first and foremost, only tangentially defined by any national affiliation.

Because of its current popularity in university classrooms, the essays herein focus primarily on *Disgrace* and secondarily on works written prior to that novel (therefore, while Coetzee lived in South Africa and during apartheid) and those written after it (since his move to Australia). As a way of bridging the space pre- and post-*Disgrace*, we suggest that two works stand in a constellated intertextual relationship with *Disgrace*, Coetzee's Princeton Tanner Lectures, *The Lives of Animals* (1999), which immediately preceded the publication of *Disgrace*, and *Elizabeth Costello* (2003), the first novel Coetzee published after *Disgrace*. *The Lives of Animals* is a work that often, because of its focus on animal rights, is referred to as a companion piece to *Disgrace*, which features animal rescue as a form of redemption. Furthermore, *The Lives of Animals* is reprinted as two of the eight "lessons" that compose *Elizabeth Costello* and hence shares links both with it and with *Disgrace*. "The Philosophers and the Animals" and "The Poets and the Animals" (the two lessons that compose *The Lives of Animals*), as well as these other lessons, subvert the form of the traditional academic lecture in that many of the lessons contained in *Elizabeth Costello* originated as Coetzee's lectures about lectures (or lectures within lectures) given by Elizabeth Costello, a fictional novelist who bears a striking resemblance to her nonfictional creator. In that Costello voices strong ethical opinions while Coetzee does not, even as he reads her lectures before his audience, her character stimulates dialogue, arouses emotion, and generates argument both among the other characters present in the narrative as well as among members of Coetzee's various audiences. Furthermore, the repositioning of these distinct lectures within the work *Elizabeth Costello* challenges the reader and instructor's ability to conceive of that work as a novel in any traditional sense. These two texts—taught either in conjunction with or independent of *Disgrace*—raise productive pedagogical questions about, among other issues, ethics, the distinction between author and character, metafiction, and genre.

The Approaches section that follows is divided into five categories beginning with "On Difficulty," which includes essays by Rita Barnard and Michael Bell. These essays will be particularly useful in providing instructors with information about overarching issues that make the teaching of a broader body of Coetzee's work, in the form of his other novels, autobiographical pieces, literary criticism, lectures, and speeches, particularly challenging. Some issues of particular interest and importance include Coetzee's status as a contemporary, living author; his move from South Africa to Australia; and the degree to which he is willing—or unwilling—to engage, either through his writing or his personal discourse, with South African politics, or if he does engage, that it is through the prism of fiction. These essays focus on both the difficulties and rewards of teaching Coetzee, an author whose works have tended to depict formal education in a less than flattering light. These essays grapple with Coetzee's resistance to "teachability" as well as his fictional criticism of the university as they seek to position Coetzee's subject matter within a workable context. These issues, particularly Coetzee's fictional critique of education and the reasons for his works' canonicity, are raised initially by Barnard's prologue. Bell's essay furthers an examination of the kinds of risks inherent in teaching Coetzee's work, even as his examination problematizes the very notion that one can "teach" Coetzee—or literature more broadly.

Second, a section called "Intellectual Contexts" accommodates essays that engage and position Coetzee's work within a variety of theoretical contexts, address generic considerations, and treat the teaching of Coetzee's work within the context of various interpretive strategies that explore the works' interaction with other modes of discourse—literary, critical, and philosophical. For example, Martina Ghosh-Schellhorn's essay situates what is perhaps Coetzee's most challenging and least critically addressed work, his second novel, *In the Heart of the Country*, within a discussion of the history of the novel. Stephen Clingman engages with questions concerning the notions of inside and outside as he addresses the multiplicity of "subjects" at play in *Waiting for the Barbarians*, and

Erik Grayson posits a poststructuralist approach to *Disgrace*, reading and teaching it via the lens of existentialism. Johan Geertsema's essay examines Coetzee's works' consistent resistance to categorization and interpretation, arguing with support from Edward Said for the "radical worldliness" of Coetzee's texts. This section ends with an essay by Pieter Vermeulen, which explores *Disgrace's* relationship to and treatment of various interextual references, particularly the works of the Romantic poets Byron and Wordsworth as the novel's protagonist, David Lurie, teaches these works to his own college students.

The third section, "Historical and Cultural Contexts," provides contexts for reading, teaching, and understanding Coetzee's body of work, as that body has been shaped by South Africa's apartheid and postapartheid milieus, as it has been repositioned since his move to Australia, and as it has been received and understood by various international audiences. David Attwell considers Coetzee's South African contexts and what it has meant to teach his work in South Africa at various institutions at various times. He begins in 1984 with his experience teaching *Waiting for the Barbarians* at the historically black University of the Western Cape, then he travels to 2004, when he taught *Life & Times of Michael K* and *Boyhood* at the University of the Witwatersrand. Like Attwell, Andrew van der Vlies and Louise Bethlehem explore South African literary and political history and the social circumstances—apartheid, colonization of South Africa by the Dutch and later by the English, relegation of black South Africans to homelands, student uprisings, the Truth and Reconciliation Commission, et cetera—that have shaped both the life of the author and his work, and Gerald Gaylard explores what it means to teach *Disgrace* in the new South Africa. Both Elleke Boehmer's and Laura Wright's essays examine Coetzee's meaning and relevance beyond South Africa, with Boehmer engaging with Coetzee's works written since his move to Australia and the ways that that move and the author's acceptance of Australian citizenship complicate and inform understandings of Coetzee and his fiction as South African and/or transnational. My essay examines Coetzee's American contexts and the way that one teaches Coetzee's "America," as depicted in such works as *Dusklands* and *Diary of a Bad Year*, to students in the United States.

The fourth section, "Ethics and Representation," consists of essays that examine the role that ethics and ethical responsibility play in Coetzee's work. The body of critical work that deals with this aspect of Coetzee's writing is at the forefront of Coetzee studies (see, in particular, Attridge's aforementioned *J. M. Coetzee and the Ethics of Reading: Literature in the Event*), and the placement of this section before the selected courses section highlights the timeliness and significance of this field of inquiry. Carrol Clarkson explores the uncanny nature of what it means to teach *Disgrace* in its fictionalized setting, the University of Cape Town, the locale that also constituted the setting for the 2008 film version of the novel. Wendy Woodward engages with the pedagogical discomfort that arises from teaching Coetzee's *The Lives of Animals*, and Robert Spencer examines another kind of discomfort inherent in explorations of representations of violence and torture in *Waiting for the Barbarians*. Patricia Merivale examines the ways that Coetzee's work engages with voicings of gendered and racial positions other than those occupied by the author, as these designations are shaped by variables such as colonization, literary production, and apartheid, and Keith Leslie Johnson's work explores Coetzee's works' politics of resistance via a biopolitical approach to *Life & Times of Michael K*.

Finally, we include "Classroom Contexts," a section that showcases several specific course contexts. The essays that we have chosen to include in this section respond to issues raised in many of the preceding sections of the text; for example, Kay Heath's essay opens this section with a discussion of teaching *Disgrace* at an historically black university in the United States and reflects some of the concerns addressed in Clarkson's earlier essay. The subject of Shannon Payne's essay similarly harkens back to Woodward's animal ethics analysis and presents a model for using Coetzee's work in the first-year composition classroom—one of the most ubiquitous contexts in which English faculty find themselves. Emily S. Davis's essay provides a model for teaching Coetzee in an undergraduate theory course, and Patrick Hayes's concluding essay calls for a return to the art of close reading as a way of getting back to the literary aspects of Coetzee's texts, works that are so often examined in the context of their ethical, political, and social import—as all of the preceding essays in our volume suggest.

NOTES

[1] Nadine Gordimer has spoken on the subject of the responsibility of South African writers in her 1984 Tanner Lecture (*Essential Gesture* 285–300).

[2] Various writers refer to the games that Coetzee plays, including Morphet, who notes in "Reading Coetzee in South Africa" that much of Coetzee's fictions played games that "seemed to be somehow at [South Africans'] expense—at the expense of our understanding of and engagement in the seriousness of our historical situation" (15).

[3] While much as been made of Coetzee's choice of this narrative perspective, Margaret Lenta notes that the third-person narrator of autobiography is "by no means new. It is not even rare" (158), and she cites several examples, including Caesar's dispatches to the Roman senate and Christopher Isherwood's 2000 autobiography *Lost Years*. Attridge, on the other hand, argues that third-person narrators are "unusual" ("J. M. Coetzee's *Boyhood*" 79) in autobiographical writing.

[4] For more on this discussion, see Barnett (particularly 293).

[5] For more on Coetzee's Australian works as well as Coetzee's acceptance as an Australian writer, see the essays in Danta, Kossew, and Murphet, many of which were first presented at a 2009 conference at the University of New South Wales on the topic "Coetzee in Australia."

Prologue: Why Not to Teach Coetzee

Rita Barnard

Wenn ihr's nicht fühlt, ihr werdet's nicht erjagen,
Wenn es nicht aus der Seele dringt,
Und mit urkräftigem Behagen
Die Herzen aller Hörer zwingt.
                    —Johann Wolfgang von Goethe, *Faust I*

If you don't *feel* it, it's hardly worth the effort
    If it doesn't issue forth from the soul
    And sway the hearts of all who listen
With a raw and potent delight. (my trans.)

In both his fiction and criticism, J. M. Coetzee has often adopted the personae of other writers in order to stage aspects of himself: Fyodor Dostoevsky in *The Master of Petersburg*, Daniel Defoe in the Nobel Prize address ("Nobel Lecture"), and T. S. Eliot in the essay "What Is a Classic?" Something of the sort is also at work in the review article "The Making of Samuel Beckett," which mentions, without explicitly referring to Coetzee's own biography, two uncanny connections with the Irish writer. To wit: that Beckett had applied for a position (a lectureship in Italian) at the University of Cape Town, where Coetzee taught for many years, and that he also expressed an interest in a job offer at the State University of New York, Buffalo, where Coetzee briefly held an assistant professorship. Beckett's sense of his own performance in the classroom, moreover, does not seem too far, mutatis mutandis, from what we are able to glean about Coetzee's, whether through academic gossip or through the multiple conversations on the subject in the recent memoir *Summertime*. "What dismayed the young Beckett most about his professorial life," says Coetzee, "was teaching":

> Day after day this shy, taciturn young man had to confront in the classroom the sons and daughters of Ireland's Protestant middle class, and persuade them that Ronsard and Stendhal were worthy of their attention. "He was a very impersonal lecturer," reminisced one of his better students. "He said what he had to say and the left the lecture room. . . . I believe he considered himself a bad lecturer and that makes me sad because he was so good. . . . Many of his students would, unfortunately, agree with him."
>
> ("Making")

The fact that Coetzee has become so very canonical, so very teachable, is therefore not without ironies. His writing, as I will show in the first part of the essay, is in many ways hostile to teaching and to teachers, even though, as I will suggest later on, an idealistic erotics of pedagogy eventually begins to take shape in it. But an erotics of pedagogy is never without perils; indeed, Coetzee spells these out in the final pages of *Summertime*: "*(a) vanity (the teacher basking in the student's worship) and (b) sex as shortcut to knowledge*" (255). Hence my somewhat perverse title. Impossible as it is in a volume like the present one, I would like to resist the relentless academicization of Coetzee's work, if only by showing the fraught and risky nature of the pedagogical enterprise as it is staged in his fiction. It is often observed that metafictional moments—scenes of reading, writing, and interpretation in novels—serve to make the reader aware of the activity that he or she is engaged in. I want to suggest here that scenes of teaching have a similar effect of simultaneous recognition and estrangement, and that, in the case of Coetzee, they alert us to the dangerous power of teaching: of bad teaching as well as powerful and good teaching.

Let me start by conceding that there are many reasons for Coetzee's canonization. For one thing, his novels are of a convenient length: students can be expected to read them over a weekend. They work well on a syllabus along with other important and teachable texts: *Foe* goes with *Robinson Crusoe*, *Life & Times of Michael K* goes with *July's People*, et cetera. They touch on many serious issues, from colonialism, to torture, to animal rights. They address the questions we dwell on in our theory courses: What is an author? Can the subaltern speak? Does speech precede writing? et cetera. And they allow us to explore issues fundamental to literary study: What is a classic? What is the relationship between the novel and history? Can one interpret without resorting to allegory? et cetera. Coetzee's work is canonical not only in the sense that it resonates in "the echo chamber of the English prose tradition" (Coetzee, *White Writing* 126); it has also become fodder for the lecture, the seminar, and the academic essay—to a degree that I myself find quite distressing, as a reader who engaged with each of his novels as they appeared, and responded to them, in the first instance, as a South African living through the anxieties and intensities of apartheid and the democratic transition. Today we can search the World Wide Web and discover canned questions for our book club's discussion of *Disgrace*; we can search the academic databases and find a proliferating number of scholarly articles, especially on those novels that seem to have a certain kind of intertextual richness or that feature fellow academics as central characters. We could even peruse, given a free hour, the blog *Soubriquet*, which narrates the labors of a diligent PhD candidate as he slogs through the dense thicket of articles on Coetzee he has to read for his dissertation, many of which he finds rather dull. (His friends write in to cheer him on when he hits a piece he actually enjoys.) It is all so very academic and industrious.

In the face of this industry, it is bracing to consider the many ways in which Coetzee's writing is suspicious of, well, school. We might recall, for starters, that in his provocative speech, "The Novel Today," Coetzee cast his opponents—Marxist critics, who insist on treating novels as though they offer "conclusions that are checkable by history"—as schoolmistresses, busily red-penciling a child's homework (3). His fiction, moreover, is rife with failed scenes of teaching. And right from the beginning, too. *Dusklands* offers, in its second section, an obtuse lecture on the adventures of the genocidal Jacobus Coetzee: an account that tames the powerful first section of the narrative by casting its protagonist as a pious Afrikaner ancestor. *Life & Times of Michael K* can be read as a moving protest against an oppressive education system, one in which teachers stand at students' desks with canes, force them to keep quiet or recite the times tables, and separate "the sheep from the goats" (110)—all with the aim of producing docile bodies for a hierarchical, racist world of camps and prisons. *Foe* offers us a more liberal, well-intended kind of lesson, but one that signally fails. Hoping to bestow a means of expression on the mute slave Friday by teaching him to write, Susan Barton discovers that the signs and codes she offers her pupil cannot elicit any free, unconstrained utterance. A word like "A-f-r-i-c-a" (which she represents, iconographically, as a row of palm trees with a lion roaming among them) is clearly fraught with oppressive preconceptions. Though Friday submits to the lesson and dutifully tries to form the letters, he does not learn in a way that gives any satisfaction to his teacher. Left to his own devices he draws on her slate "row upon row of eyes upon feet" (147) and on the author Daniel Foe's papers he inks equally enigmatic "rows and rows of the letter *o*" (152). "Friday will not learn," Barton sadly concludes. "If there is a portal to his faculties, it is closed, or I cannot find it" (147).

The list of examples continues; indeed, the scenes of teaching become all the more prevalent and complex in Coetzee's work of the 1990s and beyond. In *Age of Iron* Mrs. Curren, a retired professor of classics, finds the questions posed to her by the teacher Thabane, in the chaos of the burning shacklands, to be aggressive and patronizing: "What he is doing to me he has practiced in the classroom. It is the trick one uses to make one's own answer seem to come from the child. Ventriloquism, the legacy of Socrates, as oppressive in Africa as it was in Athens" (96). Yet she herself lectures, vainly, at a young revolutionary, who lies wounded in a hospital bed, in a manner and on a subject that he can only find intrusive and absurd. "If you had been in my Thucydides class," she sighs, "You might have learned something about what can happen to our humanity in a time of war." But her humanistic message is repugnant to her would-be student: he recoils from her touch and waits, impervious, for her to stop, just as he had waited "like a stone," through all his lessons at school (80).

The memoir *Boyhood*, finally, offers the most sustained criticism of teachers in Coetzee's oeuvre, not only of the terrifying cane-wielding Afrikaners at the school in Worcester, but of the appalling mediocrities at St. Joseph's school in Cape Town. The exegesis of the gospel by Mr. Whalen, the disdainful English teacher, is sheer banality. It is, indeed, as good an example as one can ever wish to have of a reading that ignores the literal for the sake of predetermined allegory and thereby utterly forecloses on the more radical possibilities of the text:

> "Unto him that smitheth thee on the one cheek, offer also the other," he reads from Luke. "What does Jesus mean? Does he mean that we should refuse to stand up for ourselves? Does he mean that we should be namby-pambies? Of course not. But if a bully comes up to you spoiling for a fight, Jesus says: Don't be provoked. There are better ways of settling differences than by fisticuffs.
>
> "Unto every one that hath shall be given; and from him that hath not, even that which he hath shall be taken away." What does Jesus mean? Does he mean that the only way to attain salvation is to give away all we have? No. If Jesus had meant us to walk around in rags, he would have said so. Jesus speaks in parables. He tells us that those of us who truly believe will be rewarded with heaven, while those who have no belief will suffer eternal punishments in hell.   (142)

Coetzee's mature reflections on Christ's instruction that we turn the other cheek are hinted at in a revealing interview in *Doubling the Point*, and they are clearly pitched against the interpretive domestication of such revolutionary passages in the Gospels, whether by smug dullards like Mr. Whalen, or by more sophisticated theorists: "I understand the crucifixion as a refusal and an introversion of retributive violence, a refusal so deliberate, so conscious, and so powerful that it overwhelms any interpretation, Freudian, Marxian, or whatever we can give to it" (337). But the young John, neither allowed nor able to respond, only feels himself becoming stupider as he sits through these classes. "Huddled in a ball," he makes himself small and inoffensive: "Whoever he truly is, whoever the true 'I' is that ought to be rising out of the ashes of his childhood, is not being allowed to be born, is being kept puny and stunted" (140).

Given these relentlessly repressive scenes of teaching, the wildly idealistic philosophy of teaching put forward by the John Coetzee character in *Summertime* may come as a surprise to many readers. "What I call my philosophy of teaching," he confesses to Adriana Nascimento, the wary mother of a student who seems smitten with him, "is in fact a philosophy of learning":

It comes out of Plato, modified. Before true learning can occur, I believe there must be in the student's heart a certain yearning for the truth, a certain fire. The true student burns to know. In the teacher she recognizes, or apprehends one who has come closer than herself to the truth. So much does she desire the truth embodied in the teacher that she is prepared to burn her old self up to attain it. For his part, the teacher recognizes and encourages the fire in the student and responds to it by burning with an intense light. Thus together the two of them rise to a higher realm. So to speak.   (163)

Reminiscent in some respects of the hopelessly sexist notions that the protagonist of the earlier memoir *Youth* holds about women, romance, and poetry, this eroticized philosophy is presented in *Summertime* in all its vulnerability. Indeed, it is shown to be foolish and dangerous when the rather unprepossessing John transfers his interest from his beautiful and eager student to her mother and—in a kind of deflected sexual harassment—signs up for Adriana's class in Latin dancing: something he cannot do, she tells us, *"to save his life"* (198).

Even so, I believe that we are called upon by Coetzee's oeuvre as a whole to take this philosophy seriously. Perhaps we might even see it as implied—by negation and denial—in the repressive scenes of teaching I have adduced so far. To make this case, I should note, first of all, that in Coetzee's fiction stupidity is never inherent or inert: it is a chosen or imposed condition and one with psychological, political, and ethical resonances. In the case of characters like Michael K, or Friday, or the young comrade John, ignorance is resistance: an active passion to ignore.[1] True learning and teaching, therefore, can only take place when the student desires to learn, or even, to recall the philosophy of teaching and learning from *Summertime*, tries to do so by moving closer to a teacher who seems closer than he or she to the truth. Something of the sort is implicit even in Coetzee's more cautious comments on the pedagogical enterprise. In a 1992 interview with Richard Begam, for example, he suggests that it is "a good idea for students to be exposed to the spectacle of someone else reading intently and intensively, particularly if what emerges from that reading fosters in the student a respect for close reading" ("Interview" [Begam] 429). In other words, learning occurs when the student comes to care about something the teacher cares about deeply.[2]

But Coetzee is also willing to consider the more extreme and dangerous implications of an erotics of pedagogy. "As for sex between teachers and students," concludes the meditation on pedophilia in *Diary of a Bad Year*,

so strong is the tide of disapproval nowadays that uttering even the mildest word in its defense becomes (exactly) like battling that tide, feeling your puny stroke quite overwhelmed by a great heft of water bearing you backward. What you face when you open your lips to speak is not the silencing stroke of the censor but an edict of exile.   (57)

This passage, of course, does not license us to say that Coetzee is *for* such sexual encounters. The opinion (if it even begins to be an opinion, rather than an opinion about an opinion) is voiced by a character and is included in a series of deliberately "strong" and provocative views.[3] Yet, cumulatively, Coetzee's later work does begin to put forward a protest against the prevailing pedagogical hegemony: one that would decree any circulation of desire in the classroom to be wrong. If this protest is anachronistic and unfashionable, that is part of the point: Coetzee, after all, has often cast himself in the figure of the outmoded and retrograde and has deployed his fiction to keep alive possibilities that would seem quixotic and on the verge of extinction.[4]

To grasp the outline of Coetzee's pedagogical ideals, which he begins so tantalizingly to sketch out in *Summertime*, it is useful to turn to a remarkably apt essay by Erin McWilliams, in which she proposes that we reclaim two terms, widely considered inappropriate metaphors for teachers, namely *"eroticism"* and *"seduction."*[5] Such a proposition, she recognizes, is risky, because "powerful pedagogical events are necessarily ambiguous and duplicitous, as erotic, mutually seductive encounters. The forces of desire that are mobilized in such events (the desire to teach and the desire to learn) are potentially rewarding *as well as* malevolent" (305). McWilliams's point about the ambiguity of powerful teaching immediately rings true with regard to Coetzee's oeuvre. *Boyhood*, for example, beautifully illustrates the rewarding kind of desire in the scene where the elegant Theo, the boy for whom John "will go to battle," surreptitiously teaches him ancient Greek while they are supposed to be revising a history lesson: "*Aftós*, whispers Theo: *evdemonía. Evdemonía*, he whispers back" (149).[6] The words at stake here—αυτός or *"autos"* ("soul" or "self") and εδαιμονία or *"eudaimonia"* (only weakly rendered as "happiness" or "intrinsic goodness")—permit us to hazard a guess at what the two boys might be reading: the passages on friendship of Aristotle's *Nichomachean Ethics*.[7] If I am right, the scene is all the more telling. At stake would be precisely a pedagogy of love and desire: for the "self" in the *Ethics* is intimately related to his friend, his second self (*"allos autos"*), and it is out of their reciprocal well-wishing that the desired end, the final good, of ethical excellence may be approached. But *Boyhood*, to be sure, also represents the malevolent "ungoverned passion" that can be unleashed in the classroom—as when the teacher, Miss Oosthuizen, her chest heaving, whips the handsome student Rob Hart, for reasons that the young John cannot quite fathom but intuits have to do with sex (6).

Let me risk a periodizing hypothesis at this point—one that is surely vulnerable, but also seems productive given our current concerns. (I would dare to historicize, in other words, Coetzee's untimely pedagogical philosophy.) It seems that the overall thrust of Coetzee's work shifts, around the time of *The Master of Petersburg*, from an interest in structures of domination (and how to elude them) to an interest in the dangerous irruption of the new or "the other" in various guises and valences: an interest in the *"arrivant,"* as Coetzee's Derridean readers would put it, with its unpredictable and risky consequences. This shift roughly coincides with the democratic transition in South Africa and the concomitant necessity of thinking, writing, and living through what Coetzee's Afrikaans counterpart Breyten Breytenbach likes to call *die groot andersmaak*—a concept only blandly translated as "becoming other" or "the great remaking." This radical transformation, as it leaves its mark on Coetzee's work, operates not only in the sociopolitical domain, but also, more poignantly, in the domains of the erotic and—since transformation is, after all, a "learning experience"—the pedagogical. This is certainly the case in *Disgrace, Elizabeth Costello* (subtitled *Eight Lessons*), and most explicitly, as we have seen, in *Summertime*, which stages a veritable symposium of multiple voices around John Coetzee's—intimately related—shortcomings as a lover and a teacher.

The most intriguing and touchy case to consider, however, may remain *Disgrace*, which better than any other Coetzee novel allows us to contemplate the ambivalent potency of learning and teaching. With its narrative about sexual harassment, this is not a novel that would strike the casual reader as a work that rests in any way on an idealistic philosophy of teaching and learning. On the contrary, critics have treated the sex between the professor, David Lurie, and his student, Melanie Isaacs, as a prelude or even an analogue to the gang rape of the second section. They have also, rightly, pointed to the failure of Lurie's lectures on the Romantic poets to speak to his "postliterate" students. Indeed, when he makes a rather cheap bid to regain their interest after unpacking a gnarly passage on sense perception in Wordsworth's poetry (one of Lurie's life-long passions) by speaking about "being in love," the professor himself is sickened by his pedagogical and ethical failures. His literary analysis, he recognizes, has suddenly shifted into an occasion for "covert intimacies," directed at only one member of the class: at Melanie, who, in a flash, gets his message and averts her eyes (23). Hardly a good situation. And yet I would argue that a certain idealistic pedagogy may be implied here, too. After all, Lurie's entanglement with Melanie comes in the wake of his disempowerment (he would say "emasculation") as a teacher by the university's crudely pragmatic and technical conception of its mission. The fundamental premises of Communications 101 are a far cry from the lyrical impulses that Lurie secretly believes to be the origins of human language. Moreover, Melanie Isaacs is scarcely the desirous learner imagined by *Summertime*'s avid John Coetzee. The seduction is preceded by a bland conversation between herself and Lurie, in which she confesses to a mild interest in the obvious women writers of color but scarcely a passion for literature or learning. The carefully constructed preamble to their relationship therefore suggests a transference of thwarted pedagogical desire towards the purely sexual. And the upshot of the entanglement could certainly be seen as illustrating the dynamic, mutual, and transformative potentialities of the pedagogical relationship—however perverted and betrayed it may be in this case. The trajectory of Lurie's humiliation underscores the validity of a comment from the novel's very first pages: "the one who comes to teach learns the keenest of lessons" (5). He is, indeed, "burned—burnt—burnt up" (166), the verb that recurs also in that striking passage about teaching and learning from *Summertime*. Lurie's invasion by Eros, his failure, if you will, to manage the ever-risky erotics of pedagogy, initiates even more dangerous and transformative invasions in the course of the novel: encounters with darker aspects of the new—with emergent sex-gender systems, systems of ownership, and brute power.

In *Summertime*, as I noted at the very beginning of this essay, sex is ultimately described as "a shortcut to knowledge"—a short-circuiting rather than an affirmation of the "ethical idealism" of John Coetzee's notes on pedagogy (255). There is nothing in *Disgrace* to deny this, or to counter McWilliams's caution that an erotics is not to be equated with sex or "sexual explicitness . . . or *seduction* with mere self-indulgence on the part of teachers or learners" (315). But we need to bear in mind that there is a sense in which an erotics of pedagogy necessarily involves a ceding or a failure of control. And *Disgrace* is certainly a work that despite all those books, articles, and study guides continues to present dangers to the reader, the student, and perhaps especially to the teacher. (The same may well be true of other Coetzee novels, like the cruel *Dusklands*, the revelationless *Waiting for the Barbarians*, and the treacherous *Master of Petersburg*.) There is something quite moving, for me at least, in Daniel Kiefer's account of teaching *Disgrace*: "As an openly gay professor," he notes, "I feel especially vulnerable to students' impressions of my sexual life. My immersion in David's sexual transgressions may strike them as an admission of my own perversion and further evidence that literature professors are interested in talking only about desire and violence, sex and death" (267–68). The gay teacher is especially attuned to the dangers of the teaching enterprise, with its inevitable "tangle of amorous relations" (Barthes, *Roland Barthes* 171), but we are all caught up in complexities implicit in our very enterprise. These complexities are beautifully captured by the South African academic and poet Joan Hambidge in her part-autobiographical, part-theoretical meditation on loss, writing, and sexual harrasment, entitled *Die Judaskus* (a work that Coetzee certainly read, and read with appreciation):

> Die verbintenis tussen dosent en student funsioneer eweneens volgens 'n onuitgespoke kontrak, te wete, mentor (leermeester) en student. Indien hierdie funksies oorskry word, word die basiese struktuur tussen die twee partye afgebreek. Terselfdertyd is daar implisiet in so 'n verhouding transferensie, en by implikasie dan, juis liefde opgesluit.
>
> So ontstaan vele nuanses en die verskillende funksies word verwar. Die ideale kliniese toestand tussen dosent/student word geaffekteer deur buite-tekstuele ervarings, herinneringe, en onafgehandelde sake.
>
> (23–24)

The relationship between instructor and student functions according to an unspoken contract: to wit, that of mentor and mentee. Should this function be transgressed, the basic structure defining the relationship of the two parties is fractured. And yet this is also a relationship in which transference is rife and which therefore necessarily involves love.

Thus many nuances arise and different functions are confused. The ideal clinical situation between teacher and student is affected by extra-textual experiences, memories, and unfinished business.[8]

Kiefer, in a different way, also captures our general predicament well: "Whether or not we professors are guilty of 'meddling with other people's children' sexually," as David Lurie's ex-wife puts it in *Disgrace*, "we're always interfering with them, meddling with them intellectually and emotionally" (272) — and the outcome, we must admit, is unpredictable, both for them and for us.

To speak of "risk" in the context of teaching and learning is hardly novel. Indeed, Pamela Caughie observed over a decade ago in her book, *Passing and Pedagogy*, that "no single word recurs as often in contemporary writing about identity, epistemology, and pedagogy as the word 'risk.'" Indeed, she argues, it has come to be seen as cultural capital rather than loss, "as a choice, rather than something that befalls us, a condition we are exposed to by virtue of where and who we are." "Risk in the latter sense," she adds, "has the character of an event" (62). This last curious observation will immediately bring to mind, for Coetzee scholars, Derek Attridge's much admired twin works, *The Singularity of Literature* and *J. M. Coetzee and the Ethics of Reading: Literature in the Event*, and I will close here with a gentle criticism of these works, with the aim (of which Attridge would undoubtedly approve) of suggesting a new emphasis in our approach to Coetzee. Attridge frequently insists that reading is an "event," even a "performance." He urges us to think of reading as an experience, a kind of "living through" of the literary work, and one that implies an ethic: a responsiveness or openness to the new, the singular, "the other." This way of thinking can do and has done valuable work in resisting criticism of Coetzee in terms of canned theoretical ideas and crude allegories. But there is nevertheless something in the rather repetitive formulations of *The Singularity of Literature* that finally seems, well, rather allegorical, as Brian May has playfully pointed out. The Attridgean critical parable, he notes, is "one in which Singularity, tangled in the foliage (verbiage) grown by way of a usurping Allegory, is freed by the hero Literality and restored to the throne, his weapon an Eventualizer" ("Reading Coetzee" 634). Though far from prescriptive in intent, Attridge's thought and style, sensible and genial as it is, has perhaps accrued something of a prescriptive force.

I am reminded of Adriana Nascimento's comments on existentialism in *Summertime*: she recalls how, back in the day, to be "accepted as an existentialist you had first to prove you were a libertine, an extremist. *Obey no restraints! Be Free!* —That was what we were told. But how can I be free, I asked myself, if I am obeying someone else's order to be free?" (192–93). How singular can our readings be if we always bear in mind the need for them to be singular? And what sort of an "event" or "performance" is at stake, when we are dealing (only?)

with ever-fresh restagings of the encounter of the mind with the innovative text? Where in all this is the body—the body that, as Coetzee so memorably put it in the final interview of *Doubling the Point*, stands erected as the simple standard in his fiction: the body whose power, whether in pleasure or in pain, "is undeniable" (248)?[9] And without the body, what risks do we really run in the encounter with the "otherness" of textual innovation? Is its impact upon "the existing configurations of an individual's *mental* world" (19; my emphasis) all that different, in the end, from the reordering of the literary tradition by the new classic that T. S. Eliot described for us, years ago, in "Tradition and the Individual Talent"? I am sure Attridge means the risks to signify a whole lot more. Perhaps something can be gained, however, especially as we collectively ponder our strategies for teaching Coetzee, if we were to replace the notion of an "ethics of reading" with the more embodied idea of an "erotics of pedagogy"—a concept that is staged for us, in so many wrenching permutations, in Coetzee's fiction. Thus it is that the all too abstract "encounter with alterity" can assume something of the concreteness, of the simultaneously physical, emotional, cultural, and social-political connotations inherent in the term *andersmaak*.

NOTES

I am indebted to Patricia Casey Sutcliffe for drawing my attention to the quotation from Goethe and for confirming the importance of *Faust* as yet another crucial intertext for *Disgrace* (177).

[1] For an excellent discussion on ignorance in Freudian and Lacanian pedagogy/analysis (the two practices are inextricably linked), see Felman 29–31. In Coetzee's earlier work, ignorance may, as I suggest here, best be grasped as resistance rather than repression; but the powerful idea of the irreducible of ignorance that is repression, lack of self-knowledge—in a word, the unconscious—surely underpins Coetzee's seminal mid-career work on confession, as well as his writing in *Giving Offense* on censorship (with its pervasive suspicion of the "subject supposed to know") and, more generally, his profoundly dialogic sense of the creative process. When Coetzee comments in *Summertime* on the Freudian underpinnings of his pedagogy, we may bear in mind the Lacanian idea that "the true Other is the other who gives the answer one does not expect" (Felman 32).

[2] A similar view is also articulated by the character Martin, a fellow academic in the fifth section of *Summertime*: "Students, in my experience, soon work out whether what you are teaching matters to you. If it does, then they are prepared to consider letting it matter to them too. But if they conclude, rightly or wrongly, that it doesn't, then, curtains, you may as well go home" (213).

[3] Daniel Kiefer, however, in a close reading of the passage, allows the style to make a case for risky desire, even if the passage refrains from doing so on the level of assertion: "The erotic imagery of the passage, describing utterance as frail stroke and opening lips, makes speaking itself a sexual act that will be decried as perverse. The edict of exile confronting the speaker may be a version of our students' submission to conventional moral

principles. With bitter irony in the word 'exile' Coetzee upholds the necessary, though ineffective, even dangerous act of defending sexual desire, no matter how universally it is reproved" (272).

4 I would like here to propose an analogy between Coetzee's defense of an erotics of pedagogy, skeletally present, as I am arguing, in his later work, and Roland Barthes's defense of love in the fragments of *A Lover's Discourse*. The latter text, as is well known, was born from Barthes's seminars at the Collège de France, which Barthes describes as "a space for the circulation of subtle desires, mobile desires" (*Roland Barthes* 171). *A Lover's Discourse* is animated, furthermore, by a sense of untimeliness: it finds its polemical raison d'être in Barthes's sense that there is "something scandalous—either willfully naïve or openly backward" in thinking about love in a world saturated with ostensibly authoritative and scientific and also commercial discourses about sex (Ungar 84). In other words, the critical power both of Barthes's amorous fragments and of what I describe as Coetzee's erotics of pedagogy lies in their function as a return of the repressed. My own intuitive inclination, in any event, is to view Coetzee as closer to Barthes than to Lévinas and Derrida—useful as those theorists have been to important Coetzee critics.

5 Consider the revealing notes from an ostensible diary entry, which appear towards the end of the memoir: "*To be developed: his own, homegrown theory of education its roots in (a) Plato and (b) Freud, its elements (a) discipleship (the student aspiring to be like the teacher) and (b) ethical idealism (the teacher striving to be worthy of the students), its perils (a) vanity (the teacher basking in the student's worship) and (b) sex as shortcut to knowledge. His attested incompetence in matters of the heart; transference in the classroom and his repeated failures to manage it*" (255).

6 In her essay "Ethics and Politics in Tagore, Coetzee, and Certain Scenes of Teaching," Gayatri Spivak denounces the practice of teaching children to recite things by heart. Coetzee's work, in fact, makes the learning of words by heart seem full of passion and lyricism. The eager student of *Summertime*, Maria Regina, first arouses her mother's vigilance when she begins to say such passionate and excessive things as "A drowsy numbness overtakes my sense, as though of hemlock I have drunk. Hemlock is a poison. It attacks your nervous system" (x)—things she has learned from (or for) her English teacher, Mr. Coetzee. Learning words by heart can, for Coetzee, arise from lyrical and loving impulses.

7 Note that *eu* and *au* dipthongs have become *ef* or *ev* and *af* or *av* in Modern Greek. According to Anne Marie Dziob, Aristotle uses the noun *self* ("autos") very seldom and only in his ethical treatises, where it is central to his analysis of friendship. Moreover, she continues, it is only in the chapters on friendship that Aristotle refers to another self ("allos autos") (782). Coetzee later attributes his pedagogical theory to Plato, who is a presence in these passages of the *Ethics*.

8 Joan Hambidge revealed to me that Coetzee wrote her an appreciative note in Afrikaans to tell her that he found the book very moving. The connections between *Die Judaskus* and *Disgrace* are ones that I will trace out more fully elsewhere. Suffice it to say for now that scenes of teaching are hugely important in *Die Judaskus*, and that the work consistently engages with, and to some degree emulates, Roland Barthes's *A Lover's Discourse*. Like Kiefer, Hambidge found her anxiety about her role as teacher complicated by homophobia.

9 *The Singularity of Literature* mentions the body only once and rather tentatively in the context of a discussion of responsibility: "In responsibility I respond with much

more than my cognitive faculties: my emotional and sometimes my physical self are also at stake" (126). Pamela Caughie's sharp comments seem particularly apt here: "We commonly think of risk as opposed to safety, but the moral imperative to risk ourselves has long been the safety clause in teaching literature, for the very specialness of literary language that allows us to risk ourselves in the experience of reading serves as well to contain the risk by confining it to the experience of reading" (63).

What Does It Mean
to Teach *The Lives of Animals* or *Disgrace*?

Michael Bell

I am old-fashioned enough to believe that what matters most on a pedagogical occasion is to have a clear general conception in which to accommodate spontaneously what the students may contribute. The precise pedagogical devices are less significant, although the subject matter will suggest a few along the way. The trick in teaching Coetzee may be to use his text to share, and thereby illuminate, the difficulty of teaching him. Of course, no one ever, strictly speaking, teaches literature: one can only put students in the best position possible to experience it at once internally and critically. And it must always be remembered, of course, that whatever we teach or think we teach them, our students, especially the best ones, are likely to do something quite different with it. The pedagogical ambition therefore should be not to produce clones but to give students something substantial and cogent to resist. An important part of this giving is the strategic structure: how the encounter with an individual work is framed by its place in a larger process.

Coetzee is a writer of deceptive simplicity, and his complexity lies partly in his allusion to larger histories or debates. Such allusion is often implicit, and even where there are explicit intertexts, such as in *Foe* or *The Master of Petersburg*, the relation of his text to the original is unresolved. His books lucidly exfoliate radical and painful questions without succumbing to banal answers. Much depends, therefore, on the rest of the course. So, for example, I have taught *The Lives of Animals* alongside Nietzsche's *The Birth of Tragedy* for first-year students in a philosophy-and-literature degree. Common questions in this course were the nature of argument and the status of reason and myth in relation to life values — or, more academically put, the modes of significance peculiar to philosophy and literature. In this context, the founding texts of Western philosophical thought, the Platonic dialogues, are also excellent points of comparison. I have likewise taught *Foe* in a senior seminar called Contemporary Fictions of History, in which the running analytic theme is the necessary difference between, and yet inextricability of, history and fiction. Once again, the peculiar responsibility of the writer in relation to another order of truth, in this case historical truth, helps focus students on the special claims of imaginative literature. In this course, *Foe* was paired with Jean Rhys's *Wide Sargasso Sea*: we juxtaposed the two greatest achievements of that characteristically late-twentieth-century subgenre, the rewritten classic. Finally, Coetzee's intertextual relation to masterworks of European fiction enables Coetzee to be read in the larger context of the European novel, which many of my students have covered, or are covering, as a formal requirement. This approach allows for subtle discriminations of continuity and difference of Coetzee's text with respect to the longer tradition, and the illumination applies in both directions. A truly modern writer like Coetzee helps in reading the deeper tradition of the novel in Europe.

But Coetzee's works are timely, too, because they constantly provide politically pressing and sharply focused occasions for reflecting on the nature of literary significance: What is it that imaginative literature uniquely does as opposed to those elements it may share with other modes of thinking and making truth claims? The question is especially pertinent at the present time, since the literary academy has just passed through a period in which literature was read only through translation into other terms: political, social, or ideological. Instead of being ancillary to literary judgment or appreciation, these dimensions came to substitute for it.

Coetzee has actively, yet subtly, resisted such modes of reading, and a fruitful starting point for understanding this resistance is the sense of paradox induced by reading *The Lives of Animals*. The work concerns the inability of an elderly novelist, Elizabeth Costello, despite her evident intelligence and deeply considered conviction, to convince her various audiences that animals should be respected. She was invited to lecture because of her recognized success as a novelist, but, for purposes of her chosen theme and by the nature of the occasion, she is obliged to adopt a different intellectual and linguistic register. This register, in her view, from the start falsifies or betrays what she has to say, and so she resists it as much as she can, even as she must follow its protocols. For Costello, at least in the eyes of the characters inside the story, her lecture is a failure because she cannot translate her personal belief into an objective argument. Coetzee himself cunningly adopts the opposite strategy: invited to lecture discursively on the theme of animals, he tells a story about the predicament of a fictional novelist.

Costello's problem of translation points simultaneously in the two directions that are of concern to the present volume: it indicates something irreducible at the heart of literary expression; it also suggests the futility of teaching literature, at least insofar as that teaching is understood as a matter of rational explication or translation into other terms. For the reader, who is outside the narrative frame, the true theme is not the human relation to animals but the intellectual and moral difficulty of Elizabeth Costello. Her lecture and seminar are not failures to the reader; because their elements are assembled by metaphoric association rather than by logical connection, they achieve a remarkable eloquence. This success is important in that part of the power of the work lies in the passionate conviction about the animal question, communicated through Costello. Even as the nature and communicability of this conviction are thematized as problematic, it is not reduced to an empty occasion for philosophical and literary self-consciousness. On the contrary, the two dimensions illuminate and deepen each other. For this reason, the original Princeton edition of *Lives*, accompanied by the other lectures in the series, best preserves something of the vertical irruption of Coetzee's literary narrative into the real-life academy, as well as the importance of the animal theme itself. Its later version, as lessons 3 and 4 in *Elizabeth Costello*, becomes part of a horizontal and more self-contained fiction, although the reference to lessons rather than chapters is also a fruitful point for meditation in relation to the pedagogical theme. With what degree of irony or poignancy is this term to be understood? Does fiction give lessons? Does life?

Students will often start with the assumption that the animal theme is the point of the work and that the novelist has wrapped it up in a fictional narrative to make it more engaging, but in a way that does not affect the theme's essential nature. For this reason the other lectures in the volume are useful as responses to Coetzee, which students can critique and debate, maybe grading the lectures and giving a rationale for the grades. Considering the attention to the questions of both gender and philosophical discourse in Coetzee's narrative, it seems appropriate that Peter Singer, the only male and professional philosopher among the responders, falls heavily through the delicate literary-philosophical network of the narrative as into an elephant trap. For him, the fictional frame has no meaning other than being an irritating way of expressing views without having to take personal responsibility for them (*Lives* 91). Marjorie Garber, the literary scholar, while having some pertinent observations, sees the major point only in her final, undeveloped remark that Coetzee's story throws up a question about the nature of literature (84). By contrast, the two remaining women lecturers talk about their relation to animals in highly experienced and eloquently moving ways that accept Costello's theme at face value, as if they were members of her original fictional audience (93–120). This response testifies to a certain power of felt reality in the Costello lectures. Both in their different perceptions of what is there and in what they variously miss or ignore, the subsequent lectures provide a rich set of coordinates by which students might start appreciating the intricate interrelations of Coetzee's philosophical fiction and the difficulty of communicating its power.

Because students are after all seeking to learn how to discuss literature, they might revisit Costello's own argument to assess its success or failure and to reflect on the criteria that they are using, or challenging, to make that assessment. To this end, students who are more junior could be invited to stage a debate on the topic in their own words. In doing so, they might recognize, as Costello does, that her argument cannot be made in purely rational terms. Its existential premise is based largely on feeling. Students who are more sophisticated might explore some of the many resources, philosophical and literary, on which she draws. As I have indicated in more detail elsewhere, she actually traduces a number of her sources, such as the philosopher Thomas Nagel and the scientist Wolfgang Köhler (177, 180–81). Nagel in particular makes for her the very point that she raises against him, that there is an unknowable, for us, phenomenal center of being in the animal and that we should respect that center precisely because it is unknowable. By contrast she claims simply to have the ability to feel what the animal feels — yet she is unable to identify sympathetically with the human carnivores around her, including members of her own family, so maybe her claim of sympathy is questionable. In effect, Nagel presents a so-phisticated defense of a position that she asserts more simply, or simplistically. Is she aware of this paradox? Presumably not. Does Coetzee recognize it? That is harder to say. After all, when she traduces her sources, she does so fully as the character that Coetzee has created.

Her very faults as a reader, if they are indeed to be perceived as such, may be a way of highlighting the fact that she has a deeper rightness, or exercises a more important intuition, in distrusting Nagel's and Köhler's modes of argument, so that the actual content of their arguments is inconsequential. Even when they are right, it is in the wrong way. We come back to the mode of discourse as the fundamental question reflecting the holistic nature of conviction. For her, literature is the mode through which such a holism, such an identity of thought and feeling, is known. Yet on the evidence of her own dealings with the philosophers and poets, it may be that the sheep-and-goats distinction she makes between philosophy and science on the one hand and literature on the other is also too simplistic. The form and language of Coetzee's narrative invoke poetic modes of thinking through Costello but the narrative is not itself poetic; the prose, cool, austere, far from purple, presents Costello's passion with detachment. Yet, as compared with the traditional language of philosophy, the prose clearly works in a poetic, associative way. It rhymes at the level of ideas rather than of words. Attention could be paid to key terms such as "sacrifice" and "position" to see how the apparently unbounded associations generated by Costello's arguments are woven into a tight web of mutually defining significances (e.g., see *Lives* 25, 48, 60, 68). The literary structure does not produce a practical conclusion or overall moral judgment, but it holds a complex set of competing values in mutual relation.

In this respect, a sophisticated group of students might compare *Lives* with a Platonic dialogue, such as *Phaedrus*, which is likewise concerned with the power of argument and the limits of rhetoric, and it rehearses, through the myth of Thoth, the dangers of writing in relation to authentic living thought. The Platonic dialogues, which once were thought of as vehicles for the transmission of Socratic doctrine through the writings of a disciple, are now seen as open-ended explorations of philosophical themes through a specific set of characters and social interactions. Socrates is more concerned to deconstruct false knowledge than to supply a doctrine of his own, because, as Rousseau says, it is not ignorance that is harmful but the illusion of knowing (167). Differently put, the philosophical ambition of the dialogues is now seen as significantly embedded in literature. In *Phaedrus*, when Socrates engages the nature of love, he explicitly invokes myth, where dialectical reason is inadequate. Much great fiction is implicitly philosophical, just as all the major philosophical worldviews draw on poetic means. D. H. Lawrence, whom Costello aligns with the poets, lamented the split between philosophy and poetry: they were once combined in the Platonic dialogues, those "queer little novels," but have come apart, to their mutual detriment, like a "nagging married couple," which is to say that they cannot completely separate either (Lawrence 154). By reflecting so explicitly on the interrelations of philosophy and literature, *Lives* provides a sharp focus on the irreducibility of literature as well as on its inextricable implication in the fundamental questions of life, which are elusive to reason. Just as philosophy and literature are mutually implicated even as their difference is so vital, so it is with literature and history.

Regarding the mutual implication of literature and history, it is useful to bring the insight gleaned from *Lives* to one of Coetzee's politically charged novels. *Disgrace* was written around the time of *Lives* and has some thematic overlap with it, though the formal self-consciousness of *Lives* is so unlike the tight realism of *Disgrace*. Just as *Lives* is not essentially about the animal theme so much as about the difficulty, if not impossibility, of communicating a fundamental conviction, so *Disgrace* presents a comparable difficulty, dramatically, through its two central characters: David Lurie and his daughter, Lucy. The novel was initially received in South Africa with hostility arising from its interpretation as a political allegory of the postapartheid period. Its brutal violence was a problem for some readers, not because they discounted it as a historical truth but because of its acceptance by the principal victim, Lucy, against the remonstrations of Lurie but with the apparent acquiescence of the author. The rape in *Disgrace* is like the shocking centerpiece of Costello's lecture: her comparison of the industrial production of meat with the organized slaughter of the European Jews. The redemptive hints surrounding Lurie's relationship with a stray dog has a similar sense, either tasteless or challenging, of deliberate disproportion. Meanwhile Lucy, who is not forced to justify herself, remains enigmatic. The reader may sense that there is an impersonal acceptance of what has happened to her, almost as a sacrificial victim accepts being sacrificed. An implication of this attitude lurks in the word "offering" as applied to Costello (*Lives* 45). But Lucy seems to know that it cannot be put into words, or at least not for Lurie. If the problematic of *Lives* arises from Costello's attempt to express and justify her conviction, the narrative of *Disgrace* turns on the characters' reticence. The family trait shared by father and daughter places at the heart of the story something untranslatable yet also vital and irreplaceable, while the comparison of *Disgrace* with *Lives* brings out the underlying similarity of the two texts.

Disgrace is a novel that gets people talking, which is an invaluable feature pedagogically, but the advantage is ambivalent if the argument remains too focused on the content and is uncontained by the novel's narrative structure and consciousness. The deliberate lack of authorial guidance or judgment should not be an alibi for the open-ended exchange of personal responses and nothing more. Nonetheless, it may be instructive to allow a free-flowing discussion sparked by the novel before one begins to channel it. Note that there is a challenging edge to one of the major narrative decisions. Lurie, whose consciousness drives the narrative on Coetzee's behalf, is an unsympathetic figure, which no doubt exacerbated the distaste of some early readers. One wonders what the book would be like but for this. A two-dimensional opinion piece in the mode of David Mamet's *Oleanna*? The naive default response, in the absence of overt irony, is always to identify a dominant narrative consciousness with the authorial viewpoint, just as some of Coetzee's colecturers took Elizabeth Costello as his mouthpiece. Yet Costello is not an object of irony at the level of her convictions as such, nor is Lurie. Coetzee is typically most skeptical about his own convictions. Reading *Disgrace* in tandem with *Lives* is a way of bringing out this dimension of the novel. Just as Lucy's response to the rape remains enigmatic yet suggestive and compelling, so Lurie's sacrifice of the dog hints at the novel's counterterm, *grace*, in an even more obscure, untranslatable way.

In conclusion, there are special problems and opportunities in teaching Coetzee that result from the very quality that makes him one of the most important of contemporary writers: his absolute commitment to the irreducible and irreplaceable nature of literature as a mode of moral thinking. In interviews he invariably refuses to claim any special authority either through or on the basis of his fiction. He affirms only what is in the fiction and in the form that it has already been given. Yet a great deal of literary pedagogy is essentially translation, which becomes in turn the basis of public debate. The text is turned into other modes of discourse or reference: moral, political, historical. But wherever there is an ambition to arrive at a critical judgment, and judgment usually underwrites discussion even when not intentional or conscious, the danger is that the object of critique will be no longer the literary work but the ideological interpretation of it. It is the unconscious or inarguable premises underlying rational exchange that Costello's ill-fated lecture throws into relief. Such discriminations may not trouble many authors, but they are important to Coetzee, for two reasons. The external reason is that he writes on matters of public concern that are grave, highly controversial, and already digested into ideological positions. The internal reason is that resistance to ideological translation is a primary, if not always explicit, feature of his narratives. This resistance disconcerts some readers, and the hostility it arouses may not arise from the ideological issue so much as from his intruding into public debate his lack of cooperation. He speaks of fiction as a means of "staging" a passion (*Doubling* 60–61). Argument, often one of the forms of passion, is equally staged. Coetzee refuses the possible comforts of a postmodern relativism—his issues are too urgent—yet he invests every practical judgment or action with a radical skepticism. *The Lives of Animals* and *Disgrace* exemplify in different ways that literature is the form in which the complexity of rival values is held in suspension. However a class is conducted, students should not feel they have arrived at answers to the questions posed by these works: they should rather feel the painful force of the questions.

Horizons Not Only of Expectation:
Lessons from *In the Heart of the Country*

Martina Ghosh-Schellhorn

On the Shoulders of Giants

> A careworn spinster living with her father observes with distaste his love affair with a young colored woman. She has fantasies of murdering both of them, but everything seems to indicate that she decides rather to immure herself in a perverse pact with the house servant. The actual sequence of events cannot be determined, as the reader's only sources are her notes, where lies and truths, crudeness and refinement alternate capriciously line by line.
>   ("Nobel Prize")

This faint praise is by no means an uncommon response to one of Coetzee's least popular novels, as often revealed by the first entries in my graduate students' reading journals. *In the Heart of the Country* certainly deserves better treatment, even critically,[1] and a good place to start would surely be in the classroom. I have found that an approach loosely based on the German reader-response critic Hans Robert Jauss's concept of a horizon of expectations, a postulation of the interconnectedness of texts both with each other and with a tradition in which an informed readership places them ("Literary History" 12), is particularly suited to appreciating Coetzee's narrative experiment. The horizon of expectations ("Erwartungshorizont" ["Literaturgeschichte" 173]) takes as its point of departure the threshold of (reading) experience that readers in a certain culture can be expected to have attained by the time they read a recently published literary text; it is "a 'system of references,' or a mind-set that a hypothetical individual brings to a given text" (Holub 323). Depending on the extent to which the new text conforms to previous conventions or breaks out of the frame by being innovative and unconventional, it either maintains the readers' horizon of expectations or succeeds in extending it.

Instead of downplaying students' feeling that *In the Heart of the Country* is a difficult novel, I use their frustration to encourage engagement with precisely what makes the text seem so dense — that is, with the pastiche and parody techniques so frequently used. Students are first pointed to the way Coetzee's title serves to draw us back into Africa. By placing his text in the shadow of Joseph Conrad's *Heart of Darkness*, in which Kurtz embodies the trope of the white man gone native, Coetzee prepares the ground for a contemporary, South African version of a typical colonial story. The implications this idea gives rise to lead students to hunt for further intertextual markers, and references to Erasmus's *The Praise of Folie*, Stephen Duck's *The Thresher's Labour*, Shakespeare's *The Tempest*, Daniel Defoe's *Robinson Crusoe*, Samuel Richardson's *Pamela* and *Clarissa*, William Blake's *The Marriage of Heaven and Hell*, Fyodor Dostoevsky's *The Idiot*, James Joyce's *A Portrait of the Artist as a Young Man*, and Samuel Beckett's *Molloy* are the ones they most often discover in renewed, often directed, close reading. The pleasures and frustrations of this investigative activity lead students to move further in the direction of metacommentary and to ask the next important question: What is the purpose of all this allusion? Further, we ask which literary traditions, genres, and texts an informed readership in late-1970s South Africa would, or could, have been familiar with.

A first clue can be found in the novel's publishing history. Initially most of the dialogue was in Afrikaans (with many instances of code-switching to English), and the narration was in English: Coetzee's local community of readers was ostensibly as bilingual and bicultural as he was, from this evidence.[2] This biculturality is emphasized not only by the intertextual elements just mentioned but also by the less familiar (to an international readership), South African anglophone literary tradition of farm novels, like *The Story of an African Farm* (Schreiner) and *The Beadle* (Smith) or the Afrikaans tradition of the *plaasroman*, like *Somer* (Van den Heever) or *Dawid Booysen* (Van Melle). When asked to explain this variety, students usually point to the "transitionality" of South African literature (Ghosh-Schellhorn) and therewith to Coetzee's awareness of being situated as a white South African writer who typically is in between yet very much a part of both these South African literary traditions. Taken together, the anglophone and Afrikaans literary traditions determine the kind of horizon of expectation shared by *In the Heart*'s South African readers.

By the time students are ready to read Jauss (in the original), they have established for themselves that *In the Heart* postulates an exceptionally bifocal reception. They now learn from Jauss what their goal as reader-critics should be. Jauss stipulates that the prime task of the critic is to establish what the horizon of a text is by using an "objective," threefold approach ("Literary History" 18). The class learns that the basis of objectivity is calibrated judgment. Jauss expects critics to disinterestedly judge a new text's contribution to the tradition in which its author has embedded it, by measuring it against the three distinct yet related standards of innovative excellence set by its predecessors. These criteria are

1. the "familiar standards . . . of the genre" to which the new text belongs
2. its "implicit relationships to familiar works of the literary-historical context" and
3. the "contrast between fiction and reality" with reference to "the wider horizon of [the reader's] experience of life" (18)

In class, I give students a variety of examples to help them decide what Jauss's threefold method is aiming at.

Pastoral South Africa

We next consider the history of the novel as a genre in both the British and the South African traditions before looking at the subgenres these traditions share. From the Romantic pastoral, in its specifically South African form of the *plaasroman*, to the epistolary novel, the confessional diary, the novel *à thèse*, the coming-of-age novel or bildungsroman, and the gothic romance, these narratives have usually been mediated by techniques typical of the romance, social realist, or modernist narration.

Which of these modes does Coetzee use? The closest link between the anglophone and the Afrikaans novel traditions relevant to an evaluation of *In the Heart* would seem to be the pastoral, a Romantic subgenre specific to European settler colonies like South Africa, in which arcadian elements play a central role. Students are now reminded of what *Robinson Crusoe* achieved in terms of altering its readers' horizon of expectations. As a protonovel, it retained the well-established frame story but introduced a homodiegetic first-person narrative mode typical of spiritual confessions, diaries, and journals. In doing so, Defoe ensured that the new pastoral material, that is Crusoe's establishing a realistic island kingdom far removed both from the social reality of England as well as from the imaginary islands of writers like Thomas More or Jonathan Swift, gained his readers' credence.

Well before *Crusoe*, Shakespeare exploited the pastoral genre for his meditation on power and rulership in *The Tempest*. He depicts a limited set of island inhabitants, notably Prospero, the self-acclaimed ruler washed up on the shores of Sycorax's island; Miranda, his virgin daughter; and the indigenous figure of Caliban, kept as a slave after his alleged sexual predation of the solitary female object. *In the Heart* mirrors this arrangement, with the difference that whereas

Shakespeare has Prospero leave Caliban behind on the island, it is the newly abused Magda who is abandoned by Hendrik, the monstrous-seeming, dispossessed Caliban figure forced to work hard on the farm because of his race. A further twist Coetzee introduces is that Magda's Prospero-like father is rendered powerless by her, thereby clearing the path for Hendrik's exploitation of her body, as a type of demon lover,[3] in a reversal of the power relations in South Africa.

Where is the connection between Romanticism and the *plaasroman*? Coetzee, whose reluctance to speak of his own work is counterbalanced by the acute observations he makes as a critic of the work of others, writes, "[W]hereas European Romanticism . . . sees man as a child not of cities but of nature, [the typical *plaasroman* as written by] Van den Heever presents man as a child not of cities but of the farm" (*White Writing* 87). This statement echoes Magda's final diary entry in which she expresses her complex sense of being "held captive" by the farm she equates with "paradise":

> It takes generations of life in the cities to drive that nostalgia for country ways from the heart. I will never live it down, nor do I want to. I am corrupted to the bone with the beauty of this forsaken world. If the truth be told, I never wanted to fly away with the sky-gods. My hope was always that they would descend and live with me here in paradise.   (151)

A further parallel to Shakespearean pastoral and to the omnipotent figure of Prospero, the practitioner of magic arts, is set up by Coetzee when he has Magda claim responsibility for every living being on the farm:

> How can I afford to sleep? If for one moment I were to lose my grip on the world, it would fall apart: Hendrik and his shy bride would dissolve to dust in each other's arms and sift to the floor, the crickets would stop chirping, the house would deliquesce to a pale abstract of lines and angles against a pale sky, my father would float like a black cloud and be sucked into the lair inside my head to beat the walls and roar like a bear.   (79)

Yet, as classroom discussion shows, students wonder why Coetzee questions Magda's claim to the status of creator of a farm novel, given that she is the only chronicler of farm life we have. We look for answers by reading his criticism of women writers' claims to authority in the South African farm novel context:

> For two decades of this century, 1920–40, the Afrikaans novel concerned itself almost exclusively with the farm and *platteland* (rural) society, with the Afrikaner's painful transition from farmer to townsman. Of major English-language novelists, on the other hand, only Olive Schreiner . . . and Pauline Smith . . . have taken farming life as their subject. By themselves

Schreiner and Smith cannot be said to have defined a "farm novel" genre in English to parallel the *plaasroman* in Afrikaans.

(*White Writing* 63)

The reason Coetzee gives for this failure is of no little significance for *In the Heart*: "One might even argue that neither is a true farm novelist. *As women*, as people of English culture, as free thinkers, they perhaps stood too far outside the insular patriarchal culture of the Boer farm to write of it with true intimacy" (63; emphasis added).

Note that, despite this, Coetzee chose a woman, albeit an Afrikaner, as the protagonist of his farm novel. Although Magda is a representative of her community, she is nonetheless shown to be incapable (as was Schreiner's Tant' Sannie) of being a good farmer—on account of her sex. Coetzee has her articulate her awareness of her inadequacy more than once: "If I cannot succeed in catching the sheep . . . then there is nothing for it, the sheep must perish, they must lie heaving and panting about the veld like filthy brown powderpuffs till their creator finds it in his heart to take them to himself" (104).

Coetzee thus dramatically departs from the standards he spelled out as being essential to the *plaasroman*: "[W]e find the ancestors hagiographized as men and women of heroic strength, fortitude, and faith, and instituted as the originators of lineages" (*White Writing* 83). Magda's father is not painted in saintly hues by his daughter; though depicted by her as being endowed with "strength, fortitude, and faith" enough, yet it is as the "originator of lineages" that he is denied memorialization by Magda. She derides his manhood when she writes, "Poor little thing. It is not possible to believe I came from there, or from whatever that puffy mass is below it" (75). His sole male heir having failed to survive, his only lineage is doomed to die out with a daughter like Magda who would willingly "fold him away for the night" (149).

Coetzee thus, unlike the farm novelists before him, teases out the unexplored nexus of spinsterhood and the Boer's sacred duty toward the land:

> Besides farming the land in a spirit of piety toward *voorgeslagte* and *nageslagte* (past and future generations), besides being a good steward, the farmer must also love the farm, love this one patch of earth above all others, so that his proprietorship comes to embody a marriage not so much between himself and the farm as between his lineage (*familie*) and the farm.
>
> (*White Writing* 86)

Precisely because Magda is a woman, the notion of her husbanding the farm carries several levels of meaning foreign to the *plaasroman*. Coetzee continues: "Such a marriage, which must be exclusive (monogamous) and more than merely proprietorial, will entail that in good years the farm will respond to his love by bringing forth bountifully, while in bad years he will have to stand by it, nursing it through its trials" (86). Magda is a bad husband to the farm because she has colluded with the ideology reserved for her sex by the Afrikaner myth of the *vrou* and *moder*,[4] of the woman as pillar of strength behind the farmer. As her father's firstborn she has a sacred right to the farm (as the *plaasroman* repeatedly emphasizes), but since she is merely a woman, her father neglects to induct her into farm husbandry, leaving her to carry the burden of an unwanted responsibility.

Unable to break out of the script she believes has been written for her by the Afrikaner myth of the Boer and his helpmate, Magda concedes that she is "not unaware that there is a hole between my legs that has never been filled, leading to another hole never filled either. If I am an O, I am sometimes persuaded, it must be because I am a woman" (45). The instability of Magda's character, an aspect that readers, like my students, often find dismaying, can in fact be traced back to this South African version of Jacques Lacan's "*méconnaisances* ['misrecognitions'] that constitute the ego, the illusion of autonomy to which it entrusts itself" (130). Magda hence cannot but try out various, often contradictory roles, while remaining painfully aware of a holistic lack, of the hole where there should be a whole personality: "If I am an emblem then I am an emblem. I am incomplete, I am a being with a hole inside me, I signify something, I do not know what" (10).

Women as Exceptions to the Rule

In order to understand that Magda's statements are not necessarily evidence for what the Nobel Prize press release designated a "psychotic tale,"[5] we need to turn to another critical statement by Coetzee. He commends Erasmus's *Praise of Folie* for tackling "the problematics of finding or creating a position in-but-not-in the political dynamic, a position not already given, defined, limited and sanctioned by the game itself" (*Giving* 84). Erasmus's protagonist, Moria, "need not be taken seriously because, as she says, she is a woman" (97). This "in-but-not-in the political dynamic" is exactly the position he carves out for Magda, who is made to play the Boer game. Despite her despair, she is, and she never questions it, a white Afrikaner woman, born into the privilege of farm ownership and thus having complete control over the labor force. Even in the slightly less exploitative position of mistress of the house she cannot abjure the burden of white dominance laid on her by Boer ideology.

"There is no act I know of," Magda notes, that "will liberate me into the world. There is no act I know of that will bring the world into me" (10). Her estrangement is a consequence of the status bestowed on her at birth, leaving her to speak only in commands and be spoken to in the hushed tones of acquiescence: "Why will no one speak to me in the true language of the heart? The medium, the median—that is what I wanted to be! Neither master nor slave, neither parent nor child, but the bridge between, so that in me the contraries should be reconciled" (145). When she eventually anticipates a dialectics of power in which synthesis of master and servant can be achieved, she is made to realize that neither the time nor the place is yet ripe for such an experiment: she fails miserably at winning the trust of both Klein-Anna and Hendrik. They will not call her by any name other than her hierarchical designation of "miss" (111), since no scripts yet exist with which to initiate the ménage à trois she desires. Foreshadowing *Disgrace*, the novel warns the reader against believing that the South African tables can be easily turned. Like Lucy Lurie, Magda tries to relinquish her colonially given authority as a white only to discover that she will continue to be treated as a white woman, particularly during the sexual intercourse Hendrik demands of her. Made painfully aware, especially by his humiliation of her, that she is a human being with a woman's needs and shortcomings, she still cannot assume agency for her life and seek happiness. In a truly anti-Romantic, antipastoral vein, she considers why she did not go in search of an urban modus vivendi rather than be held captive to the farm. My student-critics understand that she has invested too heavily in the contradictions of her state — privilege as the farm owner's daughter and heir, as against the self-ascribed stigma of being merely a woman, hence incomplete in herself.[6] This conflictedness, they argue, is typical of white South African identity. Magda, too, can be seen to be "validating an unquestioned right to land but expressing also the very soul of the Afrikaner's being," a blend that M. Van Wyk Smith argues to be unique to the *plaasroman* ("From 'Boereplaas'" 18).

A New Form

A text that avails itself thus of other texts is highly self-reflexive not only in theme but also in form. *In the Heart* tends to frustrate student readers who expect easy accessibility to a typical coming-of-age novel written in the first person. To induct the impatient into Coetzee's unique technique, I direct them back to the first page of his novel, and we read the opening paragraph word for word. I draw attention to the manner in which he has juxtaposed stark, sharply realistic-seeming details (placed in bold letters below) with vague, nonrealisitic suppositions (placed in italics):

> **I. Today** my father brought home his new bride. They **came clip-clop** across the flats in a dog-cart drawn by a horse **with an ostrich-plume waving on its forehead**. . . . *Or perhaps they were drawn by two plumed donkeys, that is also possible*. My father wore **his black swallowtail coat and stovepipe hat**, his bride **a wide-brimmed sunhat and a white dress tight at waist and throat. More detail I cannot give unless I begin to embroider, for I was not watching. I was in my room . . . reading a book** *or, more likely, supine* **with a damp towel over my eyes fighting a migraine**. *I am the one who stays in her room reading or*

> *writing or fighting migraines.* **The colonies are full of girls like that,**
> *but none, I think, so extreme as I. My father is the one who* **paces the**
> **floorboards back and forth . . . in his slow black boots.** *And then, for*
> *a third,* **there is the new wife.** *. . . Those are the antagonists.*   (1)

Highlighted thus, the passage enables students to step back and comment on
the impression Coetzee achieves: how each of these narrational extremes fences
in (to use an image appropriate to the colonial farms setting) the other, thereby
jostling for credibility in the eyes of the reader. The numbering of entries (ranging from 1 to 266) appears to underline the text's reliability and to promise that
a chronological narrative will unfold. As Coetzee says elsewhere of the novel,
"[It] is constructed out of quite brief sequences, which are numbered as a way
of pointing to what is not there between them: the kind of scene-setting and
connective tissue that the traditional novel used to find necessary" (*Doubling*
59). As readers, we go along with the illusion Coetzee creates of a (still un-
named) reliable narrator telling us a realistic story that has a beginning, middle,
and end. It comes as a surprise, students say when discussing this paragraph,
to suddenly learn that all Magda seems to do with her time is sequester herself
"in her room reading or writing or fighting migraines." It is even more of a
surprise to read that these unfarmlike, indeed genteel, activities are her distin-
guishing traits ("I am the one who . . ."). Coetzee makes the self-portrayal sound
even more absurd when she insists that she is the most "extreme" of them all.
By placing realistic narration alongside artificial and self-reflexive commentary,
Coetzee not only holds our attention but also raises our expectations. What turn
will this metafictionally inclined narrative take, given a central character proud
of her peculiar eccentricities?

   If Coetzee's mixed style points to instability, the establishing paragraph's narrative function is clearly overdetermined. We are informed that there are only
three characters in this stifling, conventional gothic setting: the daughter plays
the role of the heroine, while her father and his "new bride" are the "antagonists" she must face. *Agon* indicates that her tale will describe a battle against
the members of her own family, that a powerless, possibly hysterical "girl" "in
the colonies" will be in conflict with her overpowering father in his "slow black
boots" and the new, indolent stepmother "who lies late abed" (1). But as the
narrative progresses, readers find that there is no one battle, no one father, and
not even a fixed stepmother. In the few sentences of the opening entry, Coetzee
seems to have given us three motifs: a heroine, a father, and a mother figure, as
seen from the perspective of an unreliable narrator in the setting of the farm-
lands of apartheid South Africa at a point frozen in time.

   When students consider the interaction of these motifs, they see that the
novel is constructed at times in a social realistic mode, at times in a mode so
poststructural that it resists interpretation. They learn that Magda repeatedly
fantasizes about killing her father and getting rid of his corpse, that she replaces
the first stepmother with a second one before turning this figure into Klein-

Anna, with whom she believes her father is sexually engaged. Likewise, she has Klein-Anna's husband at first replace her dominant father before turning him into her companion in crime, only in order to claim that he had raped her, or to change the accusation into a declaration of his desire for his repulsive mistress.

All these substitutions can be confusing, but when students turn to the critics for help, they are usually dismayed to find that the experts are equally at sea.[7] Some believe that Magda's father does have an affair with Klein-Anna, while denying the existence of white stepmothers; some posit that none of the events occur, since all is confusion, or else that patricide is a certainty.[8] When I direct students to Coetzee's comment, "Magda is passionate in the way that one can be in fiction and her passion is . . . the love for South Africa. I see no further point in calling her mad" (*Doubling* 61), the matter is settled for some of them. For the skeptics, the stone messages, at first self-pitying and then seductive, that Magda sends to the flying planes whose pilots she believes speak Spanish take on added meaning when students consider that Spanish is the language of New World colonial conquest. It becomes clearer why Spanish should be the language that Magda, the Boer mistress, instinctively (if imperfectly) understands in her colonial settler heart. Following this line of thought, students come to appreciate that the "brave new world" Miranda so uncritically admires in *The Tempest* is reconfigured in Coetzee's antipastoral as the partly self-induced, partly inevitable plight of the Afrikaner settlers, who are landlocked on their farms and as incapable of leaving their islands[9] as Magda is of fitting herself into Klein-Anna's body or her empty self is of being filled completely by another.

The inconsistencies and indeterminacies of Magda's narrative, its mode repeatedly veering from verisimilitude to metafiction, reflect and simultaneously comment on her dilemma as heiress of a farm she is incapable of husbanding in the Afrikaner manner. By making her appear to be unhinged, Coetzee addresses the problem of rationality in the context of a settler colony's insane politics of domination. By creating a new horizon of expectations in this early novel, Coetzee could move on to the larger projects that eventually won him the Nobel Prize. *In the Heart* prepared the ground for *Disgrace*, a novel less formally complex but just as innovative as it.[10]

Coetzee's readers, in South Africa and elsewhere, have, in engaging with his extraordinary novels, significantly extended the "wider horizon" of their "experience of life" (Jauss, "Literary History" 18).

NOTES

[1] Ian Glenn mentions the negative responses by Susan Gallagher, Stephen Watson, and Michael Vaughan in his defense of the novel as an experiment in which "the play between the I-as-narrator and the I-as-subject is one of the novel's many stylistic games" (123).

[2] Only when we stop to consider the replacement of Afrikaans passages of dialogue by Coetzee's English translations when *In the Heart* was published a year later for an international anglophone readership do we begin to comprehend the high price that had to be paid in terms of the referential specificity of the South African settler context. See Wittenberg for more details.

[3] The reference here to one of Coleridge's phrases from "Kubla Khan" points us to Romanticism's innovative influence; Coleridge's contribution of exotic settings and themes significantly extended the horizon of English pastoral.

[4] "The mythology of the Afrikaner woman always stresses her role as Vrou en Moeder, wife and mother" (Gallagher 85).

[5] Head's interpretation, too, is based on the idea of Magda's turning mad (*J. M. Coetzee* 51).

[6] An example of Magda's contradictory statements is: "I was not, after all, made to live alone. If I had been set down by fate in the middle of the veld in the middle of nowhere, buried to my waist and commanded to live a life, I could not have done it. I am not a philosopher. Women are not philosophers, and I am a woman. A woman cannot make something out of nothing. However sterile my occupation with dust and cobwebs and food and soiled linen may have seemed, it was necessary to fill me out, to give me life" (130).

[7] Bartnik believes that patricide has in fact been committed (47), as do Wohlpart (221), Silvani (26), and Attridge (*J. M. Coetzee*, 25), while Stone concludes that "Magda does not succeed in permanently killing her father, even though she makes two grimly valiant efforts" (217). Briganti, on the other hand, reads Magda's account as intertextual play on the Freudian idea of women as hysterical in one of the early psychoanalytic approaches to the novel.

[8] Canepari-Labib writes, "[H]er mental confusion and her alienation have gone so far that she is not herself sure of what in her tale is true" (177). Penner sees only a "deranged spinster" (27), and he is not alone in taking a stance that fails to support an informed reading of the novel.

[9] Robinson Crusoe, to whom Magda repeatedly refers in the final sections, provides her with a yardstick by which she judges herself to triumph or fail. Unlike her, he is rescued. Coetzee has her play on the word *castaway* when toward the end she echoes Faustus in lamenting her fate, as an Afrikaner, of being one of "the castaways of God as we are the castaways of history" (147). For a more recent perspective on being cast away, especially the aspect of not being able to find a home, see Griffiths and Prozesky.

[10] To follow the extent to which Coetzee's innovation has enabled other writers to alter South African readers' horizons of expectations with regard to the *plaasroman*, see Warnes.

Teaching Coetzee's Subject:
Waiting for the Barbarians and *Disgrace*

Stephen Clingman

In J. M. Coetzee's *Waiting for the Barbarians*, we are caught up in the eternal present tense of the novel's first-person narrative. In one sense the novel has a beginning, location, and end, but in another, largely because of this form of narration, there is no beginning, location, or end. For where is this narrative located? Inside the Magistrate's mind? Or outside it? But what does *outside* mean in such a novel? The protagonist, the Magistrate, is located both at the center of the novel and at its horizon; his narrative is its inner condition, yet it also marks the limit of a world, his world. We can perform the basic analytical fieldwork: Coetzee is not the same as the Magistrate, and therefore, even from the perspective of its writing, there is an outside to the text. But this only complicates the novel further: for in what sense is Coetzee really outside *this* text? If there is, or were, an implied narrator of the novel beyond the Magistrate, would that make a difference? On these levels alone, it is worth registering an impression which I feel is probably not idiosyncratic: that approaching a novel such as *Waiting for the Barbarians* is like viewing a picture by M. C. Escher in which the hand that does the drawing is part of the image, in which staircases that lead up also lead down, in which the image establishes its own rules for experiencing its particular universe. Its orientation, from that perspective, is to be disorienting.

In *Waiting for the Barbarians* this sense of looping infinitude is emphasized in various ways. If its narrative location is both particular and unlimited, so too is its setting, both real and unreal, with echoes that range anywhere from the Roman Empire and its outposts, to the Soviet Union, to the Gestapo chambers of Nazi Germany, to the apartheid regime of South Africa, to the fictive environs of Franz Kafka's story "In the Penal Colony." From that point of view, the novel is like an uncanny haunting, evasive yet inescapable, mesmeric in its effects, its combination of the concrete and dreamlike. Most profoundly, its narrative explorations are intrinsically linked to its thematic concerns, particularly in the realms of morality and ethics. Part of the Magistrate's quest is to distinguish himself from his world, to establish his difference in a regime in which power makes the only difference. Yet how can he do so? As Magistrate, he literally administers the laws of Empire, one of which seems to be that there is no escape from its authority. Can he be both Empire's agent and dissenter? If so, it is hard to see on what grounds, because in this world of totality, the negation of difference is an overriding reality, and—as the Magistrate discovers—all gestures to the contrary are compromised. The Magistrate learns the reality of complicity, which we can also construe as a problem of inside and outside—an incorporation which may be unwilled but is inescapable.[1] In that crucial sense the Magistrate is authorized by Empire, a perspective that puts both the agency of his narrative and the narrative of his agency in a different light.[2]

And so there is concatenation. The Magistrate is an extraordinary self-scrutinizer: his subjectivity is his subject, yet so too is Empire, in ways that have a certain, if asymmetrical, reversibility. For if the narrator's subject is Empire, then he is also the subject of Empire, so that his subject is, in this doubled sense, the subject of Empire—the self of Empire in all its implications, its strange mix in which (at least in the Magistrate's case) authority is a form of subjection. Moreover, because of the rules of consciousness, the object of the Magistrate's investigation (subjectivity) is also the instrument of his investigation, and so there is another kind of multiplier. Subjectivity is a philosophical problem in the novel, and it is a problem under Empire, and these two horizons cross, constitute, and contain the narrative of the Magistrate.

What or who is Coetzee's subject? And how do teachers or students enter in? For if questions of inside/outside are troublesome from the perspective of narration, they are also perplexing from the point of view of reading (I take teaching-studying as a special case of reading). It turns out that the boundaries of a novel such as *Waiting for the Barbarians* are permeable mainly in one direction: you can get in, but it is hard to get out. This is not the normal orientation for teaching. In this light the question becomes a different one. Can we step outside Coetzee's novels and make them our subject? Or do we, conversely, become subject to them? If the latter, is there a perspective in which that may not be a problem? In other words, can we find a way of allowing the topic of subjectivity—in all its ramifications in Coetzee's writing—to become not only the content but also the form of our teaching, so that these issues become, in the words of Cavafy's poem from which the title of *Waiting for the Barbarians* comes, "a kind of solution" (19)?

I regularly teach *Waiting for the Barbarians* in the somewhat anomalous context of a general education lecture course on twentieth-century fiction (subtitle, "Writing at the Frontiers," 120 students). I teach Coetzee's *Disgrace* in very different circumstances: a small seminar class for English majors (twenty students), titled South African Literature and Politics. The modes, purposes, and frameworks of the two courses could not be more different, and yet some of the same principles I have begun to suggest apply.

What one can achieve teaching literature in a large-lecture format may be open to question, but I have arrived at a modus vivendi as well as operandi. Like many, I use *PowerPoint* (lately *Keynote*); because the course covers a range of geographic and cultural settings, I provide background, maps (past and current), artwork, music, and film clips of various kinds. In a general education course, some of this comes under the heading not only of much-needed information but of deprovincializing (or in a deeper sense, provincializing) the United States. On this basis, novel by novel, I then follow an analytical narrative through the course that weaves together its range of themes. In reading writers such as Joseph Conrad, Chinua Achebe, E. M. Forster, Jean Rhys, Caryl Phillips, Coetzee, and Zadie Smith, we are able to connect the beginning of the century with its end; we explore questions of empire and its aftermath, trace formal elaborations and developments, investigate central (and marginal) questions of identity, migration, cultural formation and knowledge, and track transitions from the modern to postmodern, the colonial to the post-colonial. In my experience, it is remarkable how novel can connect with novel, whether by way of resonance, dialogue, or difference, and how a larger kind of story seems to develop through it all.

Waiting for the Barbarians, then, takes its place in this context. The immediate question, in introducing the novel, is what and how much material is relevant. Is this a South African novel? The answer is likely to be not much, or only in some incorporative way, even though there are resonances: the Bureau of State Security (BOSS) in South Africa echoes in Colonel Joll's Third Bureau; the murder in detention of Steve Biko and others is in the background of the Third Bureau's brutal methods. But equally, some discussion with students on the novel's nameless and placeless setting is likely to be productive; they bring their own associations to the work. More relevant are other materials implicit in the novel itself: Cavafy's poem, which always provokes discussion, and extracts from Coetzee's essay "Confession and Double Thoughts: Tolstoy, Rousseau, Dostoevsky," for what is the Magistrate's narrative if not a confession of a kind? This essay is where, via Fyodor Dostoevsky, Coetzee gives his classic formulation, relevant for so much of his writing: "Because of the nature of consciousness . . . the self cannot tell the truth of itself to itself and come to rest without the possibility of self-deception" (291). And there are wider questions in the novel, of the nexus between confession and coercion, the unlicensed invasion of what one might call the space of the soul, one of the ultimate transgressions for Coetzee.

I think what I am beginning to discuss here is a theory of the immanent teaching of a novel such as *Waiting for the Barbarians*, in which the text provides the context it requires to discuss it. What this means in particular, precisely because of the novel's concerns with consciousness, identity, boundary, power, questions of inside and outside, is a form of immanent experience in the teaching-learning of the novel. I should be clear: in this I am not referring to the simple reconstitution of an older method of practical criticism or naive (at worst complicit) humanism in which the text is all, universality the easy objective, and context either irrelevant or politically suspect. Such forms of criticism, when entering into a text, always knew what they were looking for. But a novel such as *Waiting for the Barbarians* teaches us, among other things, how our forms of looking are in and of themselves the problem. Far from gazing into this novel from the outside, the novel opens up to include us, to make us part of its problem. This is what I mean when I say we become part of the novel's subject; it is our world the novel is discussing, dissecting, representing, and if there were a ready-made analysis to deal with it, it would in some way negate the reach of the novel itself. There is very little analysis we can bring to the novel that goes further than the novel does itself. It proposes a hermeneutic of following,

delving, absorbing as much as framing; a mode of interpretation that is intrinsically receptive in its very forms of analysis.

And so what follows is a strange and unusual dance of speech and silence, of
naming and unknowing, drawing students in, yet allowing them space to move
within the novel, to understand, at whatever conceptual level is attainable, its
wider and larger forms of impact. Any teacher will discuss themes. In my course
they range across the obvious and particular. We talk of torture, confession,
coercion. We discuss language under Empire, and vision in Empire's optic.
The Magistrate as a character is central, as is the relationship between him and
the woman, which encodes so many other issues: reading, interpretation, violation, the nexus between torture as a form of writing and reading its marks as a
form of complicity, the female body and/or icon, and the boundaries of Empire
(here is Conrad, and Rhys). We talk of the difference between law (which may
belong to History) and justice (a universal which the Magistrate, authorized
by Empire, abandons). There are questions of time—the time of History, the
time of Empire, the cycles of seasons, and that other existential ground always
intimated to the Magistrate yet from which he seems in permanent exile on his
"road that may lead nowhere" (152).

Within this discussion, there is for me a pedagogical axiom: not to impose too
much on the novel, not to overdetermine it, to let it—within the frameworks
I can provide—do its own work. In my experience it is remarkable, even in a
lecture setting, how many students take to the book, and how deeply. In this
there is one notable indicator. I have taught the novel through two wars in Iraq,
through detention without trial under United States rule, through revelations
about torture at Abu Ghraib and elsewhere. Here South African history meets
an American present—with extraordinary echoes for a South African teaching in the United States; and this is one of the ways in which the world keeps
on inventing contexts to match the framework of the novel. But the point is,
I barely need to say anything about it. There is scarcely a student in the room
who does not reflect on Empire at its outposts and what that means about the
center. The idea of Empire faltering in the desert against obscure and unidenti-
fiable antagonists requires no forceful allegorical reading. Rather, students take
these meanings into their lives, and work with them. More importantly, they
begin to question, in their own world, notions of complicity, of being and history
under Empire, of language, vision, and seeing under Empire's regime. To tie it
too closely would be to overdo; but the novel in this way becomes an appropriate haunting, an uncanny of the world students inhabit, in which what Sigmund
Freud suggests are the secrets of the home ("'Uncanny'"; Clingman 177–79)
take on what Conrad calls in *Heart of Darkness* "a kind of light" (11).

From this perspective some comparison with *Disgrace* is instructive. There
the topic is (among other things) also subjectivity, but the narrative mode is
different: free indirect discourse focalized on and through David Lurie rather
than a first-person account. What free indirect discourse classically stages is the
boundary between inside and outside, the perspective located both within and

without. What *Disgrace* helps us see retroactively—what it suggests—is that *Waiting for the Barbarians* is also a kind of free indirect discourse, both inside and outside the Magistrate's narration, both inside and outside his world. This helps solve the conundrum of where Coetzee is in the writing, but also where we are as readers. We are both inside and outside this novel, on the boundary between its world and ours. The trick is to take this inner form—I am speaking of both novels now—and allow it to inform our teaching. The question of subjectivity then becomes dialogic in the very constitution of our teaching. A novel such as *Waiting for the Barbarians* makes us attend to our own complicities, our own imbrication in empires of various kinds, but equally it makes us attend to our interpretive practices—the confessions we might like to coerce from a text, the ways we delve into its marks, the tautologies we might want to hear ("Prisoners are prisoners" [21]) to reinforce our subject positions. In this respect *Waiting for the Barbarians* provides not only a profound experience but also the analytical terms for understanding it, and the practices for teaching it. Like the Magistrate's experience, the novel is one that will not allow us to "settle." As teachers-readers-students we should allow ourselves to straddle the inside/outside of this book, to recognize the extent to which we are, as outsiders, inside its regions of Empire. Teaching Coetzee's subject, we are, in this doubled sense, teaching ourselves.

Teaching *Disgrace* in my South African Literature and Politics course in some ways provides an enormous contrast. For one thing, by the time we reach the novel, students are well primed with all kinds of material. We have watched the Granada-PBS series *Apartheid* (made in the 1980s), for history, place, voice, and landscape (*Frontline*). We have read Nadine Gordimer's *July's People* and Njabulo Ndebele's *Fools*, as well as the latter's essays on storytelling and the role of literature in the South African context. For drama we have studied (and on occasion watched) *The Island*, by Athol Fugard, John Kani, and Winston Ntshona, perhaps the most powerful play of the apartheid period. We have read poetry from the 1970s through to the 1990s (in Denis Hirson's anthology), and the short stories of Zoë Wicomb, and later we will read Zakes Mda's *Ways of Dying* and view *Amandla: A Revolution in Four-Part Harmony*. For *Disgrace* there is supplementary material: Coetzee's "Confession and Double Thoughts," and his views on the relation between history and fiction in South Africa. We discuss the Truth and Reconciliation Commission, as well as rape and HIV-AIDS. More recent iterations of the course include much in the way of postapartheid literature.

From that point of view, students are well prepared. But there is also a sense in which they cannot be prepared, for one way or another this is a novel that grips them. The teaching experience of the novel is for me a fascinating one. Students are both inside and outside the novel, as I am, in that initially this is a book about a professor's relationship with his students. They are, invariably, disgusted by the actions of this old man, and there is some uneasy laughter when I point out that I am, currently, in David Lurie's age range. For their part, what do they think of David's view of his students as "[p]ost-Christian, posthistorical, postliterate" (*Disgrace* 32)? Already the novel is doing its work. There is tremendous debate on the tribunal David faces: Should he confess? What is the difference between admission and confession, the discourses of law and repentance? Later there are other, related debates: on Lucy's own refusal to confess her story of having been raped, her accommodation with Petrus, and whether or in what sense David is redeemed at the end. Characteristically, opinions are divided on all these questions. As counterpoint we touch on David's banjo-strung opera, with its tale of female survival and art leading the artist. David's free indirect discourse stages his consciousness as both subject and object, inside and outside, and that too is part of our discussion in its wider implications.

But I want to focus briefly here on one major matter that concentrates, in a different way, some of the points I have been raising. This is the attack on Lucy, the fact that it is carried out by three vicious black men, one of whom may be mentally retarded. There have been denunciations both public and private of this in the South African world: as proof of white South Africans' racism, or of Coetzee's racism; as at best an unwise topic for a work of fiction in a dawning postapartheid moment. The question arises: Why would Coetzee do such a thing?

One point is clear: the form the event takes is not in any simple way an unconscious development. The iconography and staging of the scenario (black men raping white women) comes out of the copybook of hundreds of years of racial history in South Africa and beyond. Coetzee, who early in his career wrote on patterns of "blood, taint, flaw, degeneration" in the work of Sarah Gertrude Millin ("Blood"), would know exactly the provenance of such images, and their weight. He, as much as any writer, has in novels such as *Dusklands*, *In The Heart of the Country*, and *Foe* dissected the inner contours of colonial consciousness, including colonial racial and sexual consciousness. The discourse of such consciousness has been one of his primary topics. Yet here it appears to show in a different form, not as the subject of the novel but as a central part of the novel's matrix; without it, the novel, in this shape, would not exist. Is this rape the price others pay for David's redemption at the end of the novel—if that is how we are to understand his trajectory? Are there two sets of victims here, both Lucy and the men in the novel's projection who rape her? Whereas Lucy's silence in the novel is respected, what voice or presence is there in the novel for these men beyond the brutality of their actions? There is a mirroring for David Lurie in his own treatment of Melanie—the dark one, his student: "Not rape. Not quite that, but . . . undesired to the core" (25). But this event may seem of a different order.

I put the case strongly, because I feel that is how it has to be put if I am not going to gloss over it, as teacher, as reader, or simply (if it is ever that simple) in human terms. And yet I continue to teach this novel: I too am making choices. Do I teach it in the way I teach *Heart of Darkness*, as an inner exploration of the history of which we are still a part? That may get closer to it. And certainly one can have all these discussions in the classroom, putting us back on that boundary of both inside and outside. Our students too must be introduced to the price of their interpretations, their own potential complicities as magistrates of this (or any other) text. Is Coetzee's focus on the rape a way of confronting us—a way of demonstrating, through nothing less than provocation, that there is another subject in the novel, one that may incorporate it, one we will have to work hard to comprehend?

I would like to suggest a few possibilities here, and not only in a spirit of generosity. Some of them exist on more profane levels of the logical. For instance, rape, sometimes accentuated by race, is an epidemic in South Africa; this is a reality and must be faced. Or, it may be that Coetzee's focus here—deliberately, provocatively—is not on race but power and the violence that emanates in a specific moment of transition. A crucial dimension of this is male power and its abuses—just as David has abused it in his more civilized way. The rape and its aftermath may be about the link between territory and terror, or, as David suggests, the return of the repressed of five hundred years of colonial history. On one level it is about the reality and afterlife of subjection: the struggles over self, land, and placement that Petrus and (very likely) the men have confronted and that Lucy now confronts in her negotiations with Petrus. This may, in Lucy's life—and to some extent in David's—be about ways to construct a future that does not simply repeat, in altered forms, the violence of the past. From this point of view, Coetzee may be as "dogged" a writer as David is a character.[3] This is the vision that came to him, and this is the vision he will stick to. No confessions, explanations, or atonements here: this is fiction, and as Coetzee has reminded us, it follows the rules of a different "game" ("Novel Today").

The rape cannot be separated from the question of sacrifice at the end of the novel, but how is it connected? It is not simply a price but a relation, a relation between David and Lucy, David and the dog, David and the rapists, David and in some sense himself: his free indirect discourse, both inside and outside. That is one reason why there is no redemption in the novel, because there can be no ultimate, singular state, no movement beyond a grammar of the "imperfect" to the closure of the perfective (Sanders, *Ambiguities* 178). Rather there is, if anything, only the oscillating boundary suggested in the novel's title word, *dis/grace*. There are also boundaries of language and understanding. When David suggests the meanings of the rape to Lucy, she resists, and she resists through silence. Perhaps we too should allow that silence to come through. To denounce the rape is one thing, but to allegorize it may in some sense be to recommit it: the Magistrate's reading of the barbarian woman's torture. Who, in the end, will account for violence in the universe and death in our world? This is not the same question as that of responsibility, but perhaps the novel addresses the issue in a different way. David turns to the dog: what counts is an approach, a compassion, the renunciation of any claim or possession in presence for the other; and for David this is the "I" giving the "him" in "himself" up as well.

From that point of view we may have to give it up too, to allow the end of the novel to come through in the ways it does for so many, as intensely moving—and to understand the illumination in that shift: the profound nexus between suffering and attention. We may need to give up control of the text for the opera (derivation: "work") of the fiction to occur, not only as analysis but experience. In this we neither absolve nor do we stand outside. No matter the directions we come from, in following Coetzee's subject the way it has led him too as a writer, we are again tracking ourselves not from on high but inside the maze of our responsibilities and complicities. If we take it seriously, the principles that inform the novel become the form of our teaching. The novel becomes our indirect discourse, both free and unfree, the nature of our subject.

NOTES

[1] My use of *complicity* in this chapter is inflected by a reading of Sanders, *Complicities*.

[2] For a more sustained analysis in this vein, see Clingman, ch. 6.

[3] A suggestion made later about John Coetzee by one of the characters in Coetzee's *Summertime* (197).

Coetzee's Other Other:
An Existential Approach to Teaching *Disgrace*

Erik Grayson

As an instructor of existential literature courses at a large research institution, I have had the opportunity to teach students schooled in the postmodern traditions favored by research professors educated during the 1970s and 1980s heyday of poststructuralism, students accustomed to deconstructing texts and locating the possible social, political, gender, and economic (among others) codes that have shaped them. Whether it is the result of the often abstruse, anfractuous language common among theorists or the distant (or hypothetical) cultures discussed in their texts, those of my students familiar with postmodern, poststructural, and postcolonial theory often complain of feeling disconnected from what to them seems an overly academic, hyperintellectualized, and in some cases irrelevant body of thought. Enter J. M. Coetzee, whose fiction indisputably appeals to the same theorists my students claim not to get. Coetzee, an author whose work regularly includes references to Franz Kafka and Fyodor Dostoevsky and who wrote his doctoral dissertation on Samuel Beckett, is an easy—if unconventional—addition to a syllabus, foregrounding existential theory that is more accessible (and, some would argue, more relevant) in a class populated by disaffected poststructuralists.

A central concern for existentialists, poststructuralists, and postcolonial scholars is the figure of the other. The other happens to be a prominent topic in the literary criticism pertaining to Coetzee's Booker Prize–winning *Disgrace*. Thus, whether the focus is on David Lurie's inability to be the woman or on his fixation about how he appears to another person, a discussion of the other in *Disgrace* enables students to trace a distinct conceptual lineage from the phenomenological-existential concerns of Jean-Paul Sartre through the existentially oriented lens of Simone de Beauvoir's gender studies into Emmanuel Lévinas's Derridean-filtered existentialism and into the postcolonial studies of Edward Said and Gayatri Spivak. Ultimately, the intensely individual-focused, consciousness-centered concerns of existentialism help students better appreciate the alienation of Coetzee's characters, while the more sociopolitically oriented foci of poststructural and postcolonial studies help them perceive the often hidden catalysts for the existential malaise of the characters.

Course Rationale and Development

Existential Literature, like many 300-level courses offered through my English department at Binghamton University, is a reading-intensive, discussion-based class targeted at upper-level English majors and similarly advanced undergraduate students. Although it is listed in the university's course catalog as a literature seminar, Existential Literature has clear interdisciplinary implications and so requires students to read philosophical writing alongside the novels and plays one would expect to find on an English syllabus. Since Existential Literature is a seminar, I have been able to design and teach it with the assumption that many of the English and comparative literature students enrolled have already been exposed to a wide range of theoretical approaches to literary study. I also assume that the handful of registered nonmajors anticipate that they will be facing material more difficult than what is encountered in an introductory or intermediate English class. Even so, I expect students who enter my classroom to have only an elementary idea of existentialism. I devote the first third of the class to introducing the movement through a combination of philosophical readings, student presentations focused on key figures and theoretical issues, and the works of literature most closely associated with existential thought.

We begin with Sartre's "Existentialism Is a Humanism," which succinctly introduces such crucial notions as the presupposition that an individual's existence precedes an individual's essence, that humankind is condemned to freedom, that anxiety is a central component of existence, and that there is no fundamental moral code providing the individual with a blueprint for proper or right action. We build on this foundation with selections from Sartre's *Being and Nothingness* that discuss the figure of the other, playacting, and bad faith, all of which become unifying themes in the course. We move to Albert Camus and the question of absurdity before doubling back and visiting the ideas of Søren Kierkegaard, Friedrich Nietzsche, and Martin Heidegger, on which Sartre, Camus, and the group of mid-twentieth-century French intellectuals most commonly associated with existentialism built their systems of thought. When students have been given concepts like the leap of faith, angst, alienation, the collapse of moral authority, and the unswerving certainty of individual finitude, we examine canonical texts by Beckett, Camus, Sartre, and Kafka that dramatize them.

Why Teach Coetzee in an Existentialism Course?

When I began developing Existential Literature, I first had to address the question, What makes literature existential? Many instructors understandably limit themselves to canonical texts by the widely anthologized existentialists active during the middle part of the twentieth century, especially philosopher-novelists like Camus and Sartre. Courses on existential literature include pre-existential writers like Kafka. But few teachers actively challenge the boundaries of the existential canon by integrating postmodern literature into their classes. Perhaps they perceive nineteenth- and twentieth-century existential philosophy as anachronistic, not applying to works that came later. Believing this approach to be too narrow and wanting to examine the ways in which existential philosophy can illuminate the complex problems of human life in any epoch, I decided not to confine myself by constructing a course solely out of the literature traditionally anthologized in collections such as Linda Patrik's *Existential Literature: An Introduction*. Instead, I drew on texts from any era that addressed the concerns of existential philosophy, giving particular emphasis to the postmodern and postcolonial literature my students were likely to encounter in other English or comparative literature courses; in this way I hoped to encourage a broader range of interpretation in their future reading. The final two-thirds of the course challenges the traditional understanding of existential literature by incorporating texts by Horace McCoy, Chuck Palahniuk, Kurt Vonnegut, and Coetzee. In our discussions, students question canonical existentialist views on nihilism (through McCoy's *They Shoot Horses, Don't They?* and Palahniuk's *Choke*), on role-playing (through *Choke*), on individual freedom (through Vonnegut's *Slaughterhouse-Five*), and on how the other influences one's identity and consciousness (through Coetzee's *Disgrace*).

From the Postcolonial Other to the Phenomenological-Existential Other

The figure of the other has been a major topic of discourse among postcolonial theorists since at least the publication of Frantz Fanon's *Black Skin, White Masks* in 1952. Discussions of the role of the other frequently consider how literature confronts and interrogates the inability or calculated unwillingness of the colonizing power to comprehend the reality of the subaltern, the colonized. Postcolonial readings of Coetzee's fiction tend to emphasize the difficulties that figures such as Jacobus Coetzee (in *Dusklands*), the Magistrate (in *Waiting for the Barbarians*), the medical officer (in *Life & Times of Michael K*), Susan Barton (in *Foe*), Elizabeth Curren (in *Age of Iron*), and David Lurie (in *Disgrace*) have in accepting the alterity of and coexisting with the racially, religiously, linguistically, culturally, and sexually dispossessed—respectively, the Hottentots, the barbarian girl, Michael K, Friday, Vercueil, and Melanie Isaacs. Many critics of Coetzee's oeuvre seem to agree with Spivak, who argues that "the project of imperialism has always already historically refracted what might have been the absolutely Other into a domesticated Other that consolidates the imperialist self" ("Three Women's Texts" 253); they read *Disgrace* as fundamentally about the failure and consequences of the colonizer's impulse to negate the agency of the colonized.

Not surprisingly, those of my students familiar with postcolonial theory tend to read David's aggressive sexual pursuit of the reluctant Melanie as an allegory of the refusal of South African whites to recognize the autonomy of the Rainbow Nation's colored population in the postapartheid era. Allegorical readings of the book do appear to answer key interpretive questions, but this approach to Coetzee's fiction rarely satisfies students who have come to know and feel for the characters. Their dissatisfaction, I find, originates in the widespread use or misuse of literature to illustrate highly contentious and politicized concepts such as Spivak's of the imperialistic drive to tame the uncivilized other, a tendency that has, as David Attwell notes in an early essay on *Disgrace*, resulted in "an over-heated discussion about what is the *least complex*—and arguably least interesting—area of the novel's performance: its socially mimetic function" among many of Coetzee's readers ("Race" 332).[1] Incorporating the phenomenological-existential ideas of being toward death and being for others (with the anxiety one experiences on recognizing that the existence of others threatens one's sense of self) into a discussion of Coetzee's fiction encourages students to shift their focus from deciphering the author's meaning or message to exploring human experience at its richest and most nuanced. It also prevents the artist from being reduced to a pedant.

Disgrace: *The Problem of Sex and the Problem of the Other*

In Existential Literature, I usually begin our discussion of *Disgrace* by asking my students to reexamine the scene in which David Lurie forces himself on Melanie Isaacs in an act that the narrator informs us is "[n]ot rape, not quite that, but undesired nevertheless, undesired to the core" (25). As we discuss the professor's impression of himself as a libertine driven by passion, I encourage students to find the root of David's seemingly unchecked libido so that we may better understand what motivated him to assault the girl. With the help of a few guiding questions (What do we know about David's attitude towards sex? Does anything in the text suggest that his pursuit of women is motivated by something other than sensual gratification?), our discussion generally turns to David's arrangement with Soraya, the prostitute with whom he spends his Thursday afternoons at the outset of the novel. I like to draw my students' attention to the novel's opening line, in which the narrator informs us that "[f]or a man of his age, fifty-two, divorced, he has, to his mind, solved the problem of sex rather well" (1), a passage that suggests that David views sex less as a pleasurable activity than as a knot he must untangle. The next question I pose to the class is, Why is sex a problem for David? When students look more closely at the text, one possible answer emerges: David senses that it is difficult "for a man of his age" to find a woman to sleep with him. Evidence of this anxiety emerges at the beginning of the second paragraph, when we see him attempt to justify the broad age gap separating him from Soraya: "Technically, he is old enough to be her father; but then, technically, one can be a father at twelve" (1).

At this stage in the analysis, my students draw on two readings from earlier in the course: Martin Heidegger's discussion of being toward death in *Being and Time* and Sartre's concept of being for others in *Being and Nothingness*. In reference to the former, my students point out that when David begins to notice how "[g]lances that would once have responded to his slid over, past, through him," he entered into "an anxious flurry of promiscuity," a phrase that highlights the unease that has taken over his sex life (7). His "flurry of promiscuity" is like the last-ditch sprint of a runner afraid of losing a marathon or a shopkeeper's drastic lowering of prices in an effort to help pay the bills. David can feel the sand draining from the hourglass, so he attempts to bed as many women as he can before the last grain is emptied. In other words, the "problem of sex" he claims to have solved in the first sentence of the novel is also the problem of his approaching death. Having discussed selections from Heidegger's *Being and Time*, my students are quick to suggest this connection.

The theme of aging continues throughout the first third of *Disgrace*. Indeed, long before Rosalind calls him "[s]tupid and ugly" for presuming to "think a young girl finds any pleasure in going to bed with a man of [his] age" (44), David perceives himself as "on the point of joining . . . the tramps and drifters with their stained raincoats and cracked teeth and hairy earholes" on account of his "clinging to the last to [his] place at the sweet banquet of the senses" (24) as he pursues the uninterested Melanie.

I encourage students to recall Sartre's being for others. The existence of the other, Sartre tells us, implies the "permanent possibility of *being seen* by the Other," the awareness of which leads the individual to see himself or herself as the other might (344). Once the individual enters this state, the individual passes judgment on himself or herself as an object whose foundation remains firmly in the other's control. The unsettling sense of self as object that re-sults through the recognition of the other's gaze moves the individual toward being for others. David enters his "flurry of promiscuity" only after feeling that "[g]lances that would once have responded to his slid over, past, through him." His abundant use of sight-related language throughout the text reveals how painfully aware he is of the other's look. He reflects that "[p]erhaps it is the right of the young to be protected from the sight of their elders in the throes of passion" when Rosalind insists it is impossible that "a young girl finds it good to watch [a man of David's age] in the middle of" sexual activity (44). His internal-ization of the negative assessment of his appearance by the other is so power-ful that, by the time he sleeps with Bev Shaw toward the end of the book, he disparagingly describes himself in terms like those he first feared Soraya would apply to him: "Let her gaze her fill on her Romeo, he thinks, on his bowed shoulders and skinny shanks" (150).

Since David begins defining himself as an unattractive old man only after he imagines how others—particularly younger women—see him, we can say that he exists in a state of bad faith, because the other is the source of the iden-tity he has embraced. In Sartrean existentialism, the individual living in bad faith will often attempt to recover freedom of self-definition by assimilating the other's freedom. Significantly, Sartre cites sexual desire as a prime example of this dynamic. The carnal impulse, for Sartre, represents the individual's efforts to reduce the other to a purely corporeal form and, furthermore, to make the other recognize his or her fundamental objectivity. So it should come as no sur-prise that David attempts to convince Melanie that "her beauty does not belong to her alone. . . . She does not own herself" (16). When his flirtation fails and the young woman expresses no reciprocal desire for him, he begins to wrestle with the possibility that he is "an ugly sight" (9). Moreover, as our discussion of Heidegger highlights, because David views sexual conquest as evidence that he need not "turn his mind to the proper business of the old: preparing to die" just yet (9), it is reasonable to ask if it is the state of bad faith into which Melanie's lack of interest thrusts him that leads to his violence toward the girl, a violence that sets the entire novel's action in motion.

One of the challenges I face in teaching Existential Literature is finding a way to show how what many people regard as a dated philosophical movement can be a valuable tool in understanding the motivations behind the sociopolitical realities of the contemporary world. *Disgrace*, with its deeply political implications about race and gender relations, is an ideal addition to the course. When contemporary postcolonial literature is introduced into a discussion of ideas more commonly associated with nineteenth- and twentieth-century Continental philosophy, students are able to appreciate fiction as part of a larger exchange of ideas that, while often separated into studies of specific periods or thematic schemas, need not be so rigidly segregated. It is my hope that Existential Literature will prompt my students to challenge accepted readings of literature and be more willing to take the sorts of critical chances that result in new ways of thinking about important texts.

NOTE

[1] For a comprehensive analysis of this "over-heated discussion," see Easton.

Reading Coetzee's Worldliness

Johan Geertsema

How are we to read Coetzee and teach his work? His novels strongly resist our attempts to fit them into neat interpretations. Thus any attempt to read *Disgrace* as an allegory of postapartheid South Africa or, more broadly, of the postcolonial nation is doomed. The text may lend itself to such an allegorical reading, and students are often keen to read it this way, but *Disgrace* works to disrupt an allegorical reading by refusing to answer the unsettling questions that it raises. Why does Lucy decide to keep the child after she is raped? Why does she accept the offer by Petrus to become his third wife or concubine? What are we to make of the ending of the text, when David Lurie gives up the dog to which he has become so attached? If the text is an allegory of racism, apartheid, or the nation, what does the prominent presence of animals in it signify?

Despite this disruption of reading in *Disgrace*, the act of reading is as central in it as in Coetzee's other texts. For instance, *Summertime*, the most recent of his fictionalized memoirs, is made up of fragments and interviews to which the reader, who is also a writer figure, must try to lend coherence. The text takes up the story of a young writer, Coetzee, who has returned from the United States to Cape Town, where he now, in the 1970s, lives with his father in straitened circumstances. The first of the interviews, being conducted for a book on Coetzee by a young English biographer, is with Julia Frankl, who supposedly knew Coetzee at the time. Attempting to explain why she seduced Coetzee, she refers to the actions of characters in a novel, then asks, "What are books for if not to change our lives?" (34). Julia's rhetorical question insists on the power of reading. It is pedagogical: reading can change our lives. This idea is central to Coetzee's writing. Despite critics' tendency to read *Disgrace* as allegorical, even otherworldly, I argue in this essay that Coetzee's work is marked by a radical worldliness of the kind insisted on by Edward Said, who consistently sought to change the lives of those who read him. Coetzee's writing, however, when placed alongside Said's, shows the easy anthropocentrism of Said's humanist vision.

My emphasis on the pedagogical character of Coetzee's work may at first glance seem surprising, because for a long time, since the dark days of 1980s South Africa, his work has stubbornly opposed attempts to co-opt it into any particular agenda. It seems anything but didactic.[1] Yet pedagogy is evident everywhere in it. "Now my eyes are open and I can never close them again" (95), Mrs. Curren, a retired classics professor, thinks to herself in *Age of Iron* during her confrontation with the Socratic Mr. Thabane, who has shown her the horrific reality of army violence in a township under emergency rule. But once she has seen, the novel considers the question of what she can do in response. *Elizabeth Costello*'s subtitle is *Eight Lessons*, though what exactly these lessons teach is unclear. *Disgrace* starts off as a campus novel that then, after Lurie's fall from grace, traces a reversal of roles: it is the professor now who must learn or, rather, unlearn. As Michael Marais has pointed out, "there is much evidence in *Disgrace* to support the claim that Coetzee has furnished this work with the structure of an anti-*Bildungsroman*, a novel which involves the forfeiture rather than consolidation of the protagonist's sense of self" (*Secretary* 175). Coetzee's complex texts, whether *Disgrace*, *Elizabeth Costello*, or *Age of Iron*, which ends in an embrace from which "no warmth was to be had" (181), have lessons, though these lessons are anything but straightforward. But then how might such a text affect a reader? How might it change our lives? Change occurs, I would argue, through its unsettling character, which is a consequence of its resistance to an allegorical reading that would buttonhole it and close it off. That is, Coetzee's work is powerful precisely in its resistance to straightforward readings, in its refusal to provide the reader with a comforting (a warming) embrace.

Readings that allegorize Coetzee, and in particular *Disgrace*, are common. In what is one of the most important scholarly contributions to date on Coetzee, Derek Attridge has analyzed what he terms "the urge to allegorize Coetzee" (*J. M. Coetzee* 39).[2] Attridge's argument is that allegorization smoothes over disjunctures, gaps, and differences and thereby reduces the rich, concrete experience of reading Coetzee's texts (see 46). Peter D. McDonald notes, with reference to the controversies the novel elicited shortly after publication, that the racialized African National Congress reading of the novel assumed that *Disgrace* was an allegory, an assumption also evident in the way the Booker Prize committee characterized this text ("*Disgrace* Effects" 326). But consider how *Disgrace* insists precisely on what is overlooked when readers, whether the Booker Prize committee or the ANC, or indeed our students, insert it into such preformed systems of interpretation: namely, the concrete materiality with which the text is concerned, a materiality that does not lend itself to some or other readily available meaning for the simple reason that what the text means, though it certainly means something, escapes our final grasp. But that returns us to the question of how to read and teach Coetzee if his texts escape reading and teaching.

It is here that Said's concept of worldliness can become useful. By *worldliness* I understand what Said would call a text's "circumstantiality" or "circumstantial reality" (*World* 34): its embroilment in the world, its irreducible connection with the work of culture and hence, through action, politics. In terms reminiscent of Hannah Arendt's use of this concept, Neil Lazarus glosses it with reference to Said's work as "an active searching out and public presentation of connections, contrasts and alternatives that shades necessarily and ineluctably into the framing and articulation of political demands" ("Representations" 117). Lazarus's definition points to the activist character of worldliness, its disturbing emphasis on material conditions and particular actions that can be universalized in the struggle for justice, which, for Said, is enabled by a critical distance to institutions.

I have taught *Disgrace* with Said's *Representations of the Intellectual*. Said draws out connections between literature and the real world and asks students of literature to become more self-aware in their reading practices. One needs to "universalize the crisis," to make links between texts and the concrete "sufferings of others" (44). Although allegorical readings certainly draw connections between a work and the real world, Said's reading practice insists not on characters and events standing in for real-world analogues but on the materiality with which the text is concerned. For Said, as for Coetzee, reading has an ethical dimension that is quite different from the universalizing of allegory, which tends precisely toward the elision of the particular. Coetzee's worldliness lies in the force of his work's resistance to dogmatic positions, in its constant querying of assumptions.[3]

My approach to *Disgrace* thus turns on the importance in it of the idea that conceptual abstraction means a reduction of concrete experience. The Russian formalist Viktor Shklovsky counteracts such "automatization" of experience with art: "in order to return sensations to our limbs, in order to make us feel objects, to make a stone feel stony, man has been given the tool of art" (6). He wants to poeticize the world by using the formal strangeness of poetry (which he deems the most concrete art) to reverse the alienation from the world attendant on, paradoxically, being immersed in it. For Shklovsky, the reader can experience the world anew through art, thereby becoming aware again of its materiality, and that awareness, that change of the reader's consciousness, can have liberating social consequences. Overly intellectualized abstraction for Said is the enemy of concrete worldliness. In *Representations*, he asserts that "activity in this secular world of ours—where it takes place, whose interests it serves" demands a consideration of material particularity. "[A]bstractions or orthodoxies" are quite literally otherworldly, in that they forget the materiality of the world (120).

Laura Wright observes that Coetzee's fiction works through a "performative displacement" that involves estrangement or deautomatization by insisting on the concrete materiality of being, of the "presentation of the animal as animal" (*Writing* 14, 15). She reads *Disgrace* alongside *The Lives of Animals*, paying particular attention to Coetzee's gendered performance of Elizabeth Costello as well as her subsequent displacement from the discourse of male critics who read the text (109–13). Wright interestingly connects this performance with the question that Lurie asks himself: "[D]oes he have it in him to be the woman?" (*Disgrace* 160).[4] This sentence appears in a passage in which he tries but fails to imagine the experience of rape from the perspective of Lucy, his daughter (though distressingly enough he finds himself successful in entering the perspective of the rapists).

It puzzles and unsettles readers of *Disgrace* that Lucy decides to keep the child she is carrying as a result of the rape. When I delivered a lecture on *Disgrace* at the University of Zurich in 2001, female students were in agreement that Coetzee could make Lucy do this only because he is male. But the text does prepare us for her decision to keep the baby: by refusing to press charges after the rape, she rejects her father's reading of the attack. Lurie's reading is that the rape is "revenge" (110), "vengeance" (112) for what Farodia Rassool, one of the committee members before whom Lurie earlier had to appear after his own sexual misconduct against the student Melanie Isaacs, calls a "long history of exploitation" (49). Lucy appears to be "meekly" accepting what has happened to her, thereby hoping, Lurie suggests, to "expiate the crimes of the past by suffering in the present" — in other words, the decades if not centuries of gendered racial oppression in South Africa. Yet Lucy responds, "No. You keep misreading me. Guilt and salvation are abstractions. I don't act in terms of abstractions. Until you make an effort to see that, I can't help you" (112).

Lucy is here rejecting Lurie's allegorical reading of her. This reading goes beyond the event and Lucy's bodily experience of it to see it as something else, part of a "long history of exploitation." Such allegorization works by eliding the concrete specificity with which Lucy must deal. But this specificity, Coetzee is suggesting, is something that neither Lurie nor the reader may render abstract by making it part of some larger, historical narrative. Respecting the specificity is an ethical imperative, as Marais has perceptively argued ("'Little'" 180–81).

To grasp the point we need to pay attention to the metafictional aspect of *Disgrace*, which is not immediately evident: Lucy characterizes her father as a reader when she asserts that he keeps "misreading" her. The novel thereby draws a parallel between Lurie and the readers of the text, who are reading not only the novel but also her response to the rape. Thus the readers are warned not to allegorize her experience.

Such an approach seems counterintuitive at first. Wouldn't the historicization that puts the rape of Lucy in a larger narrative of injustice and suffering make her plight more understandable? But Said's work helps us see that her refusal of this abstraction is an insistence on materiality. She will not be co-opted into any preformed system of signification. In its enigmatic alterity, her refusal is worldly in the most radical sense of that word. It indicates a respect for the suffering experienced by a particular person.

This respect for suffering is evident in all the work of Said, a suffering that knows no national or cultural boundaries. He defines an intellectual as

> [one who is] endowed with a faculty for representing, embodying, articu-
> lating a message, a view, an attitude, philosophy or opinion to, as well as
> for, a public. And this role . . . is publicly to raise embarrassing questions,
> to confront orthodoxy and dogma (rather than to produce them), to be
> someone who cannot easily be co-opted by governments or corporations,
> and whose *raison d'être* is to represent all those people and issues that are
> routinely forgotten or swept under the rug. The intellectual does so [i.e.,
> represents] on the basis of universal principles: that all human beings are
> entitled to expect decent standards of behavior concerning freedom and
> justice from worldly powers or nations, and that deliberate or inadvertent

violations of these standards need to be testified and fought against coura-
geously.   (*Representations* 11–12)

This passage suggests that Said's worldliness has an ethical blind spot; despite
his admirable insistence on the concrete materiality of political struggle and his
concomitant suspicion of the abstractions of "orthodoxy and dogma" that would,
in a Manichaean way, classify people as belonging to either of two sides—the
"innocently good" and the "irreducibly evil" (113)—his intellectual is concerned only with human beings.

The increasingly important place of nonhuman animals in Coetzee's work is
of a piece with the resistance to conceptual abstraction in his writing. Therefore the resistance of his work to allegorizing may be read as a more radical,
more stringent worldliness than Said's. Coetzee's preoccupation with suffering
exceeds Said's in its attention to animal life.[5] In *Disgrace*, this preoccupation
manifests itself in two striking ways: Lurie's changed attitude toward nonhuman
animals—from supposing that since he eats them, he must "like them, some
parts of them" (81) to being so moved by the mercy killings in which he assists
that he breaks down (142–43)—and Lucy's understanding of herself as animal.

If Lucy rejects her father's reading of her position, what might her own reading of it be? It is firmly grounded in what we might call, with Elizabeth Costello,
"the unabstracted, unintellectual nature" of "animal being" (*Elizabeth Costello*
111). This grounding is evident from her enigmatic agreement with Lurie's
characterization of her situation: in accepting Petrus's protection she is "like a
dog" (205). This phrase of course directly invokes the final sentence of Franz
Kafka's *The Trial*. It evinces, as David Attwell has remarked, Coetzee's "emphasis on ontology . . . shorn of system, and therefore inimical to philosophy"; this
is a "consciousness of what it means to be alive, sharing the precariousness of
creation's biological energy" ("Race" 340).

Disgrace by no means limits its concern to human suffering: it insists on "the
fact of a biological existence" that "humanity shares with all the earth's creatures" (339). It thereby questions Said's humanist prerogative. In its attention
to ontology, to the concrete materiality of animal existence, including that of human beings, *Disgrace* subverts the human-nonhuman hierarchy. But that then
returns us to the question as to how we will be able to read Coetzee's work at all,
if what it reaches toward is the unabstracted, unintellectual nature of not only
animals' but humans' concrete, entirely nonfigural animal being.

For what is reading if not the figuration of allegory? Reading as allegory
involves the "translation of other things, other lives, into the work of human
consciousness" (Levine 263), thereby making them accessible to that consciousness. But although human beings are animals, animals in their biological ani-
malness transcend human consciousness, which in George Levine's reading is
precisely the point of Elizabeth Costello's invocation in *Slow Man* of William
Blake's tiger (229) and in *Elizabeth Costello* of the frogs in which she proclaims
her belief (217).

Given the inevitable allegorization that the process of reading entails, we need as readers of Coetzee's work, when translating the irreducible other into human consciousness, to face the paradoxical challenge of reading the texts against themselves. Consisting as they do of words, they tend toward the very abstraction that reading Coetzee's worldliness places in question. In insisting on Coetzee's worldliness, not only can we understand his work better, but that work also may unwork itself in order to change readers by bringing them in touch with the concrete materiality of the suffering of others, and not only human others.

NOTES

In December 2010 I presented an earlier version of this essay to students and faculty members at the University of Paderborn, and I would like to offer my thanks to Christoph Ehland for the invitation to do so. Thanks are further due to student audiences in Singapore and Zurich with whom I have had the privilege of exploring Coetzee's work.

[1] In the 1980s and 1990s, Coetzee was a controversial figure in South Africa precisely because of the lack of the explicitly political in his work. In the short address "The Novel Today," delivered in 1987 in the context of the struggle against apartheid and the injunction by ANC-aligned organizations that writers use their work to further that struggle, he responded by expressing the belief that the novel is a "rival" to history rather than a mere "supplement" to it; therefore it is not a "handmaiden" in support of the power politics that shapes history (5). Art opposes politics; it offers a different kind of truth and in fact works to subvert the truth of politics. In other words, Coetzee was repudiating the instrumental use of art.

[2] Attridge demonstrates that allegorical readings reduce a text in two ways. First, they universalize it. Thus Coetzee's writing cannot be about anything in particular: for instance, *Disgrace* is not about the suffering of animals but about suffering as such. Second, an allegorical reading limits a text to one particular meaning: for example, *Disgrace* is an exemplification of South Africa's postapartheid condition (33). Because of this reductiveness, Attridge, though not entirely rejecting allegorical interpretations of Coetzee's work, argues for what he terms literal reading (39). It grounds "the experience of reading as an event": treating the text not as an object but as an entity that comes into being in the act of reading. By paying attention to the process of reading Coetzee's complex work, by being "responsive" to the text and immersing ourselves in it, "we participate in, and perhaps are changed by" it (48).

[3] Coetzee, like Said, opposes the dogmas and naturalized truths of rationality. Referring to the idea of the "new economic world order" — market capitalism — that most if not all governments and citizens accept as inevitable, he makes the point that an intellectual should confront these supposed "realities . . . precisely because they so confidently proclaim themselves realities." Coetzee calls them "a house of cards, a huge confidence trick" ("Critic" 110). Since 2007, the new economic world order has been exposed as questionable if not delusional.

[4] Wright takes this question as posed by a third-person narrator, not by Lurie. But a case could be made that this is an instance of free indirect discourse, that the reader is

being given access to Lurie's mind while, at the same time, standing at an ironic distance from his thoughts.

[5] As Coetzee puts it in an often quoted interview, "I, as a person, as a personality, am overwhelmed, [and] my thinking is thrown into confusion and helplessness, by the fact of suffering in the world, and not only human suffering" (*Doubling* 249).

Teaching the Critique
of Romanticism and Empire in *Disgrace*

Pieter Vermeulen

One of the challenges facing teachers of survey courses in literature written in English is to find teachable textual examples that ground the long-term narratives of modern literature that invariably subtend such a course. Teachers of modules on the contemporary novel or postcolonial literature face the same challenge, even if a grand literary-historical narrative is often only implicit in such a module. How do we let students appreciate the stakes of the historical shift from a narrowly English to a global or even planetary perspective? How do we trace literature's changing relation to the ethnic or sexual other? Or the way in which literature has registered its implication in networks of colonial, patriarchal, and anthropocentric power and attempted to develop strategies to reconfigure those networks?

One of the things that makes *Disgrace* such a rewarding novel to teach is that a detailed discussion of it will raise literary-historical and ethicopolitical issues in close connection to its plot. I have found that the strong responses that the plot invariably provokes in students can fruitfully be channeled toward complex questions of literary history and theory. Teaching a few passages in detail can present those questions in an exceptionally concrete and vivid way. This essay sketches the outlines of a class—or a series of classes—that begins by paying attention to the two scenes early in the novel in which David Lurie, its main character, is teaching Byron and Wordsworth. This in-depth reading lays bare the parallels and interactions between these intertexts and other important themes. It also opens onto theoretical and ethicopolitical questions and the long-term dynamics of modern literary history. *Disgrace* makes it possible to combine these two pedagogical purposes. Not only does it evoke Wordsworth and Byron in a way that identifies them with a particular ethics, aesthetics, and politics but it also clearly embodies this Romantic position in the character of Lurie at the beginning of the novel. As the plot, keeping its focus on Lurie, tracks the disintegration of his perspective during his confrontation with the new South African reality, we can track the fate of a particular ethics and aesthetics in a postcolonial, globalized world in a way that points more broadly to the historical dynamics of modern literature. While the plight of the disgraced and displaced Lurie reflects the fate of the literary ethos he embodies, the surprising trajectory of his engagement with Byron in the course of the novel underlines why an older literary ethos is widely felt to have become obsolete and also gestures toward a less grandiose literary practice and a more worldly and inclusive ethics. This story is one of the stories of modern literature.

It may seem that I am teaching *Disgrace* as an allegory because I am teaching it in parallel with literary history. The appropriateness of an allegorical approach has been a main bone of contention in Coetzee criticism. Allegory is often criticized for its derealization of historical and political contexts and its tendency to lose itself in metafictional abstraction. In my experience, such reservations hardly apply in pedagogical contexts, because a course designed to cover a particular genre, a particular phenomenon (such as postcolonial literature), or a part of literary history will always locate particular works or passages in an overarching framework. The challenge is to engage students on the particular and general levels at the same time.

Through the association with Romanticism in the passages in which Lurie is teaching Wordsworth and Byron, two poets to whom he also feels a personal affinity, his imminent disgrace suggests that the canonical literature he teaches has suffered a backlash in the age of postcolonialism and inspired literary projects that aim to rewrite that tradition or write back to it. His disgrace illustrates the untenability of an ethos and poetics that have not adapted to the altered circumstances in which contemporary literature functions. Because his teaching of Romantic poetry is thoroughly implicated in the plot of his affair with Melanie, these passages also allow students to appreciate how literature is always open to the ideological and pedagogical uses and abuses of power. I confront Lurie's interpretations with brief excerpts from the two poems he is teaching (Wordsworth's *The Prelude* and Byron's *Lara*), to highlight the importance of a critical approach that is attentive to textual detail and to demonstrate how that detail can reveal a text's implication in networks of power.

First I ask students to locate Lurie's classes in the novel's plot—that is, their relation to his evolving relationship with Melanie and his functioning in the university community. Then I put these intertexts in a broader context by explaining that they can be linked to two complementary positions, imperialist and orientalist: the imperialist denies the other's difference (*Prelude*); the orientalist treats the other as exotic and strongly gendered (*Lara*). I ask students to sum up the lessons Lurie derives from (or imposes on) these texts, in order to identify the ethos that characterizes his desire and failure to take into account the resistance that reality and other people put up against that desire. In graduate or in advanced undergraduate courses, I compare Lurie's facile interpretation of the poems with their actual text to show that his distortion of the poetry is in line with his disregard for reality. The connection between his colonization of reality and his careless reading method gives students a sense of what motivates contemporary critiques and revisions of traditional literary practices.

The novel's two scenes of teaching do not require much specific knowledge about either Byron or Wordsworth. As Lurie—not Coetzee (Beard 59–62)—initially projects a rather commonplace image of these two poets, a couple of key elements are sufficient: Byron's association with Don Juan, Wordsworth as the poet of nature or as a political apostate, and so on. It is clear from the beginning that Lurie closely identifies with Wordsworth's poetry, with what the novel calls "the harmonies of *The Prelude*" (Coetzee, *Disgrace* 13). His disgrace signals the distortion of those harmonies: Lurie is called a "disgraced disciple" of

Wordsworth, and the novel stammers phrases from the "Infant Babe" passage, one of the key scenes in *The Prelude*: "Blest be the infant babe. No outcast he. Blest be the babe" (46; see Wordsworth, *Prelude* 2.232–66).

Lurie's class on Wordsworth (21–23) immediately follows a scene in which Melanie has for the first time dared to refuse him, citing a theater rehearsal as an excuse (20–21)—which will not prevent his unsolicited visit to that rehearsal in the scene following the class (23–24). For the class on Wordsworth, I underline two things: first, the relation between reality (or the senses) and the imagination in the passage from *The Prelude* that Lurie teaches; second, his infelicitous attempt to translate Wordsworth's English account of a European experience (of Mont Blanc) to South Africa. That the interpretation is overdetermined by the scene's place in the novel's plot reminds us that all interpretation is shaped by ideologies and desires. I emphasize that the demotion of sensory experience in Wordsworth's and Lurie's theory of the imagination is linked to the failure to appreciate the difference between an English-European and African perspective. Because that failure is linked also to Lurie's indifference to Melanie's perspective in their illicit relationship—an indifference underwritten by the novel's relentless first-person perspective—we can see how Lurie's disgrace also signals the demise of the Romantic literary ethos, and of the questionable geopolitics such an ethos has historically sustained.

Wordsworth describes his perception of Mont Blanc as a process in which "a living thought" is "usurped upon" by "a soulless image" (6.527–28; Coetzee, *Disgrace* 21). Lurie remarks that Wordsworth is looking for a way to allow the imagination and "the onslaughts of reality" to coexist (22). Yet when he fast-forwards to Wordsworth's famous invocation of the imagination as a power that compensates for the shortcomings of sensory experience (593–609), it is clear that he is aiming not for adequacy or consistency but rather for a covert justification of his own pursuit of sexual gratification. In line with his earlier attempt to seduce Melanie with the help of references to Byron and a spectacular mobilization of the first line of Shakespeare's first sonnet (15–16), he is willfully reading into Wordsworth a theory of the imagination in which reality's resistance to imaginative transformation counts for very little. A corollary of this disrespect for that resistance is his disregard for Wordsworth's actual phrasing: even if the second passage "perhaps even contradicts" the first, he declares that Wordsworth is "[n]evertheless" moving toward a resolution (22).

The irony of Lurie's conviction that the imagination can counterbalance "the onslaughts of reality" is clear in the light of the rest of the novel, in which the reality of the new South Africa hits Lurie hard indeed. Belief in the transformative power of the imagination is of course a staple of Romanticism—one can refer to Coleridge's theory of the imagination in his *Biographia Literaria* or to Jerome Christensen's helpful formula for the quintessential Romantic ethics and poetics: "to live a life in which those accidents that befall us do not make us despondent . . . a life self-governed by the restorative application of poetic form to what appears as given" (205). Wordsworth is a prominent example of this ethos. Book 12 of *The Prelude* is entitled "Imagination and Taste, How Impaired and Restored," a phrase that captures the dynamic of the whole poem and points to the limited role that real-life accidents play in the strain of Romanticism that Coetzee's novel criticizes.

Romantic commitment to the resilience of the imagination in the face of historical disaster is an English coinage, and one aspect of cultural imperialism is surely the assumption that this coinage unproblematically works in alien contexts. Lurie's class offers an example of this mind-set when Lurie compares Wordsworth's Alps with the Drakensberg or Table Mountain (23). His life on the farm will teach him that this ethics and aesthetics is a product of an essentially European landscape experience. To defamiliarize the mutual exaltation of nature and self that marks the European sublime, it is instructive—and entertaining—to refer to Aldous Huxley's essay "Wordsworth in the Tropics," which both recognizes the formative role of a Wordsworthian aesthetics for the English mind and marks the limits of that aesthetics. Huxley notes that "most serious-minded people are now Wordsworthians" but that a Wordsworthian belief in a person's communion "with the field and waters, the woodlands and the hills" is seriously challenged when one visits the tropics, where nature is "always alien and inhuman, and occasionally diabolic" (113, 117). "The Wordsworthian adoration of Nature" is possible only "in a country where Nature has been nearly or quite enslaved to man"; in the tropics a person "is an alien in the midst of an innumerable throng of hostile beings" (116, 115). I link Huxley's insistence on "the diversity and utter strangeness" of nature (128) to Coetzee's remarks, in his book *White Writing*, on the insufficiency of a Wordsworthian aesthetic to cover the vastness and emptiness of the South African landscape. This insufficiency resonates with Lurie's disorientation and sense of loss after his displacement to his daughter's farm. Huxley's tropics underline the superabundance of nature, but Coetzee's South Africa highlights nature's paucity: the land "remains trackless, refuses to emerge into meaningfulness" (*White Writing* 9). Nor can the emphasis on verticality in the European sublime find any application on the South African plateau (52). Again, *Disgrace* showcases the insufficiency of a particular aesthetic and the need for contemporary literature to develop new strategies. One new strategy is followed in the development of Lurie's Byron project.

The class on Byron's *Lara* is situated at a charged moment in the plot: it is a coded attempt at self-justification directed not only at Melanie but also at the rest of the students. That Lurie has just been confronted by Melanie's boyfriend, who shows up in the lecture hall (30–31) adds resonance to Lurie's discussion of Byron's stranger (32), a resonance that multiplies in the light of Lurie's equally incongruous attendance at Melanie's rehearsal just before. *Lara* is rarely part of a course in which *Disgrace* is taught, but a few markers can implicate it in the literary-historical narrative that *Disgrace* teaches. One of Byron's *Oriental Tales*, *Lara* is an important document in the history of orientalism. This intertext makes it possible to teach a face of empire that differs from the one we saw before: whereas Lurie's class on *The Prelude* illustrates the suppression of difference, his take on *Lara* illustrates the construction of difference (Davis 198–201). The excerpts from the poem's eighteenth canto that are printed in the novel show that Byron presents Lara—traditionally considered a typical instance of the Byronic hero—as an exotic other, "[a]n erring spirit from another [world]" (32; Byron, line 316). Lurie's interpretation irons out the ambivalences and tensions that constitute the Byronic hero in order to sell Lara as an advocate of desire and therefore as an apology for his own pursuit of sexual gratification. Lara is "a being who chooses his own path, who lives dangerously," yet for all that "we are not asked to condemn this being with the mad heart" (32–33). Lurie's doctored version of Lara—the similarity of the two names deserves to be noted—has clear affinities to the Wordsworthian ethos, in which the transformative power of the imagination is not hindered by the claim of reality: indifferent to moral law or custom, Lurie's Lara just follows his instinct in the pursuit of his desire.

Yet the forty-seven lines of the section Lurie is teaching make clear that Lara's indifference and world-weariness are not a freely adopted posture but rather the painful result of his experiences. Byron's poem, in other words, is not a canonical source that can provide authority for Lurie's behavior. I use this realization to reemphasize that, first, the transmission and reception of literature often have an agenda and, second, that a properly critical approach pays attention to textual material that exposes agendas. Lurie excerpts lines that present Lara as a "thing of dark imaginings, that shaped / by choice the perils he by chance escaped" (32; Byron, lines 317–18) but fails to note that the next line of the poem adds that these willful transformations try to escape reality "in vain" (319). The passage Lurie skips (317–37) explains that Lara became a solitary figure not by choice but because the events of his life crushed his initial "capacity for love" and his "early dreams of good" (321, 323). Lara's indifference is a matter of despair rather than of desire; his character illustrates not the consequences of the decision to live by one's own rules but the traumatizing impact that reality can have on the mind; his is "[t]he stinging of a heart the world hath stung" (74).

The irony is that when read properly, *Lara*, instead of supporting Lurie's case for the rights of desire, accurately prefigures his condition after his disgrace, when Lurie is ruthlessly exposed to a South African reality for which Romanticism fails to prepare him. The novel's names for the fate of his desire after his disgrace are *despair* and *indifference*: after the attack against his daughter, Lurie is "without desires, indifferent to the future" (107); "[t]he blood of life is leaving his body and despair is taking its place" (108). He discovers that solitude and silence are not always a matter of choice—as in his refusal to confess in front of the committee—but can come from a radical inability to communicate with and relate to others. Again, a turn of the plot allows us to apprehend a literary-historical dynamic: Lurie's displacement coincides with the moment when an English literary tradition proves incapable of addressing complex new realities, and this incapacity motivates contemporary critiques and revisions of that tradition. Note the novel's development of the line from Wordsworth that Lurie uses to excuse his sensual behavior: ". . . the light of sense / Goes out, but with a flash that has revealed / The invisible world" (22; lines 601–03). The image of the flash is soon literalized in the rather dismal special effects in the play in which Melanie is playing a part (24, 192), and during the assault on the farm Lurie himself becomes the candle that "leaps up one last time," "at the moment of expiry" (22, 96, 99). In contemporary South Africa, a flash reveals not the invisible world but a reality that demands to be addressed in new terms.

I have outlined some connections among the novel's plot, its critique of Romanticism, and its negotiation of an imperialist legacy. A complete account of the novel needs to complement this approach with a discussion of the novel's tentative indications of an alternative for the positions that it criticizes. As many of its different thematic threads develop in parallel, this modest reconstructive movement can be connected to the critique that was implied in the earliest passages: the role of animals, Lurie's Byron project. Animals figure as metaphors that serve as discursive support for Lurie's pursuit of desire but then become a palpable reality in the dogs Lurie encounters on Lucy's farm. These decidedly real animals puncture the legitimizing fictions that sustained his initial outlook and begin to suggest the possibility of an ethics and aesthetics that are both more modest and more appropriate to a changed reality (L. Wright, *Writing* 21–50). He compares his relationship with the prostitute Soraya in the first chapter to that of a predator hunting a vixen (10) and his relationship with Melanie to that of a fox killing a rabbit (25), only to end up as the "strange beast" that is hunted by the university committee (56). On the farm, however, the dogs he encounters begin to stare back and to disrupt their recuperation as metaphor (81, 85, 142). Once they are liberated from the dictates of productivity (146) and the confines of a discourse that is complicit with their mass destruction, they make possible a generous, affective relationship between man and animal (205, 215). The very last passage in the novel indicates that this affective bond can inform a more ethically attuned imagining of community: Lurie sacrifices one of the dogs "like a lamb" (220), a simile that, like the earlier "like a dog" (205) and unlike the almost casual metaphors from the beginning of the novel, does not smoothly reinscribe animals as part of a discourse of desire. Instead it marks the fact that the creation of a discourse that aims to be true to a new South African reality must recognize rather than suppress the violence that is intrinsic to all symbolization and to all imagining of community.

The development of Lurie's Byron project follows a parallel pattern: it begins as a routine academic exercise, then morphs into the high cultural form of a chamber opera written from the perspective of Byron and thus of desire and passion (4, 180), until Lurie begins to conceive of Teresa as a "dumpy little widow" instead of Byron's "young, greedy, wilful, petulant" love interest (181). Again, self-serving fiction gives way to the sobering facts of life, which demand a different kind of symbolization. Like his groundless concern for the dogs, he does not conceive of the project "as a service to mankind" (146) or as a profitable activity (188–89) but as something much less grand — and much more faithful to Teresa, who "demands a music of her own" (183). This music is not that of the piano but of the banjo (an African instrument) and is more faithful to history and to a new reality that calls not for the erotic or elegiac but for the comic (184–86). Lurie's apparent pastiche of religious sacrifice in the novel's last passage can be heard in this minor key that announces a contemporary alternative to Wordsworth's European sublime. Even if the contours of the alternative ethics and aesthetics toward which the later parts of *Disgrace* gesture are much less determinate than the positions it criticizes, the novel is well suited to teach the need for that alternative.

Teaching Coetzee, Then and Now

David Attwell

Cape Town, 1984

A frequent point of departure in Coetzee criticism is to attack the naïveté of a handful of mainly South African critics who, in the 1980s, responded to his early fiction by saying that its political credentials were weak. Indeed it proved convenient for the authors of the critical monographs that began to roll out from the 1990s on (including a book of my own) that a clutch of essays had appeared that brought to bear on Coetzee the historical materialism that drove so many historians and critics of the period.

Historical materialism was the most powerful paradigm in the social sciences and humanities in South Africa in the 1970s and 1980s. It provided strong intellectual resistance to the politically dominant ethnic nationalism, and it helped weaken the gradualist liberal ethos that until then had characterized the English-speaking universities. It is now also more obvious that it gave white middle-class intellectuals the means to act on the overwhelming ethical demands associated with the injustice and violence happening around them. But as a mode of reading, the criticism that was part of this intellectual movement could be a blunt instrument; its default move was to point out what features of society literary texts failed to address and, in that failure, what was revealed about the ideological positioning of those texts.

When applied to Coetzee, this mode of symptomatic reading came up short because it could not match the generic, epistemological, and aesthetic self-consciousness of his novels—in fact, it was unequal to the *historical* sophistication of his writing. Coetzee's self-consciousness and sophistication were a boon for a literary criticism that was increasingly hungry for nonmetropolitan texts and anxious to deploy interpretive methods that had developed with the institutional expansion of literary studies leavened by the successes of critical theory.

By comparison with the later criticism it facilitated, the early critique of Coetzee was hardly an enterprise, since it consisted of only a few essays. Some of the work that provoked the later criticism had not even been formally published.[1] Since that period, for every published article critical of Coetzee on political grounds, there have been at least two that take the article to task. It is true that there were some politically judgmental reviews — by Nadine Gordimer writing in the *New York Review of Books* ("Idea"), by an anonymous reviewer (Z. N.) in the *African Communist*, for example — but they too have facilitated, and have been superseded tenfold, by criticism that has been only too eager to expose their shortcomings.

Coetzee's writing itself has absorbed and answered the political judgments that have at times been ranged against it. A passage from *The Master of Petersburg* is an example. "You see how the poorest of our black poor of Petersburg have to live," rails the revolutionary assassin Nechaev against the fictional Dostoevsky of Coetzee's novel. "But that is not seeing, that is only detail! You fail to recognize the *forces* that determine the lives to which these people are condemned! *Forces*: that is what you are blind to!" (180). "Black poor" is a metaphor for the people who live in the slums of the Haymarket district in Petersburg, but the adjective is undoubtedly double-coded with South Africa in mind. More important, Nechaev's outburst is cast in historical-materialist terms, suggesting the prevailing outlook in Coetzee's immediate academic context (historical materialism of this kind reached the Russian revolutionary movement only after Dostoevsky's time).

In response to Nechaev, Dostoevsky "is still not sure what Nechaev means by lines [of force]. He does not need to be told that bankers hoard money, that covetousness makes the heart shrivel. But Nechaev is insisting on something else. What? Strings of numbers passing through the window-paper and striking these children in their empty bellies?" (182). This peevish response of Dostoevsky is one of many moments in Coetzee that register the helplessness of the writer-intellectual in the face of an overwhelming political demand. Coetzee as a serious novelist in the public gaze represents the conditions under which he works and signals his discomfort with the terms in which accountability is measured, but the critic deriving vicarious support from such a representation, that is a different matter. Critics are fortunate not to be accountable in the ways in which South African writers of the late twentieth century were. But if criticism is seldom answerable, in any society, as writers of serious fiction are, it remains answerable to its role in higher education, which provides its material base, because students and fellow scholars are the bulk of its readership. The present volume presents a rare opportunity to rearticulate the pedagogical function of Coetzee criticism.

When one examines the reception of Coetzee's early fiction in South Africa from the point of view not of criticism but of pedagogy, a different narrative begins to emerge. The difficulty lies in accessing this history. Past course lists, which are easily recoverable, will not tell us how the work was actually received, so we have to rely on personal testimony and anecdote, which is the mode I adopt here.

My first encounter with Coetzee's writing was as a student. Having failed to find a publisher among the established presses for his first novel, *Dusklands*, Coetzee published it with Ravan Press in Johannesburg in 1974, an oppositional publisher that had grown out of the left-liberal Christian Institute. The book soon became required reading for undergraduates in English at the University of Natal in Durban, a bold decision on the part of a handful of exceptional staff members, among whom were Mike Kirkwood, later Coetzee's publisher at Ravan, and Tony Morphet, who moved into adult education but continued to review, and interview, Coetzee. Book adoption, crucial to Ravan's precarious financial situation, gave Coetzee his first sizable readership. I was in that group of undergraduates and in 1976 responded to a dissertation topic set by the staff, "Western Man as Colonizer," which required one to write comparatively on Joseph Conrad's *Heart of Darkness*, William Faulkner's "The Bear," and *Dusklands*. Postcolonial studies *avant la lettre*.

When subsequent criticism repeats the story of Coetzee's politically compromised first reception, it ignores the fact that his early work was rarely read this way. *Dusklands* was a shattering text for many readers, and its politics were part of the package. It put South Africa's contemporary woes (and America's experience in Vietnam) firmly into the history of colonial violence, in prose that positively assaulted. As an exposé of colonialism cast in existential-phenomenological rather than materialist terms, it stood alongside Frantz Fanon and Albert Memmi. Like them, it had been inspired in part by Jean-Paul Sartre (as was the next novel, *In the Heart of the Country*, which refers freely to *Being and Nothingness*). The Marxist critique that later came from critics like Michael Vaughan, Paul Rich, and Peter Kohler was really an attempt to reassert in literary studies the priority of materialist and class-based analysis in a rather internecine struggle inside a broad-church left. Such contestation was taking place across the range of social science and humanities disciplines.

Much more representative of Coetzee's reception was the first sustained review that *Dusklands* received, from Jonathan Crewe, who, writing in the journal *Contrast*, spoke of the book's matching the best of contemporary world fiction and bringing the energies of modernism into a fresh engagement with South Africa's history and traditions. The materialist critique was therefore one position among others in which Coetzee's was generally seen as a startling and liberating voice, a view that was confirmed as *In the Heart of the Country*, *Waiting for the Barbarians*, and *Life & Times of Michael K* rolled out from Ravan.

In the light of this history, the acrimony that characterized the debate over *Disgrace*'s portrayal of South Africa a quarter of a century later seems lamentable, to say the least. We could ask how *Disgrace* might be continuous with Coetzee's early fiction, not a departure from it, and what changed in the public reception of Coetzee in the intervening years. We could observe that the political culture around the South African transition, from 1990 on, was unreceptive to the cultural legacy of the 1960s. Existentialism, Marxism, feminism, the cultural revolution, structuralism, poststructualism, the counterculture of the West that flowered in 1968, all this was remote from the pragmatic nationalism of the climate in which the transition was negotiated. *Disgrace* seemed to come out of an angry European past; its ethos was unfathomable to the heirs of the new South Africa, an unfathomability that was exacerbated by the novel's apparent topicality.

I turn to an actual experience of teaching Coetzee's writing during the late apartheid years. In 1984, I began teaching *Waiting for the Barbarians* at the historically black university in Cape Town, the University of the Western Cape (UWC). Although the university had been established for colored students in 1959 on compromising terms, by an act of parliament that segregated higher education, by the early 1980s the activism on campus ensured that the university would become a locus of resistance and a beacon of transformed higher education, a reputation it still enjoys. Among students and younger black staff members, the prevailing political position had been defined by the Black Consciousness Movement of Steve Biko and SASO (South African Students Organization), but it was shifting toward the nonracial ANC (African National Congress). By the time the UDF (United Democratic Front) was formed in August 1983, the Congress position was dominant, although Cape Town's community politics was never uniform — another significant voice was the Unity Movement, which had Trotskyite roots. The University of the Western Cape was, all told, an empirically secure basis for testing the reception of Coetzee among politically astute students.

The novel was not the kind of text that one could teach to large lecture halls of undergraduates, so it didn't occupy the same place in the curriculum that was given to Shakespeare's *Macbeth*, Arthur Miller's *The Crucible*, Graham Greene's *Brighton Rock*, or Chinua Achebe's *Things Fall Apart*; it was taught in upperlevel seminars and featured in dissertations. There it more than struck a chord. It was self-evident to these students that the fictional Empire of *Waiting for the Barbarians* was analogous to the dispensation and mentality that had produced the P. W. Botha government's policy of "total strategy," a response to the perceived "total onslaught" of military resistance, economic sanctions, and social ungovernability that had been under way since the late 1970s. That the novel could be about both the local situation and all similarly paranoid empires at almost any point in recorded history was well within the grasp of the students.

It was also clear to the students that the episode in the novel when an elderly man is tortured to death and his corpse is left in a cell overnight draws on reports of Steve Biko's murder in 1977 by security police and on the subsequent inquest: "During the course of the interrogation contradictions became apparent in the prisoner's testimony. Confronted with these contradictions, the prisoner became enraged and attacked the investigating officer. A scuffle ensued during which the prisoner fell heavily against the wall. Efforts to revive him were unsuccessful" (6). On a campus where leaflets were distributed providing guidance to students in the event of their being put in solitary confinement, the malevolent target of this parody of circumlocution was easily recognizable.

Jeremy Cronin, the poet who had spent seven years in prison for ANC activity, later a parliamentarian, was to argue that activists and soldiers of the resistance found it demeaning to be associated with the faceless barbarians of Coetzee's novel, as if their actions took place obscurely at the bottom of the garden. I never encountered students who felt that they or their avatars were being represented in this way: Why *would* they be linked to the nameless barbarians? It was clear to them that the novel was about the Empire and its representations. For these students, Coetzee came over as a kind of intellectual spy who had succeeded in infiltrating the obscure world of the Empire, with its oddly perverted fantasies and motives, and was reporting back with knowledge of these mysteries. Coetzee was a comrade.

The challenge of teaching *Waiting for the Barbarians* was not to point out the novel's relevance, which was self-evident, but to lead students toward the more complex reaches of the text: the Magistrate's historical research and what it signified, his obsessive fascination with inconclusive signs, whether marks on the body of the tortured or an ancient, indecipherable script on slips of poplar wood. One could point to Coetzee's professional interest in language, to the rise of semiotics, the early years of deconstruction, all of which provided students with a sense of intellectual context. But these explanations proved less significant to them than the demise of an imperial culture observed through the bewildering dissolution of its signs. Students were interested in the novel's ability to open that experience to them from the inside.

They were also interested in the Magistrate as a representative of the white liberal who is beset by dilemmas, insecurities, and prevarications and who is losing power to the more brutal incarnation of colonial authority, Colonel Joll. That the Magistrate and Joll are two sides of the same coin was not difficult for them to grasp, but that the Magistrate too could be vulnerable, could fall in love with a barbarian girl and not know what to do about it, could be at the receiving end of torture and marvel at his own reactions to pain, could have unfulfillable longings in a world that was collapsing around him—all this was instructive. The students knew such men of culture, the ameliorators—teachers, ministers, newspaper editors, liberal politicians—who were unable to do much about the brutal racism that defined their world, but to share their corrupted, hopeless desires from the inside was eye-opening.

I am walking with Patrick Cullinan, a poet, across the sandy lawns and paved walkways of Freedom Square in the center of the UWC campus, in early 1985. At the university entrance, a war is being waged between students and the police. Hurled stones are being answered with tear gas, rubber bullets, and occasionally buckshot. A familiar face engages us, a student we know from classes, on his way to the gate, his hands tucked behind his back. "Mr. Cullinan, when is the Chaucer assignment due?" "The twenty-third," says Patrick. "Thanks," the student says and turns to leave. Behind his back he is hiding half a brick.

Johannesburg, 2004

Twenty years later, literary studies requires us to discourage students from making crude connections between the texts they read and the world in which they live. Or, if they make such connections, they are required to place a special kind of light filter between themselves and the text, one that reveals the conditions under which the text purports to be meaningful. To the question, How are they to acquire this filter?, there is no direct answer: one acquires it over the course of an entire degree.

Simon Gikandi addresses this phenomenon in an argument that has postcolonial theory specifically in mind. He proceeds as follows: postcolonial theory has its origins in the Western or metropolitan or First World academy of the 1980s. It arose in the slipstream of poststructuralism, with which it has much in common although it emphasizes introducing into metropolitan theory and criticism the historical testimony associated with the colonial experience. Therefore at the heart of postcolonial theory lies a contradiction: it is antimimetic, and its disciplinary intuitions are antipathetic to—or at best it has no language for—the work of cultural recovery, restitution, and redress. Its discourse is out of tune with its historical project.

The source of this anomaly, Gikandi continues, is poststructuralism's reluctance to embrace mimesis. He cites Paul de Man:

> Literary theory can be said to come into being when the approach to literary texts is no longer based on non-linguistic, that is to say historical and aesthetic, considerations or, to put it less crudely, when the object of discussion is no longer the meaning or the value but the modalities of production and reception of meaning and of value prior to their establishment—the implication being that this establishment is problematic enough to require an autonomous discipline of critical investigation to consider its possibility and its status. Literary history, even when considered at the furthest remove from the platitudes of positivistic historicism, is still the history of an understanding of which the possibility is taken for granted.   (qtd. in Gikandi 166; de Man 7)

What de Man says of theory, and what Gikandi says of postcolonial theory, is consistent with what we have come to expect of both criticism and good teaching. We are more interested in the medium than the message ("message" has become a shibboleth; my students lose marks for using it). The purpose of our teaching, then, is to focus students' minds not on the historical meaning of the text but on "the modalities of production and reception of meaning and of value." We do this because we are primarily responsible to "an autonomous discipline of critical investigation," and we have a particular responsibility to avoid "the platitudes of positivistic historicism." In a South African university, especially when one is teaching Coetzee or any other historically and ethically engaged writer, the climate is not auspicious for this task.

The students I taught at Wits (the University of the Witwatersrand in Johannesburg) were the children of the generation I encountered at UWC. They had reached consciousness, as we say, entirely in the era of Nelson Mandela's release. Reading literature, studying film, is not necessarily something they would have experienced as countercultural, even if the syllabus included *Blade Runner*, Jeannette Winterson's *Oranges Are Not the Only Fruit*, and Yvonne Vera's *The Stone Virgins*.

We wrestled the entire curriculum into a new shape at Wits in the early 2000s, a task that every English department in South Africa has done regularly in the previous two decades. One reason for the constant syllabus revision is structural: all students take a core curriculum, with some options and electives in small groups. With staff-student ratios of seventy or even a hundred to one (in the United Kingdom, the average is about eighteen to one), there is no alternative but to teach in large groups, with some small-group teaching added on. Each department, therefore, has to create, and continually re-create, a consensus among the staff about what should be taught.

There are also cultural reasons for the constant syllabus revision: most students are second- or third-language speakers of English, with a range of backgrounds reflecting the diversity of Johannesburg as an African metropolis. The solution we hit on at Wits was to construct a contrapuntal curriculum—I use *contrapuntal* with apologies to Edward Said's *Culture and Imperialism*. In practice, it meant that when we taught a canonical text or movement (still part of our responsibility to the discipline), alongside it we taught something from world or South African literature that extended the geographic range. Augustan satire—Pope's *Rape of the Lock*, for example—is taught alongside *Propaganda by Monuments*, a postapartheid satire by Ivan Vladislavić. Traditions don't have self-evident authority; Milton has to work as hard as Zakes Mda to reach his readers.[2] This pedagogical equality may be true to some degree even in Britain, but it is particularly true of postapartheid South Africa.

Although we share a proper sense of responsibility to the discipline as defined by de Man, we are careful to choose texts the students will find meaningful, even if we are cautious about what *meaningful* means. The texts we prefer when Coetzee is put into the curriculum, for undergraduates, are *Life & Times of Michael K* and *Boyhood*. *Disgrace* is reserved for the South African literature option at the honors (fourth-year) level, for two reasons. First, it is required reading in the literature syllabus of independent schools throughout the country, so those students who arrive at the university from private school backgrounds (a not insignificant number) have already encountered it (*Disgrace* is more than likely their only encounter with Coetzee at this stage). Second, because the press has insisted on polarizing Coetzee and the ANC, it will take maturer minds and more time to sift through the confusion.

So I am lecturing on *Michael K* and *Boyhood* to as much as a hundred and fifty students at a time, repeating these classes at different days and hours in the schedule. With *Michael K*, I share with students Gordimer's unfavorable review, which criticizes the novel's politics, and Coetzee's responses to it in "The Novel Today" and in some of the dialogues in *Doubling the Point*. We talk about the novel's indebtedness to Franz Kafka, its orientation toward an imagined future, the blending of realism and allegory, and about K's gardening. I assure them that this is not a novel about environmentalism, that gardening is part of a symbolic system in which it is juxtaposed to the camps, to confinement.

As we follow Michael's fortunes closely, we soon reach the subject of resistance, and I try to convince students that the novel proposes a model of resistance that is conceptual and textual. The terrain on which it conducts its struggle, I tell them, is cultural: we might feel for Michael, but we must remember that he is a fiction. Coetzee's notion of freedom is existential rather than political. The novel proposes that politics is the problem; it develops an ethical language that imagines humanity renewed by ontological awareness and that invests writing with the ability to achieve this consciousness. I realize that I am treading on thin ice and that some of my colleagues might not approve of so strong an interpretation, of such meaningfulness, but I press on in order to reach the students. They dutifully write it all down, store it up for the exams. None of it seems to disturb them.

Boyhood is an accessible route into Coetzee—assuming that its representation of childhood will have a mimetic function for students, that they will see themselves in John. There is some basis for making this assumption, since much of the narration is poignant, but the third-person mode tends to undercut strong identification. The self-directed irony and cultural diagnosis tend to work more effectively on older readers. There is a further layer of difficulty that is beyond the ability of many students to appreciate fully: this is not an empirical account of a South African childhood but the retrospective imagining of the possible childhood origins of a certain writerly persona. To understand the text properly, we need first to have a sense of the writer Coetzee has become; we need to read *Boyhood* through *Michael K* and other novels. The identification with the mother in *Boyhood*, for example, acquires more weight when seen in relation to Coetzee's use of female narrators or to his preference for the margins of culture.

I persevere, to open the oeuvre for the students, but I have the feeling that I am on the defensive. What I am saying comes over as canonical, authoritative, even official—and boring. My intuition is confirmed when a student (female, socially adept, with an air of private schooling, black) asks me rather familiarly after one of these lectures why Coetzee gets all the attention. I ask her which writers she would prefer the attention to go to. "Zakes Mda," she says.

NOTES

[1] See Vaughan; Kohler; Rich; and to a lesser extent, since his work was not historical-materialist, Knox-Shaw. Kohler's essay had appeared only in the unpublished papers of the University of the Witwatersrand's History Workshop.

[2] For readers unfamiliar with Mda, he is a South African novelist, playwright, and poet, the author of over twenty works. He currently teaches at the University of Ohio. He has won numerous literary awards, including the Commonwealth Writers Prize and the Sunday Times Fiction Prize for his 2001 novel *The Heart of Redness*.

"[From] Whom This Writing Then?" Politics, Aesthetics, and the Personal in Coetzee's *Age of Iron*

Andrew van der Vlies

Age of Iron has proved for me to be one of the most successful and rewarding of J. M. Coetzee's novels in the advanced undergraduate classroom. This essay offers some reflections, based on my experience of teaching the novel, on how it allows for informed discussion of the sociohistorical contexts of Coetzee's work in the late 1980s, while also encouraging students to grapple with the difficulty of the author's conception of a literature that complicates expectations about the relation between politics and fiction (and between the personal and the political) in a time of historical emergency.

There are a number of reasons, I believe, why *Age of Iron* is taught less frequently than Coetzee's other novels. Are those of us who elect to teach his work so wedded to the sense of Coetzee as an author of complex, allusive, and suggestive allegories (allegories that disavow their status as such) that we prefer to focus on the novels that immediately precede this work of 1990? These earlier works are the novels that attracted criticism for the author's apparent reticence about representing directly the conditions in the South Africa in which he found himself—P. W. "Rubicon" Botha's late-apartheid pariah state—during the years of the total onslaught, the tricameral parliament, so-called independent homelands, political assassinations, and state-sponsored township vigilantes. In the midst of this turmoil, *Waiting for the Barbarians* seemed to offer itself as an allegory set in no particular time or place (though suggesting central Asia sometime in the later centuries of the common era). If *Life & Times of Michael K* appeared to acknowledge an undeclared civil war—or war by the white-minority regime against the majority of the population—in South Africa, it was set teasingly in the future, even if one no less dystopian than the country and time in which it was written. *Foe*, offering a re-visioning of the circumstances of the writing of Defoe's *Robinson Crusoe* and *Roxana* in eighteenth-century England, seemed to some as far removed as it was possible to be from a South Africa in the grip of a state of emergency.

If I overemphasize the extent to which these novels are not about South Africa in the late 1970s and early 1980s (many readers and reviewers at the time apprehended keenly their political energies), it remains true that teaching these earlier texts does not require that students engage in great detail with the historical contexts that critics accused Coetzee of ignoring. Forgoing that engagement allows us too easily to be only liberal humanists; it suggests the ongoing power of fiction to speak to changing circumstances, to teach lessons about language and liberty (Philip Glass's opera adaptation of *Waiting for the Barbarians* proves this point, I think) or, if we are more theoretically self-conscious, about discursive constructions, canonicity, gender and race inequities, and the dangerous inevitability of speaking for the silent subaltern.

Age of Iron, on the other hand, invites students to consider both historical contexts and the question of the relation between the life and art: it poses challenges regarding definitions of metafiction, realism, and protest, and it invites—at the same time as rendering problematic—speculation about the novel's relation to the life of its author. From what one might term Coetzee's middle period, *Age of Iron*, itself a liminal novel about states of liminality, also presages key themes and concerns of Coetzee's most celebrated and controversial novel, *Disgrace*.

Balancing Context and Allegory: "[M]indful That the Storyteller . . . Claims the Place of Right"

Age of Iron is often described as the first of Coetzee's fictions to address directly contemporaneous circumstances in South Africa. It ends tantalizingly with a run of dates, *"1986–89"* (198).[1] Who, I ask my students early in a class on *Age of Iron*, is the author of these dates? Is it Mrs. Curren, who wrote the letter that, in the fictional frame, forms the body of the novel's text? Or is it Coetzee? Does the fact that the dates are italicized place them outside the frame of the fiction (are they paratextual, in other words)? Does the novel's final paragraph, which some students read as suggesting Mrs. Curren's asphyxiation at the hands of Vercueil, render at least the end date impossible? While "The Vietnam Project," the first half of *Dusklands*, also ends with a run of dates (*"1972–73"*), there it seems clear that the reader is invited to interpret these as appended to the narrative by the fictional narrator, Eugene Dawn. The addenda to the second part of *Dusklands* and to *Elizabeth Costello*—the "Deposition of Jacobus Coetzee" and "Letter of Elizabeth, Lady Chandos, to Francis Bacon," respectively—are also dated, but here the documents are part of their respective texts' fictional, and historically remote, universes.

That *Age of Iron*'s historical occasion can be precisely located in August and September 1986 complicates the question: Mrs. Curren writes while "sitting in bed," her "knees pressed together against the August cold" (55 [students in the northern hemisphere may need to be reminded that August falls during the winter in the southern hemisphere]); her narrative draws to its close soon after "September 23, the [Spring] equinox" (190); Mr. Thabane tells her that he was born in 1943 and is forty-three (99). Can we assume that Mrs. Curren survives three years past the few months narrated in her extended letter?

What pedagogical payoff is offered by giving this context such close attention? Mid-1986 saw some of the worst civil unrest in South Africa. On 12 June, President Botha declared a state of emergency that, among other things, allowed the presence of the military—those young white men whom Mr. Thabane derisively calls Mrs. Curren's "boys . . . here to protect you" (101)—in the townships. A badly affected area was Crossroads, a slum of corrugated iron, wood, and plastic shacks on desolate, sandy flatland (the Cape Flats), which had become one of the largest such settlements in the country, serving as home for thousands of black migrants to Cape Town, many from the Eastern Cape. When these residents resisted removal to Khayelitsha in late May and early June 1986, much of Crossroads was destroyed by vigilantes—known as "*wit-doeke*" (89) for the white headcloth they wore as a badge—loyal to a local strongman, Johnson Ngxobongwana.[2] These, the "incendiaries" Mrs. Curren observes in part 3 of the novel (95), were armed and abetted by the apartheid state: Florence tells Mrs. Curren they are being given guns (89); Thabane tells her that the bullet that killed Bheki will have been approved by the South African Bureau of Standards ("SABS"), in other words provided by the South African military (103). The violence continued for months as Ngxobongwana's thugs cleared neighboring settlements and served as proxy for the state's opposition to local residents affiliated to the United Democratic Front and, through it, to the outlawed African National Congress. Bheki and John are among these residents.

A great deal more might be said about the discernible historical and geographic locations to which Coetzee appears so carefully, if obliquely, to direct the reader: this is work for the assiduous student to pursue. Yet it remains a challenge to encourage students generally to weigh the significance of the invocation—and disavowal—of allegory that attends contexts that are so historically specific and also so allusively limned. Mrs. Curren muses that watching Florence walk with her daughters, Hope and Beauty, is "like living in an allegory" (90). Many of the names are suggestive: Vercueil might also be "Verkuil," suggesting the Afrikaans *verkul* ("to cheat") or *verskuil* ("to hide"), Mrs. Curren concedes to Florence (see 37); Dr. Syfret, Mrs. Curren's oncologist, shares the name of a then-prominent investment and asset management company (taking care of the financial health of a morally diseased society). Her foray into the settlements out in "the bush" (90) on "the Flats" (134) is, as many critics have observed, like a descent into the underworld—with a laconic Thabane serving as Aeneas to her Vergil (and Florence is a sybil). Crossroads is a historical place but also an aptly named liminal space representing a challenge: Mrs. Curren, too, has reached a political and personal crossroads, as she is obsessed with images of the liminal and the idea of crossing from the living to the dead. The historical and geographic context is therefore also allegorical. When, after Bheki's friend John has been killed in her yard, Mrs. Curren spends the night under a flyover or "overpass" (157) on nearby Buitenkant Street, a real street (near the real Mill Street, from whose post office she imagines Vercueil will post the letter to her daughter), we see one more location whose name underscores her political choice: it is, literally, the "outside" street, having run along a border of the Dutch settlement in what is today Cape Town's City Bowl. Mrs. Curren has placed herself on the fringes of her community, that of suburban anglophone "liberal-humanist posturing" (85). (There is no evidence, as some have averred, that she is an Afrikaner; fewer white South Africans are as easily classified as one thing or another as northern hemisphere students might believe.) She declares to the police gathered at her home to apprehend John that she stands not on their side (*"Ek staan nie aan jou kant nie"*) but "on the other side" (*"aan die teenkant"*) (153–54); she might have said *buitekant* ("outside").

But Mrs. Curren also stands against demands made on her by those who oppose the state. That she regards Bheki and John's "comradeship" as nothing more than "a mystique of death" (150) suggests her desire to escape the polarizing discourses of the moment. She declares to Thabane that what she thinks of what she has seen on the Flats she "must say in [her] own way" (98). This statement speaks to the difficulty of relating art and politics in a period of political and humanitarian crisis. It is an issue that concerned Coetzee deeply during the middle 1980s and one that *Age of Iron* mediates for students perhaps better than any other of his fictions. The novel in fact seems to engage directly with two significant statements he made about politics and aesthetics from the 1986–89 period: a speech delivered on the occasion of receiving the 1987 Jerusalem Prize; an address delivered at the *Weekly Mail* book fair in Cape Town, in the same year, and published in a South African journal under the title "The Novel Today" in 1988.

In the Jerusalem Prize speech, which appears in *Doubling the Point*, Coetzee noted a hollowness in the love white South Africans profess for the countryside, one often figured in an exaggerated veneration directed at *"the land*, that is, toward what is least likely to respond to love: mountains and deserts, birds and animals and flowers" and not the heterogeneous population that shares it (97). This love, insufficient in the past, will continue to be so, he suggested. Shortly after Mrs. Curren has recalled singing the utopian anthem *"Jerusalem! . . . And was Jerusalem y-builded here?"* (24), perhaps a wry intertextual, frame-breaking reference to Coetzee's speech, she offers an opinion not dissimilar to his: that the country was "not loved enough" by those whose actions ravaged it. For her, such love has become impossible (121).

In his address, Coetzee gave a forthright defense of his desire to resist what he called a "powerful tendency, perhaps even dominant tendency" in the country at that time "to subsume the novel under history" ("Novel Today" 2). Attempts to construe "the novelistic text" as "a kind of historical text," merely a supplement to history, meant that some novels had "greater truth" attributed to them by some critics. But he insisted that it was not to distance himself "from revolutionary art" that he made this defense (4). Rather, it was in order to stake a claim for a space in which art was able to speak in its own way and not only in a manner endorsed by the dominant (by which he meant both apartheid and antiapartheid) discourses of the day.

Encouraging students to consider these admittedly taxing ideas requires perseverance, but the rewards, particularly in classes that go on to read Coetzee's later works, are many. They include fostering a more nuanced sense of his idea of the resistance of the literary to the encroaches of political discourses (which is not to say that students ought not to be encouraged to interrogate the coherence or usefulness of this position) as well as of his use of figures of alterity in later fictions (*Disgrace*'s dogs being the most obvious). Most important, this strategy offers students a clearer sense of how Coetzee's broad and ongoing project of contesting, complicating, and refusing the binaries of colonial and anticolonial discourse plays out in the very form of his fictions: in the recurrence in his oeuvre of unreliable narrations, contingent or structurally impossible occasions of narration, and the foregrounding of the material circumstances of a text's putative production. All occur in *Age of Iron*. Students who focus on the novel's immediate historical and political contexts, on the complicated imbrication of sociohistorical allusiveness with allegory in the novel, and on Coetzee's own statements about the discourse of literariness and the discourse of history will be singularly equipped to engage more competently than otherwise with Coetzee's later fiction.

"Nothing Is Private Anymore": Personal Paratexts and the Question of Autrebiography

Given its metafictional suggestiveness, *Age of Iron* invites readers to draw a connection between Coetzee's own investment in an aesthetics resistant to the demands of dueling political ideologies and Mrs. Curren's belief that, in order to give an account of what she has experienced, she cannot resort to mere reportage. (There is perhaps some irony, and also an answer to his critics, in John Coetzee's having his protagonist write, "John" is "a *nom de guerre* if ever I heard one" [147].) Mrs. Curren's representation both as keen student of a particular classical canon of humanist scholarship—numerous intertextual references include those to Homer (85, 140), Hesiod (50), Ovid (the leitmotif of metamorphosis throughout) and Vergil (especially book 6 of the *Aeneid* [89, 92, 192]), Cervantes (18), Shakespeare (40, 189), Wordsworth (168), Hawthorne (114), and Tolstoy (14)—and as a writer, literally as one trying to write in (and out of) difficult historical circumstances, make it very tempting to read her as an analogue for the author.

My students frequently infer this connection, and some critics make a case for the same congruity, though it is not straightforward. Coetzee seems rather to be staging Mrs. Curren as a performer of a certain set of opinions and literally as a writer in a particular context—one that he shares (the novel's motif of ventriloquism, highlighted chiefly in her interest in the *Aeneid* with its sybils, emphasizes the complex performativity). Nowhere does the novel give Mrs. Curren's first name: critics frequently call her Elizabeth Curren, drawing on Coetzee's reference to her as such in an interview with David Attwell (*Doubling* 250) conducted after he had completed the novel but before its publication, or on the novel's paratexts.[3] In the novel, she is only "Mrs. Curren" (148) or, as she signs herself in a note to Florence, "E.C." (41). That she shares Elizabeth Costello's initials, of course, suggests that she is a precursor of this other performer, who also shares a set of concerns and contexts with the historical Coetzee. But Coetzee is clear: after suggesting in the interview with Attwell that *Age of Iron* deals with what it means to "speak from a totally untenable historical position," with "*history* and *authority*" and the "contest" that is "staged" between them in mind, he offers this comment: "What is of importance in what I have just said is the phrasing: the phrases *is staged, is heard*; not *should be staged, should be heard*. . . . Elizabeth is the one who believes in *should*, who believes in *believes in*" (*Doubling* 250).

This issue of authorial context (and intention) remains a thorny one for students. Having canvassed concerns with contexts and allegory, aesthetics and politics, as outlined above, I return them (and readers of this essay) to the issue by suggesting that I have not lost sight of the novel's concluding run of dates. These seem to draw attention to a period immediately preceding the novel's publication. Imagine Vercueil as the enabler of this reading; perhaps, in the logic of the narrative, he has dated the pages himself and sent them into the world, to the daughter in North America, to a transnational global reader who stands in our place. This period precisely defines the last gasps of the late-apartheid state (F. W. de Klerk's speech to parliament on 2 February 1990 can be taken as a marker of the start of the interregnum that followed). It is a run of dates corresponding to Coetzee's own growing public status as outspoken critic of the near-impossible conditions for writers of conscience in the Manichaean context of the political space. However, another set of dates, suggesting the complex imbrication of Coetzee and his fictional writer-figure, also occurs in the novel: the dedication "For V. H. M. C. (1904–1985) / Z. C. (1912–1988) / N. G. C. (1966–1989)."

I am usually surprised by how few students pay attention to the peculiarity of this triple dedication. Those familiar with Coetzee's *autre*biographies (esp. *Boyhood*, which I have taught in the same course as *Age of Iron*) recognize the first two sets of initials as belonging to Coetzee's mother and father.[4] The third dedicatee is Coetzee's son, Nicolas, who died as *Age of Iron*'s manuscript was in its final stages. Coetzee has never spoken of this personal tragedy; the authorized biographical outline, produced for the occasion of the Nobel Prize award (by Tore Frängsmyr), merely confirmed the death (*J. M. Coetzee — Biographical*), though the recent (2012) publication of J. C. Kannemeyer's *J. M. Coetzee: A Life in Writing* offers more detail on Nicolas's life and the tragedy of his untimely death (452–57). Such personal tragedy lends poignancy, certainly, to Mrs. Curren's anguished negotiation of the meaning of dying at a distance from her daughter, "We embrace our children to be folded in the arms of the future, to pass ourselves on beyond death, to be transported" (5), or her plea to Johannes/John that "Fifteen is too young to die. Eighteen is too young. Twenty-one is too young" (143). *Waiting for the Barbarians* was dedicated to Coetzee's daughter and son, the latter then alive; the dedication in *Age of Iron* is unique in Coetzee's oeuvre to date in memorializing the dead.[5]

One way of prompting students to think further about the significance of the

dedications is to consider the material instantiation of the text in two different editions.[6] The United States Penguin paperback (1998) places a half-title
page between the dedication and the first section of the novel, which is marked
with an Arabic numeral and not given its own page. The British Penguin paperback (1991) has no half-title page; the dedication immediately precedes the first
section number, which stands on its own page and is given in Roman numerals.
There appear to be contradictory impulses here. The United States paperback,
in its presentation of the prefatory matter, suggests that the dedication stands
apart from the body of the novel whose text, under the title "Age of Iron" (repeated on its own half-title page), is the single body of writing that follows; this
decision emphasizes the text as Mrs. Curren's narrative and has the dedication
serve purely as publication information, part of the novel's paratextual matter:
it is the dedication of Coetzee, the author. In the first British Penguin paperback edition, by contrast, the division between the author's and the putative
fictional narrator's inscriptions is less clear. These two approaches to how the
fictional narrative should be framed return us to questions about metafiction
and realism. They are given added urgency in the context in which Coetzee was
writing, where playful postmodernism might have risked relativism and opened
him to charges of reaction. On the other hand, a straightforward realism would
too easily subtend a political message, making of the "novelistic text" merely "a
kind of historical text," in the terms of "The Novel Today."

Intertexts and Impossible Narration: "[H]old[ing] the Letters of the Word Apart"

Age of Iron serves well as a precursor to themes and issues encountered in
Disgrace, including shame and guilt, the sublime, hospitality and the nature of
the gift, translation, and the demands of others (alterity also figured in animal
terms). Many of these seem self-evident in retrospect; nonetheless, it is fascinating to note the early occurrence of disgrace represented as a condition into
which a subject is thrust, for a term apparently without limit, through complicity with injustice (86, 165). Only an unwarranted, unsolicited, and unpromising
"wager on trust" (130) in another—here, Vercueil, the abstruse other, and his
silent ministering—promises a way out of this limbo.

Mrs. Curren's frequent allusions to a classical and Western canon highlight
her commitment to an aesthetic tradition constructed by the radical left as being at odds with the requirements of realism in a time of emergency. But there
is another body of intertextual reference that draws attention to the novel's
engagement with the nature of writing itself. Mrs. Curren thinks of her de-
caying, unkempt house as "a late bourgeois tomb" (150), alluding surely to Nadine Gordimer's *The Late Bourgeois World*, in which another female narrator
contends with the demands of activism and with complacency. Mrs. Curren's

comparison of Bheki's body to "pig iron" (124) and her "feeling of walking upon black faces" (125) echo recurring motifs in Gordimer's *The Conservationist*, while her obsessive shortwave radio listening (23, 181) echoes the Smaleses' in *July's People*. If the trajectory of Gordimer's characters is almost always from liberal-humanist optimism to a disillusionment that sometimes prompts an acceptance of active identification with the revolution, *Age of Iron* appears to foreswear those alternatives—just as Michael K resists revolutionary agency in a novel that attracted a mixed review from Gordimer in the *New York Review of Books* in February 1984 ("Idea"). *Age of Iron* is thus, in some senses, Coetzee's apparent writing back to the politics of writing in Gordimer's oeuvre: in fact, very early drafts of the novel, from August 1987, feature the (then-male) first-person narrator telling his domestic servant that the writer Gordimer wrote about people like them ("Age").[7] No direct references remain in the published novel, but there are wry allusions: Gordimer is famously a cat owner, and Mrs. Curren's invocation of a late bourgeois tomb is prompted by the "smell of cat urine" (150).

Above all, the comparison with Gordimer emphasizes Coetzee's novel's concern with the strangeness of the literary (about which Derek Attridge writes so suggestively in *J. M. Coetzee and the Ethics of Reading*). Gordimer's narrative voices, often in the conspicuously difficult, late-modernist free indirect discourse, are not those of writers per se. Mrs. Curren *is* a writer, and one who draws frequent attention to the problem of realism: she questions the status of her own narrative after describing (in fact, imagining) Florence's meeting with her husband William (43–44). She dwells on the difficulty of words—John does "not believe in" them, she charges (145). Delirious, she scrawls "sprawling, sliding characters, meaningless" on her walls (182).

Mrs. Curren's cancer is also like a word, one "living inside" her, "another word," one that cannot be spoken (145). Words—or the impossibility of their conveying truth—are ever in the forefront of her mind. Early in the narrative, Vercueil spits at her feet, and she thinks: *"The thing itself. . . . His word, his kind of word. . . . A word, undeniable, from a language before language"* (8). The italicized phrase, much debated in philosophical discourse ever since its use by Plato in the so-called philosophical digression in his seventh letter (in the *Dialogues*), taken up by Kant (for whom it was a synonym for the noumenon), Hegel, Husserl, Heidegger, and Wallace Stevens, involves a tension between ontology and representation. Giorgio Agamben offered this gloss in a paper published in English translation in 1987:

> The thing itself is not a thing—it is the very sayability, the very opening which is in question in language, which is language, and which in language we constantly presuppose and forget, perhaps because the thing itself is, in its intimacy, nothing more than forgetfulness and self-abandonment.
>
> ("Thing" 25)

Age of Iron's complex layering of context and allegory, the perhaps impossible occasion of narration, the tension between its fictional point of composition and its dates, its status as artifact dedicated to the dead, as a thing offered to the other as reader, a personal and political enactment of memory and embodiment set against the threat of forgetfulness and self-abandonment, make the novel a meditation not only on the difficulty of being a writer in a state of emergency but also on the difficulty of representation in general. It is this suggestiveness that fits the novel for inclusion in any college syllabus concerned not only with South African or postcolonial or world literatures but more generally with realism, politics, and ethics.

NOTES

[1] This date range was inserted, the manuscript records, during late revisions in early 1990 ("Age").

[2] For more on the apartheid government's policy of contramobilization, students might consult the *Report of the Truth and Reconciliation Commission* (vol. 2, ch. 3, par. 555).

[3] Attwell refers to her as Elizabeth in his conclusion to *J. M. Coetzee* (125). Coetzee may have approved the first edition jacket blurb description in which she is named Elizabeth Curren.

[4] See Coetzee, *Boyhood* 27, 49, 105, 106, 115–16 ("Vera"), and 152 ("Z. Coetzee"). Coetzee's own unambiguously biographical statement of his parents' names occurs in the biography included in his University of Texas, Austin, dissertation: "John Maxwell Coetzee was born in Cape Town, South Africa, on February 9, 1940, the son of Zacharias Coetzee and Vera Wehmeyer Coetzee." See "'Worlds.'" Kannemeyer's biography, published after the completion of this essay, confirms Coetzee's parents' full names—Vera Hildred Marie, born Wehmeyer, and Zacharias—and discusses the dedication in this novel (443).

[5] This was the case until Coetzee dedicated *Scenes from Provincial Life* (2011; comprising *Boyhood, Youth,* and *Summertime*) to his late brother ("In memoriam D. K. C."). David Keith Coetzee died the previous year (see Kannemeyer, *J. M. Coetzee: A Life* 603–04). Coetzee's most recent novel, *The Childhood of Jesus* (2013), contains a similar dedication, "For D. K. C."

[6] Book-historical pedagogy is generally too little used in teaching Coetzee. For some examples of scholarship engaging in teachable ways with book-historical methodologies in relation to Coetzee, see Flanery; Van der Vlies, "Local and Global Lives."

[7] I have relied for this detail on notes made on the manuscript drafts of *Age of Iron* by Patrick Flanery, who consulted them at Harvard's Houghton Library in 2009 (the materials have since moved to the Harry Ransom Humanities Research Center at the University of Texas at Austin). I am indebted to Flanery for his assistance and his engagement with this essay.

Refusing Adamastor:
Lucy Lurie and "White Writing" in *Disgrace*

Louise Bethlehem

In the aftermath of the rape of his daughter, Lucy, David Lurie, the protagonist of J. M. Coetzee's postapartheid novel *Disgrace*, speculates that her assailants "will watch the newspapers, listen to the gossip. They will read that they are being sought for robbery and assault and nothing else. It will dawn on them that over the body of the woman silence is being drawn like a blanket" (110). Early responses to the novel in South Africa were anything but silent concerning its depiction of interracial rape. Rape was central to the controversies that the novel generated. The reception of the work tied different interpretations of the representation of rape to a set of moral assessments in thrall to the anxiety of the transition to democracy.

Disgrace achieved notoriety then precisely because it resonated with the still unresolved tensions of apartheid. This notoriety is a distinctive part of what Edward Said called the "wordliness" of the novel (*World* 35), and I set forth that worldliness for my students early on in my presentation of the work. In my teaching of *Disgrace* to undergraduate and graduate students at the Hebrew University of Jerusalem, I have found it useful to begin with an account of the conflicting appraisals of it in South Africa. I emphasize that local readers apprehended rape less in the context of a form of sexual violence endemic to South Africa than as the occasion for drawing inferences closely bound to the work of moral censure. These inferences circulated in and between groups, generating different consequences as an effect of their very circulation.

For many white readers, Coetzee's depiction of Lucy as a victim who chooses to remain silent intersected a broader pessimism regarding the viability of whiteness in postapartheid South Africa. The acclaimed antiapartheid playwright Athol Fugard stated in January 2000, "I haven't read it . . . but I could not think of anything that would depress me more than this book by Coetzee — *Disgrace* — where we've got to accept the rape of a white woman as a gesture to all the evil we did in the past" (qtd. in Marais, "Very Morbid Phenomena" 32). This interpretation, and others like it, reflected a sense of unease at odds with the reconciliation that democracy in South Africa promised to inaugurate. Lucy, whose rape conferred on her the status of quintessential victim in some quarters, was held to model self-abasement and voluntary marginalization as proper conduct for white South Africans seeking to atone for the collective guilt of apartheid.

The rape of Lucy would provide the basis for a very different set of judgments by other South African readers. In April 2000, representatives of the ruling African National Congress (ANC) submitted the novel to the South African Human Rights Commission's inquiry into racism in the media, because *Disgrace* was considered to perpetuate the racist stereotyping of black South Africans. The novel, it was claimed in an oral deposition, reverted to long-standing white perceptions of the black South African as a "faithless, immoral, uneducated, incapacitated primitive child" (*ANC Submission*; see also P. McDonald 323), thus reproducing apartheid ideology. Coetzee, the ANC deposition argued, "represents as brutally as he can the white people's perception of the post-apartheid black man" (*ANC Submission*; P. McDonald 324). This reading saw the novel as evidence of ongoing racism in the white media, bypassing its literariness and its studied, if ambiguous, poetics (P. McDonald 323–27). In a recapitulation of Lucy's reflections on the rapists, "I think I am in their territory. They have marked me" (158), the deposition articulated its own version of white fear at the prospect of continuing to be "in 'their [i.e., black] territory' as a consequence of which the whites will lose their cards, their weapons, their property, their rights, their dignity. The white women will have to sleep with the barbaric black men" (*ANC Submission*). Contemporary reviews of the novel for a black readership would reproduce this reading. Writing in the *Sowetan*, its editor, the influential black journalist Aggrey Klaaste, found the "story of black men raping a white woman . . . quite offensive" (qtd. in P. McDonald 325; for further discussion of the ANC's response, see Attwell, "Race").

The contested reception of the novel shows the tangle of moral judgments and emotions of the South African readership at the time of its publication. This account is in itself a valuable archive to bring to the attention of our students, but additional concerns of importance for the teaching of *Disgrace* should be articulated. In presenting *Disgrace* to my students, I have found it useful to reframe the reception of the novel in terms of the "affective economies" that have coalesced around it (Ahmed 117). In my classroom discussion of the novel, this reframing serves as a prelude to setting out some of the historical determinants that have made the responses to *Disgrace* so volatile.

Sarah Ahmed develops the view that emotions play a performative role in structuring social space. Emotions "*do things*": "they align individuals with communities—or bodily space with social space—through the very intensity of their attachments" (119). Ahmed argues that the circulation of emotions between "bodies and signs" (117) plays a role in the demarcation of individual as well as of collective identity. In this reading, *Disgrace* becomes the occasion for the circulation of intense attachments in the South African public sphere. Boundary lines between historical communities—white South Africans, black South Africans—are redrawn, with an anxiety that flies in the face of the emergent unity of the Rainbow Nation. It is the submerged intertextual as well as social history of these attachments that informs my attempts to augment the literary and cultural competence of our students. I introduce them to one of the formative texts of what Jonathan Crewe terms white "cultural memory" in South Africa ("Recalling" 75): the Portuguese Renaissance poet Luíz Vaz de

Camões's 1572 epic work *Os Lusíadas* (*The Lusíads*, i.e., the sons of Lusus or the Portuguese).

Camões's text is testament to the early history of the Portuguese in Africa. The infante, Prince Henry the Navigator, a fifteenth-century junior prince of the kingdom of Portugal, was a central figure in promoting and financing Portuguese maritime exploration to open a sea route to the East and challenge Mediterranean Islam. The Portuguese were also inspired by the expectation of encountering the lost white domain of Prester John, fabled ruler of a Christian kingdom in the Orient (Van Wyk Smith, Introduction 6–7). In 1488, Bartolomeu Dias rounded the southern tip of Africa, which he is said to have named the Cape of Good Hope, Cabo de Boa Esperança (2). The expedition reached its farthest point in March 1488, when it anchored off the coast of the Eastern Cape and erected a *padrão* or stone cross. Dias met his death in these waters in 1500, aptly termed the Cape of Storms, Cabo Tormentoso. The Portuguese enterprise was continued by Vasco da Gama, who sailed from Lisbon in 1497 with four ships and made landfall on the African coast on 4 November. Da Gama proceeded past the point at which Dias had turned back, giving the name Natal to the coast in the region of the Kei River on Christmas Day. At Malindi, on the coast of Kenya, da Gama took on board a Muslim pilot whose navigational skills enabled the Portuguese to reach the Malabar coast of southern India in May 1498. Although da Gama returned from India without valuable cargo, he opened the riches of the Indian spice route to the Portuguese, thus ensuring the success of their trading empire.

The Portuguese initiated European contact with southern Africa but did not establish permanent settlements there. Instead they preferred harbors along the east coast of Africa, north of modern South Africa, where gold, ivory, and slaves could be acquired (Ross 21). Travelers shipwrecked off the coast of South Africa gave reports of their contact with indigenous peoples (M. Wilson 78–85). The killing of the Portuguese admiral Francisco de Almeida, viceroy of India, by indigenous South African hunter-gatherers, the Khoikhoi (called Hottentots), in retribution for the Portuguese theft of cattle after the Portuguese anchored in Table Bay in 1510, further discouraged settlement (Ross 21). The deeds of the Portuguese seafarers in Africa are central to *Os Lusíadas*. The author of the epic, Camões, himself traveled to Africa and the East half a century after da Gama.

The fifth canto of *Os Lusíadas* depicts da Gama's landing at the Cape of Storms during the course of the famous circumnavigation that would open the sea route to India. Da Gama and his mariners encounter a vengeful apparition, the Titan Adamastor, who recounts his lineage and fate. He has been turned to stone for lusting after the white nymph Thetis (Tethys in Landeg White's translation [stanza 53, line 5]), the immortal wife of Peleus. Betrayed before the consummation of his passion, Adamastor finds himself transformed into the landmass of the Cape peninsula itself. "I am that vast, secret promontory," he tells the sailors, "[y]ou Portuguese call the Cape of Storms" (stanza 50, lines 1–2). He shapes the white South African cultural imaginary by cursing the European invaders for their incursion into his territory and prophesying the retribution that will be the consequence of the white presence at the Cape.

Camões invests Adamastor with anachronistic knowledge in order to render concrete the vengeance promised. The poet has the Titan foretell the death of Viceroy de Almeida in Table Bay—an event that postdates da Gama's voyage. Adamastor also details the fate that will be meted out to Don Emmanuel de Souza and his wife, Leonora De Sà, who would be shipwrecked off the Transkei coast in 1552. The couple and their three children, together with other survivors of the wreck of the *São João*, were portrayed in the sources on which Camões drew as having journeyed into the South African interior, where they were initially received with generosity by their indigenous hosts but then robbed, stripped naked, and driven into the bush to perish. In his introduction to an anthology of writing on Adamastor, which traces the evolution of the topos in the work of approximately fifty poets, Malvern van Wyk Smith reconstructs the allegorical treatment of the couple in the sixteenth-century Portuguese romantic epic *Shipwreck of Manoel de Souza de Sepulveda and Dona Lianor de Sa*, by Jeronimo Corte Real (1594). His conclusion, "The young knight and his wife become the lost flower of Portugal's nobility, perished on African shores. . . . Dona Lianor particularly becomes the prototype of all fair white women despoiled in the desert" (Introduction 19), is resonant with the theme of interracial rape that I seek to have my students address (see also Brink, "Myth" 43).

The fate of Don Emmanuel de Souza and Leonora De Sà is presented in canto 5, stanzas 44–48, of *Os Lusíadas*. A consideration of this portion of Camões's text returns us to the crucial role of the white woman's body for the management of affective economies in what Mary Louise Pratt has called "the contact zone" (8). The epic implicitly sets the "naked, matchless body" of Thetis, the white nymph whom Adamastor desired (canto 5, stanza 55, line 4), against the involuntary nakedness of Leonora as we witness how "harsh, grasping people / Tear her clothes from the lovely lady" and her "body of such crystal beauty" is "Exposed to frost and the scorching winds" (stanza 47, lines 3–6). Camões rehearses a fatal conjunction of flesh and stone as the Portuguese couple meet their death in the African wilderness: "After softening the very rocks / With tears distilled from grief and pain, / They embraced, their souls already flown / Their wretched gaol of exquisite flesh and bone" (stanza 48, lines 5–8).

The formative desire of a subsequent tradition of "white writing," as Coetzee puts it in his critical volume of the same name, to establish reciprocity with the South African landscape by "mak[ing] the landscape speak" (*White Writing* 176) is foreclosed in *Os Lusíadas* through the annihilation of Don Emmanuel and Leonora. Indeed, it is a hallmark of the topos that Adamastor will spawn a "poetry of dread" in the analysis of Jeremy Cronin, a poet and former political prisoner under apartheid (77). In the writing of Roy Campbell, a reactionary South African modernist poet, and elsewhere, Adamastor is seldom other than a synecdoche for South Africa figured as a "land of violence and sadism" (Gray 32).[1]

I call my students' attention to the persistent interweaving of both race and gender in the anxious "myth of origin" (Brink, "Myth" 41) that the topos of Adamastor inaugurates. "Camões's Adamastor," writes Andries Walter Oliphant, a South African scholar, "is widely interpreted to represent the racial apprehensions of white settlers regarding Africans. This is associated with the colonial prohibition of sexual intercourse between white women and black men in South Africa" (61). Oliphant confirms the dominant reading of the topos, which has largely gone unchallenged in South African literary scholarship. The Adamastor myth, states Dorothy Driver, a feminist critic, "has always been taken to be about race, and specifically about the black man's frustrated desire for a white woman" (455)—a desire rendered comically graphic in André Brink's 1993 novella *Cape of Storms: The First Life of Adamastor*.

Brink's short work explicitly challenges dominant European mythology (Brink, *Reinventing* 21–22). The challenge emerges partly through the explicitly metafictional nature of a text that self-reflexively interrogates the transmission of the topos, partly through Brink's bawdy exaggeration or "send-up" (22) of the sexual anxieties of white men. The tale is told by a Khoikhoi man whom Brink names T'kama ("a slang-word for the male member" [*Cape* 4]). The ribald plot is largely devoted to T'kama's failure, on account of his size, to consummate sexual intercourse with the white woman Khois ("woman") whom he abducts. But Brink's playfully erotic revision of Camões substitutes union for coercion as T'kama and Khois eventually have a child together. That the mixed-race child holds out the possibility of redemption after T'kama's capture by the Portuguese at the end of the novella—"somewhere in the land, I knew, somewhere . . . was the child. He would live on" (128)—should not be overlooked. This motif is central to Brink's deliberate deconstruction of colonial anxieties about miscegenation, anxieties that would result in the infamous Immorality Act of the apartheid state.

Yet Brink's burlesque departure from the dominant mythology underscores, through the strenuous elaboration of an alternative, the resilience of that which it resists. Precisely in its thwarting of T'kama's desire, Brink's text offers oblique testimony to the power of the fantasy of interracial rape that haunts Camões's epic. This point returns the class discussion to Coetzee's novel. To invoke Camões in the context of *Disgrace* is to ask students to consider that violation of the white woman has an even earlier provenance than is implied in its characterization as "the colonial nightmare *topos*," the phrase that Peter McDonald uses in his discussion of the novel (326).

Whether Leonora was raped or not, I suggest to my students, is beside the point. My intervention here is a form of troping on what Coetzee has Elizabeth Costello term the "madness of reading" (*Elizabeth Costello* 174), and it intersects the concerns I have staged earlier in classroom discussion regarding the affective economies that congeal around *Disgrace*. The similarities between the topos of Adamastor and its intertexts in the white cultural imaginary, on the one hand, and between Coetzee's novel and the controversy surrounding it, on the other, are now recast for my students with respect to two additional references. The first arises from the paradigm of postcolonial studies: Jenny Sharpe's analysis of discourses of interracial rape in the wake of the Indian Mutiny in 1857. The second returns us to a specifically South African setting for the consideration of interracial rape, however geographically remote from Coetzee's Eastern Cape, through the work of Charles van Onselen, a South African historian.

Sharpe describes how the figure of the Indian as a docile and pliable colonial subject in British colonial discourse was supplanted, after the mutiny, by the figure of the Indian as the savage rapist of British women. This transformation, she argues, was a response to the social and political challenge of the mutiny. British authority, severely tested by popular resistance, reconsolidated around allegations of rape, whether or not white women were in fact raped. A crisis in British authority was managed and controlled through the recirculation of the violated bodies of English women as a sign for the challenge to colonial rule. Sharpe's analysis shows how rape constructs white womanhood as a crucial "cultural signifier" (4) in the consolidation, management, and reconsolidation of colonial power.

In South Africa, this same use of allegations of rape by the white government should not be underestimated. I remind my students of the black-peril scares that swept across the Witwatersrand between 1890 and 1914. Typically, these waves of collective hysteria followed accusations by white women of rape or sexual molestation that were made on what Van Onselen terms an "unprecedented scale" (45). Van Onselen points to the genesis of this hysteria in relations between masters and servants on the Rand, where for a time working-class white women were employed as servants alongside black men. He argues that public hysteria coincided with "periods of stress or acute tension within the political economy of the Witwatersrand as a whole" (51). Writ large as a collective fantasy that we might parse, alongside Frantz Fanon, as "A Negro is raping me" (*Black Skin* 178), Adamastor's barely cloaked threat would be mobilized in the rhetoric as well as in the political and economic instrumentality of the white women's accusations.[2]

This historicizing analysis applies to the management of white power in South Africa, whether the emergence of "the colonial nightmare *topos*" of Dutch or British colonialism in South Africa is considered in *The Lusíads*, *avant la lettre*, or whether whiteness is scrutinized in the "cusp-time" of the transition to democracy there (Boehmer, "Endings" 45). My teaching of *Disgrace* insists that the analysis of discourses of interracial rape must take cognizance of the construction of white womanhood in a given context, together with the regulatory effects of that construction.

In Camões's text, as in *Disgrace*, the white woman's body becomes the site where hierarchies of race are articulated, where inclusions and exclusions are forcibly enacted—whether or not violation actually occurs. Representations of interracial rape in the contexts we have examined stage the violation of the white female body and simultaneously the violation of that body as boundary. I suggest, in conclusion, that we consider how such boundary violation is complicit with what Anne Pellegrini has called the "racial economy of compulsory heterosexuality" (23), in whose framework power accrues differently and differentially to white and black men across the boundary that is constituted by the white woman's body. Numerous canonical texts, ranging from William Faulkner's depictions of the deep South in the United States to Coetzee's renderings of the South African hinterland (consider "The Narrative of Jacobus Coetzee" in *Dusklands* [51–125], and *In the Heart of the Country*), can be referenced for our students to promote critical discussion of the racialized and gendered power relations that have legitimated white patriarchy. Pellegrini suggests that the disproportionate attention given to interracial heterosexual rape involving black men and white women masks the fact that under slavery and colonialism white men had virtually unlimited access to women of color (223). Lucy Lurie's queer sexual agency stands outside the framework that Pellegrini describes. Her willingness to become a third wife or concubine along the terms Petrus suggests (*Disgrace* 204) unsettles the racial dynamics of this sexual dispensation but not its patriarchal dimensions. Nevertheless, Lucy's queer desire, staged between the lines of a text that does not do it justice, points to a vision of the "rights of desire" (89) that is more emancipatory than the one her father enacts (see Bethlehem, "Aneconomy"). Adamastor casts a pall over Coetzee's *Disgrace*, but a dissident reading of Lucy that betrays the letter of the text in which she subsists might enable our students to begin to consider the political and ethical consequences of refusing to give Adamastor the last word.

"I have told the whole story," insists Lucy Lurie. "The whole story is what I have told" (110).

NOTES

[1] For additional discussions of Adamastor in South African literary scholarship, see Bethlehem, *Skin Tight* 38–54; Crewe, "Recalling" and "Specter"; Cronin; Driver; Murray and Voss; Van Wyk Smith, Introduction; Wade; as well as the collection of essays edited by Vladislavić *T'kama-Adamastor*.

[2] For a differently weighted allusion to the black peril in the context of *Disgrace*, see L. Graham, "Reading." For a thorough exploration of the intersection between rape and race in South African literature from the colonial period to the present, see L. Graham, *State*.

Countering Context:
Teaching *Disgrace* in the New South Africa
Gerald Gaylard

> **Sympathy** *n*. (Capacity for) being simultaneously affected
> with the same feeling as another; tendency to share
> or state of sharing another person's or thing's emotion
> or sensation or condition . . . mental participation
> *with* another in his trouble or *with* another's trouble;
> compassion (*for*); agreement (*with*) in opinion or
> desire . . . having, or as a result of, sympathy with
> another, by way of sympathetic action.
> —*Concise Oxford Dictionary*

> **Empathy** *n*. Power of projecting one's personality into (and
> so fully comprehending) the object of contemplation.
> —*Concise Oxford Dictionary*

South Africa, perhaps especially the South Africa of public institutions (including schools and universities), effects certain closures, not least in the realm of affect. Teaching Coetzee in and against this context offers the potential to begin to counter some of these closures, on both sociological and affective levels.

These closures range across a broad spectrum. Firstly, South Africa's heritage as a British colony survives in a certain Anglo-empiricist materialism and instrumentalism. Literature and the reading thereof are not exempt from this heritage; because literature can relatively easily delve into worlds beyond the material, functional, and empirical, it is often subjected to a reductionist reading that sees it as merely an avenue into the exploration of "real" social issues. This is evident in the tendency of many students to read *Disgrace* sociologically. A second closure is the sociopolitical overdetermination of South African society, culture, and literature. This seems to be a result of what Louise Bethlehem has called a "rhetoric of urgency" ("'Primary Need'"), an extremely complex discourse composed of a plethora of grim sociohistorical exigencies, Dark Continent otherings, condescending media portrayals, and so on. The rhetoric of urgency tends to endorse the simple materialist reading of society and literature, regarding anything that is not productively engaged in the reduction of African poverty as being indulgent and ethically dubious. Art and aesthetics in this reading are often irresponsible. Thirdly, these interlinked discourses in South Africa were exacerbated by the struggle heritage of the apartheid years, which, understandably, considered only the raison d'être of political enfranchisement. For literature, this prioritizing meant that writers should focus on historical realities and political injustices, write accessibly, and see culture as a weapon of the struggle. Fourthly, these compounded tendencies to see sociopolitical realities as preeminent have been made more extreme by globalization in the postapartheid era, which cemented the development of a consumer culture and various forms of what is referred to in *Disgrace* as "the great rationalization" (3).

If *Disgrace* as a teaching text potentially disrupts these closures, how does it do so? Perhaps some buttressing via the text's reception is required. If the ways in which *Disgrace* was read in this context are initially foregrounded, then the assumptions underlying such readings become apparent. In the context of the so-called new South Africa, various South African critics and teachers have tended to read the text in a realist manner. Indeed, the novel may well be regarded as inviting such a reading. If read as a realist text, the novel appears to be an unrelentingly grim portrayal of the more unfortunate social aspects of postapartheid South Africa, and reviewers consistently focused on them when the novel appeared in 1999. Shaun de Waal called it "unremittingly bleak"; Timothy Trengrove-Jones saw "no redemption in a bleak tale of colonialism reversed"; Andrew O'Hehir described it as a "sober, searing and even cynical little book"; while Matthew Blatchford excoriated it thus: "[T]he tale is narratively framed by explicit racism, implicit sexism and homophobia. It gives a distorted image of contemporary South Africa . . . cheered by Afrophobes overseas." These negative receptions were crowned by the ANC's similar dismissal of the text (see Attwell, "Race in *Disgrace*"; P. McDonald). There were also many overseas criticisms of the text that echoed these local responses. More substantial reviews, which have read *Disgrace* sociologically or have considered sociological critiques at length, include those by Grant Farred, Peter McDonald, and Mary Eagleton. Despite this negative reception, the novel was prescribed on the secondary-school syllabus for some years, usually being taught in the vein of the reviews—that is, as providing a window onto South African society and its problems in the aftermath of apartheid. In other words, the temptation with the novel and the teaching thereof is to focus less on its narrative trajectory, characters, formal aspects, theoretical interventions or metafictionality than on the sociopolitical issues it raises, which range from sexual abuse to political enfranchisement.

Fully confronting the pedagogical challenge of explaining realist reading ideally requires a theoretical excursus into realism and its social and political history, quite a challenge for a secondary-level classroom and out of the reach of most students at that level as well as some junior undergraduates. Moreover, it would also require a close reading of the text to make its complex web of intertextuality apparent, again a hard task for students with scant acquaintance, if any, with the intertexts utilized by Coetzee (I count over twenty intertexts in the book, primarily Romantic, ranging from Blake to Byron to Wordsworth and beyond). Both of these pedagogical approaches suggest that the prescribing of the text at the secondary level was somewhat optimistic. Nevertheless, it is possible, by outlining the critical reception already mentioned, to begin to ask questions about reading texts and what assumptions underpin any reading. There are obviously a number of instrumentalist and nationalist assumptions underlying the reception of the text in the new South Africa, particularly in the primary criticism of the text as racist and morale damaging. At this point in the class, Coetzee's Jerusalem Prize acceptance speech is surely crucial for student understanding of his project, particularly Lurie's quixotic refusal of historical realities and "the great rationalization."

All these observations have been made by pedagogues well outside South Africa—for instance, in the University of Redlands (USA) collaborative project *Encountering Disgrace: Reading and Teaching Coetzee's Novel*. In this volume, however, Daniel Kiefer suggests what I think is the most challenging aspect of the text and its teaching: not only does the novel challenge its historical context and reception but it also suggests that new modes of reading, indeed of feeling, are required. As Kiefer's article "Sympathy for the Devil" indicates, the deep challenge of the text is for readers to feel for David Lurie, an anachronistic, entitled, proud, and irritable roué whose self-serving ethics and feckless diffidence do not inspire identification, especially not from students whom he dismisses as "post-Christian, posthistorical, postliterate, they might as well have been hatched from eggs yesterday" (32). What I have been calling closed readings are summarily judgmental and condemnatory in South Africa today, particularly of Lurie and his ilk. This raises issues of political correctness, consensual normativity, the fashionability of the new, and (dis)taste. For Kiefer, pedagogical success with the text involves his condemnatory students gaining some sympathy for Lurie. Sam Durrant explores similar territory, albeit from a literary rather than pedagogical angle. For Durrant, "while the author himself is able to imagine his way into the consciousness of a limited array of narratorial personae, these personae are themselves unable to imagine themselves into the lives of those less privileged" ("J. M. Coetzee" 120). Indeed, the extent that Lurie manages to imagine himself into the lives of others, even nonhuman animal others, is probably close to the distance that students have to travel to imagine themselves into his life.

Clearly it is no mean feat to get students full of righteous indignation not only to develop some empathy *for* a character they find repellent, someone who signifies all that they reject at this point in their lives, but also to feel some sympathy *with* this character. There is no pedagogical answer to this difficulty, but the cognitive theories of Jerome Bruner, Lev Vygotsky, and Jean Piaget advocate starting from where students are. If the text is to hold any interest, it must be shown to question the ethicalization of the sexual, asking whether sexuality can be reduced to the biological imperative of identifying and protecting procreation and progeny. The text, through Lurie's arguing for "the rights of desire, . . . the god who makes even the small birds quiver" (89), asks whether sexuality outside of reproduction and the nuclear family is really evil, dramatizing this fundamentalist perspective in the Isaacs family. Many students feel disgust from the beginning. Further progress depends on the extent to which they feel the horror of Lurie's rake's progress through dismissal, rejection, violence, and abjection to a kind of quiet acceptance. The text abounds with images that suggest this abject path in somatically potent ways: the contrast between the flourish of the signature and the stark binary columns of the report that turns the lovers to foes (40), the burnt scalp (a scalping?), the image of the dog psychopomp, the amelioration of the grand opera to a plinky-plonk banjo paean. Lurie evokes a fearful, sympathetic vertigo in us: we know that with just one slip we could easily slide down just such a slippery slope, we know that all is fragile on planet Earth. Moreover, he gets his full karmic comeuppance for his Byronic sexual excesses via Lucy's rape and her choosing to bear the child of the rape; suddenly the ethicalized biological imperative of verifiable parenthood through controlled sexuality does not seem so gray, bourgeois, and unattractive to him. The pathos of this ironic reversal should not be lost upon those who were initially disgusted by him.

Whether we want to call this a process of developing the sympathetic imagination is a moot point. For some Coetzee commentators the affective dimension is really a question of ethics (Attwell, "Race"; Marais, *Secretary*; Helgesson). For Durrant, Lurie's descent makes it "clear that stupidity…has always constituted the ethical destination, or anti-*telos*, of Coetzee's fiction" ("J. M. Coetzee" 121) in the sense that Lurie's sympathy for the dogs is preverbal, something he describes as "stupid, daft, wrongheaded" (146). Durrant continues:

> As soon as the sympathetic imagination acquires a content, it forgets the difference of the other. To remember the other is to place the imagination in abeyance: it is only in his stupefying work with animals that he avoids imaginative projection and enacts a singularly *un*imaginative sympathy. . . . In place of the traditional concept of the sympathetic imagination, in which the self attempts to mentally inhabit the position of the other, Coetzee's fiction works to other the self, to deprive the subject of its privileges until it is reduced to an approximation of the other. In place of the mental process of imaginative *pro*jection, Coetzee's subjects undergo a bodily process of *ab*jection.   (130)

What happens in *Disgrace* is not so much empathy, or projection of the imagination in order to achieve understanding, as sympathy, in terms of feeling with, emotions that are not sought. I agree with Durrant that *sympathetic imagination* is probably not the right phrase; *visceral sympathy* may be more accurate. There is recent neuropsychological evidence, the "mirror neurons" in the brain (Ratcliffe 12), that suggests sympathy has visceral origins, even though social and cognitive factors are probably just as important. A postcolonial transculturation of the idea of the sympathetic imagination is called for. As Elleke Boehmer says of David Lurie, "[W]e see him taking the quality of sympathy beyond its conventional limits, the divides between the living and the dead, between humans and other animals, without being precisely sure why he is doing so" ("Sorry" 141). A somatic sympathy certainly short-circuits a socially conditioned cognitive response. In *Disgrace* this is a minimalist negative sympathy; there is no feel-good redemption here, no outcome or reward or expectation attached to sympathy. This sympathy is not only not chosen, it is also not strictly required; it is a pure generosity.

Moreover, as Lurie's decline suggests, the text is not merely asking the reader to sympathize with Lurie's character as a real person; after all, Lurie is a character in a book. It might be regarded as naive, even dangerously so, to treat characters in books as though they are real people. *Disgrace* builds upon the work of Matthew Arnold and the Victorian and later humanists that advocated identification and sympathy, primarily with characters, as a means to enlarge emotional and imaginative range, expanding toward a more textual understanding of empathy and sympathy. Lurie is not just a character, he is also a textual function in that he embodies the text's narrative trajectory to humility, even to humiliation. The fall into moral and physical disgrace that just one slip could precipitate for any of us is the narrative path of the tragedy. The novel might be said to play on fear in this respect; it conjures with the will to survive and flourish, as do all texts with primitivist and pastoral tropes, and asks us what happens to our sympathies when we are at rock bottom. This is probably a difficult thing for young learners to grasp, but surely this makes a grappling with the unglamorous difficulties of danger, decline, and mortality all the more worthwhile.

Furthermore, not only does the text provide an avenue into the exploration of affect but it also opens the door to metafictional and metapedagogical questions about literature and the value of literature and literariness. Given that students move from a likely dismissal of Lurie toward some sympathy, albeit grudging, there is the opportunity to discuss how literature works and what it might achieve, particularly in a context that routinely forecloses sympathy and reaching out to otherness. In particular, the text's foregrounding of fear and the effects of closure allow students the opportunity to consider the mechanics of moving beyond fear. Finally, these questions of literature's affectiveness and effectiveness can also be brought full circle back to the context of South Africa today, a nation that is struggling with globalization and the imposition of what Coetzee calls "a business model," not least on its universities (Interview [Poyner] 24). *Disgrace* asks probing questions about South Africa's place within global economies and what effects those have upon the local. These questions may have a salutary effect upon current South African students, who are deluged with global media and who like to think of themselves as citizens of the global.

Hence my argument has been that *Disgrace* enables a pedagogical intervention into South African contextualities via affect. In this respect the novel builds upon the character-based sympathy of humanism, significantly extending it into a more visceral and textual sympathy where feeling is architectonic, not just related to the individual, and involves radical responsibility and generosity. This extension is arguably vital if our feeling is to move beyond the individual and take on any social relevance.

Teaching Coetzee and Australia

Elleke Boehmer

If we looked back with the benefit of hindsight, we could say that J. M. Coetzee's *Disgrace*, published in 1999, ended a dark and withdrawn chapter in his writing. It was his last novel set wholly in South Africa and the work that preceded his move to Australia. *Summertime* (2010), the third volume in his autobiographical *Scenes from Provincial Life* (2011), is set in South Africa but styled as a memoir. For a novelist most of whose work had up to this point been deeply informed by the landscape and colonial history of the Western Cape region, this closing of a South African thematic in his work, coincident with his immigration to Adelaide in 2002, represented a profound though also carefully weighed change. On 6 March 2006, on the opening day of the Adelaide Writers' Week festival, Coetzee was publicly sworn in as an Australian in a tent in his chosen city, whose "grace," he said in an interview, had deeply attracted him when he first visited it. "Coetzee pledged his loyalty to Australia, its people whose democratic beliefs he now shared, whose rights and liberties he respected and whose laws he would now obey," observed an Australian journalist of the event. Taking the duties and obligations that came along with his new citizenship seriously, he was soon to bring the meaning of human rights and democracy in Australia under mordant scrutiny in the third novel of his Australian period, *Diary of a Bad Year* (Debelle).

Yet despite Coetzee's formal and carefully considered adoption of his new nationality, Coetzee is still widely taught and studied in the academy as a South African and not an Australian or even a transnational writer. It is as if the worldwide success of *Disgrace*, that novel often hailed as definitive of the postapartheid period, coupled with the award to him of the 2003 Nobel Prize for Literature, for his South Africa–situated oeuvre, has embedded the idea of a South African Coetzee in readers' and teachers' minds (an approach that the publication of *Summertime* in 2009, with its South African setting, might be seen to have confirmed). Against this idea, my essay pays heed to the particular choices of national location and naturalization the author has made in the past ten years. It considers what it is to teach his Australian work and how that work in fact composes or "[makes] up" its Australian context, as he puts it (*Elizabeth Costello* 12), given that he not only actively espoused Australia but in interesting ways also anticipated it in his fiction. Even some of his essays in the 1988 collection *White Writing*, about explorer and settler writing in South Africa, seem to be in dialogue with what we might call the matter of Australia or conventions of representing Australia. Certainly, in his Australian phase, he has written in ways that respond, however obliquely, to a certain mainstream and masculine tradition of contemporary Australian writing—as we find, for example, in the work of Peter Carey or Tim Winton.

Coetzee, in short, is one of those writers who has, if unusually late in life, exchanged the accident of his birth location, South Africa, for another, formally chosen place, Australia. How should this choice affect the way we approach the later, transnational Coetzee in the classroom? What does his new home-land mean to him? How productive is it to teach his Australian-period work in conjunction with some of Australia's prominent native-born writers? What is the significance of Australia to him as a writer, how is it represented in his fiction, and, most of all, what effect has his move had on his work? Even in his most rooted South African period (reflected in *Age of Iron*, for example), he never was a writer particularly devoted to realism, geographic or otherwise. If Australia in its environmental, historical, national, and literary qualities has shaped his fiction since 2002, how does this shaping manifest itself? How does he imaginatively approach his new land—that is to say, as a symbolic prospect or a complex of territorial memory and national tradition?

In asking these questions and presenting Coetzee's Australian context to stu-dents, it is important from the outset to bear in mind that Australia was once a British settler colony (or a combination of settler colonies, federated in 1901) and therefore had a status in the British Empire that was comparable to South Africa's (united in 1910). The colonial trajectories of the two countries run in close parallel. In literary and mythographic terms, Australia and South Africa together form part of the antipodes, which in colonial writing was often set in negative contrast to the enlightened north on the one hand and the brave new world of America on the other. As the South African writer JC in *Diary of a Bad Year* observes, "Australia was never a promised land, a new world, an island paradise offering its bounty to the new arrival. . . . Life in the Antipodes was meant to be a punishment" (112). He could equally have been speaking of South Africa. Whereas South Africa's twentieth century was marked by the establishment and then dismantling of the policy of a state-sanctioned racism called apartheid, which oppressed the black majority, Australia's history as a nation has been profoundly shaped by the exclusion and in some cases near eradication of the Aboriginal minority, a racist policy partially redressed in re-cent years by various rehabilitation programs (such as the Sorry campaign). The Aboriginal condition, however, has never been one of Coetzee's chief Australian concerns, perhaps because the plight of the colonial other is something that he already explored in some depth in previous work, most notably *Foe*. Instead, the influence of the new settler world of Australia on Coetzee is registered in his mode of imagining the country: in the how rather than in the what of his repre-sentation. His Australian period work, *Elizabeth Costello*, *Slow Man*, and *Diary of a Bad Year*, produces a recognizably Australian world yet in a way that is often sporadic and sometimes even perfunctory and unconvinced. In this essay I probe that intermittent quality of his Australian representation and observe in particular how he imagines space (topography, city sites) as a means of both disconnection from and affiliation to his new country.

It is important to note that in his actual *and* imaginative move to Australia, Coetzee did not so much exchange one literary tradition for another when he immigrated as shift national location within the genre of settler realism. He was always preoccupied with the ways in which reality is established in a work of fiction and therefore with the codes through which literary realism is at once constituted and undermined. In fiction after fiction, wherever set, he involves his reader in scrutinizing the operation of these codes of "embodying" afresh, as Elizabeth Costello puts it (*Elizabeth Costello* 9; see Attridge, *J. M. Coetzee* 102). He has always been aware that realism must be taken by the reader as just as unreliable and constructed as other modes of representing reality.

For Coetzee, this problem of embodying, of bringing the real world to mind in writing, is particularly acute in a colonial and settler context, given that the language and imaginative schemas that a colonial white writer has at hand for interpreting the world bear little connection to the surrounding landscape and its peoples. In the classroom, *White Writing* can be used to pinpoint the estranged quality that an imported language has in a settler nation, be it South Africa or Australia. As he writes, "The [South African] poet scans the landscape with his hermeneutic gaze, but it remains trackless, refuses to emerge into meaningfulness as a landscape of signs" (9). As in South Africa, so too in Australia, the white writer is locked inside the foreign, imported ideas and symbols through which he attempts to imagine his new place. Despite the move from South Africa to Australia, Coetzee's work after 2000 has continued self-consciously to confront these narrative demands of settler writing, of embodying afresh.

The difference is that in Australia, a country acquired by conscious adoption rather than through the accident of birth, Coetzee has been more noticeably concerned not only to establish the country fictionally as a space but also to realize that space as an actual, recognizable location. He has arguably represented Australia with a greater directness of reference than he ever showed in the imagining of South Africa. If in novels like *Life & Times of Michael K*, as well as in the critical essays in *White Writing*, he was concerned with how to represent the arid South African hinterland, his Australia is more strongly registered although similarly conceived as a land of the mind, a space relayed through intellectual schemas.

In Australian-born authors like Carey and Winton, the relation of land and voice, or of (Australian) context and language, is generally taken as definitive of their writing (as Carey demonstrates with his ventriloquism of folk hero Ned Kelly's voice in *True History of the Kelly Gang*). For Coetzee, a writer who has always been something of a skeptic regarding national affiliation, this national tradition and definitive relation do not or cannot operate in the same way. The difference emerges when he is taught alongside these typical Australian writers, his new literary compatriots. It is significant that from *Waiting for the Barbarians* (1980) on, he has chosen to write at a distance from region and vernacular, indeed from most forms of territorial identification (*White Writing* 7–8, *Elizabeth Costello* 199–200). His voice was always a stripped-down, standardized, global English. Even when he decided to adopt the identity of Australian writer through his alter ego Elizabeth Costello some years before he physically settled in Australia, he did not modify this voice. Becoming an Australia-located writer, writing Australia as if as an Australian, "[making] up" Australia, as Costello says, was an intellectual, not linguistic, challenge that interested him. One of the most important elements of his connection to Australia, therefore, is the way in which the link between writer and land is established.

Australia insinuates itself into *Elizabeth Costello* in the form of journalistic outline or sketchy reportage, or as a kind of visual shorthand, where precisely conceived images or scenes are made to designate a wider social world. "So real," Costello observes metatextually (if also archly) in describing Marijana's domestic interior in *Slow Man*—an interior that features white leather furniture, a lurid abstract painting, and a ceiling fan (241–42). Coetzee has apparently kicked away some of the abstract metafictional schemas that in South Africa underwrote his visual imagination. His referential vocabulary, at least on the surface, has a less distant or mediated relation to the world that is being described. It may be that his purpose is, to a degree, to embed himself as a naturalized writer in that tradition of Australian writing strongly identified with the land and the nation.

Coetzee's interest in accurately evoking Australia is reinforced at the level of his writing style and at the level of his generic choices. In the classroom, we might juxtapose the direct, straightforward realism of the first part of *Slow Man*, at least until its self-reflexive halfway break, and the essayistic and diaristic commentaries of *Diary of a Bad Year*. Even when Australia is designated in the relatively transnational *Elizabeth Costello*, a functional, minimalist language is employed—not so much dry and sere, as is the language in *Disgrace*, as less than literary. It is a language grown impatient with the task of description. Costello refers, in passing, to the "Irish-Catholic Melbourne of her childhood," assuming that this phrasing is sufficient to evoke an entire context (*Elizabeth Costello* 179, 125). In *Slow Man*, the language of minimalist denotation is spun out in the thin strand of scene setting that runs through the novel. The vocabulary designating South Australia is dominated by street names, basic topographic features, and the urban commonplaces of Adelaide: "He will never stride up Black Hill again, never pedal off to the market to do his shopping, much less come swooping on his bicycle down the curves of Montacute" (25); "Years ago he used to cycle through Munno Para on the way to Gawler. Then it was just a few houses dotted around a filling station, with bare scrub behind" (241; see also 151). Magill Road, repeatedly mentioned as the site of Paul Rayment's accident, is built up across the novel into a metonym for accident, a sign of how brutal reality can interrupt the dulling rhythm of the everyday.[1]

The language of dry reportage insinuates itself also into the quasi-academic prose of the essays that make up *Diary of a Bad Year*, in particular into the uppermost strand of the first part, "Strong Opinions," JC's jaded pronouncements on public life. Here Australia, specifically Sydney, after 2001 and after the Iraq War, is a land of compromised liberal idealism, reduced moral decency, and withering national pride (120). The nation is thus in several ways a perfect backdrop and foil for JC's exposition of his "pessimistic anarchistic quietism" as against the "hurly-burly of politics" (203, 171). Because JC wishes to speak a greater truth about public affairs to "ordinary people" than that supplied by politicians, "strong opinions" changed him from being a novelist who dispenses lessons to being "a pedant who dabbles in fiction," one given to a dry, nondramatic style (125–26, 191).

Coetzee's concern with how to evoke reality in Australia relates to other interests that have become prominent in his Australian-phase work, such as his wish to live from the heart, as he puts it, and not only through the verbal constructs of literary fiction. This desire is poignantly expressed in Costello's eighth lesson (*Elizabeth Costello* 193–226). Understanding life through the medium of the body is important to Australian writing: consider Winton's harsh West Australian realism (*Breath* and *Dirt Music*). As a symptom of Coetzee's preoccupation with the quality of reality and how to represent it, *Diary of a Bad Year*, the more candid second section especially, is overwritten with words signifying the real or the true: "really," "truth," "truly," "authority effect," as well as "love," the "truth" of "the heart," the "thing itself," "love itself." The writer-narrator JC several times expresses his fascination with the effect of "indisputable certainty" called up by a realist writer like Lev Tolstoy (234–35, 119, 126, 196, 198, 149–51, 185). Throughout the novel, it is the evocation of the real in the manner especially of Tolstoy—how it is done, why it is important—that motivates the narrative (192).

During the decade of his residence in Australia, Coetzee appears to have learned well that in Australian literature the nation, its society and landscapes, is brought into being through certain figures and conventions. Paul Rayment in *Slow Man* says of himself, "I can pass among Australians. I cannot pass among the French. That, as far as I am concerned, is all there is to it, to the national-identity business: where one passes and where one does not" (197). In Australia Coetzee wishes for his imagination, or for his constructs of Australian reality, to pass. He goes so far as to engage with some of Australia's foundational stories and exhibits his habitual cool correctness in the process. *Slow Man*, for instance, takes on the stock figures of the maimed white hero and the fake or forgery, such as we find in Patrick White's *Voss* and Carey's *Theft*, respectively. Both *Slow Man* and *Diary of a Bad Year* touch on Australia's history of new immigration, from Croatia in *Slow Man* and the Philippines in *Diary*.[2] What is particularly intriguing about *Slow Man*, his first fully Australian novel, is that he feels obliged to assert a characteristically Australian interest in "fictional truths and truthful fictions" (Attridge, *J. M. Coetzee* 199). In a novel preoccupied with how Rayment's life becomes Costello's creation and how she, as his creator, becomes his doppelgänger, Coetzee overdetermines our reading by stamping the novel with the sign of the fake, in the homonymic Fauchery forgery incident. When Rayment allows Drako Jokić to make free with his photograph collection, Drako abuses Rayment's hospitality by making amusing photoshopped copies of Rayment's precious prints and replacing the real things with the fakes.

When Coetzee immigrated to Australia, he approached the country with many of the definitive preoccupations of literature ready-made, as if carried in his suitcase. He referenced the standard representational conventions and commonplace reality effects in order to announce himself as a writer of Australia. He sought to do justice to his new country as it is most typically defined, yet he also remained deliberately knowing and paradoxically distancing. The opening of *Slow Man* is unequivocal on the tug of the real, on cutting life to the quick. The novel begins with Rayment literally in medias res, flying through the air, the cause of the accident at this point not given. The impact of the opening, however, remains tantalizingly out of reach: reality cannot be relived. From *Slow Man* to *Diary of a Bad Year* the trajectory is clear. In order to write Australia, Coetzee has been involved in rounding up the various standard referents of a colonial dystopia. He exhibits these commonplaces in his work, demonstrates that he understands their uses, but then finally discards them as inadequate to embody a true Australian reality, as inadequate as any self-referential postmodern trope.

NOTES

[1] On the novel's multiple metafictional turns, see Kossew, "Border Crossings."

[2] Reference is to the cultural-historical and literary studies of, among others, Carter, *Living* and *Road*; Hassan; Healy; Huggan, *Australian Literature* and "'Greening'"; Schaffer; and R. White.

Teaching Coetzee's American Contexts; or, How I Teach America — and Africa — in Cullowhee, North Carolina

Laura Wright

In *Youth*, the second volume of J. M. Coetzee's *autre*biography, the narrator tells us that in South Africa in the 1960s,

> [t]he songs on the radio all came from America. In the newspapers the antics of American film stars were obsessively followed, American crazes like the hoola hoop slavishly imitated. Why? Why look to America in everything? Disowned by the Dutch and now the British, had South Africans made up their minds to become fake Americans, even though most had never clapped eyes on a real American in their lives? (90)

Here as elsewhere, the idea and question of "America" haunts Coetzee's work. It looms as the entity that "will swallow" Eugene Dawn, the mythographer-narrator of "The Vietnam Project," the first part of Coetzee's first novel *Dusklands* (9); it is the residence of Mrs. Curren's daughter in *Age of Iron*, a place where Mrs. Curren says her grandchildren "will die at seventy-five or eighty-five as stupid as they were born" (195). In *Youth*, it is the place that John will not go because "he knows what America does to artists: sends them mad, locks them up, drives them out" (151). And in *Diary of a Bad Year*, JC finds it "impossible to believe that in some American hearts the spectacle of their country's honor being dragged through the mud does not breed murderous thoughts" (40). For him, America is a place of dishonor, "selfish and cruel" in its government's support of torture during its "so-called war on terror" (122, 39).

In the work of a writer often accused of being evasive and indirect in his treatment of South Africa, its people, and its politics, throughout his oeuvre, there is nothing indirect or evasive about the novelist's rendering of the abstraction termed "America": in Coetzee's fiction, America is the monolithic imperial power responsible for the silencing of the rest of the world; it is a safe haven that nonetheless requires homogeneity and submission to a consumer-driven ideology of ignorance. And for Coetzee and his various authorial personae who do not fall for its allure, America constitutes a locus of resistant and often covert protest. As the narrator says of the young John in *Boyhood*, "preferring the Russians to the Americans is a secret so dark that he can reveal it to no one" (26). Finally, with the exception of *Dusklands*, which took shape while he lived in the United States, America as a setting is a conspicuous absence in Coetzee's work: in his trinity of *autre*biographies, *Boyhood*, *Youth*, and *Summertime*, for example, there is no account of the author's time spent in America, the period from 1965 to 1971 during which Coetzee obtained a PhD from the University of Texas, Austin, and went on to teach at the State University of New York, Buffalo, and during which he applied for—and was denied on the basis of his anti–Vietnam War activism—United States citizenship.[1]

Yet within Coetzee's fiction, indeed, in his life, the relationship between South Africa and America and Coetzee's relationship to both loci is invoked to posit not so much a kind of oppositional duality that frames "America" as the other to South Africa but a lens through which one place learns about its uncomfortable likeness to the other's often oppressive social and political regimes. And largely for this reason, I feel that Coetzee's works have proved so popular to American scholars. The violence that Coetzee witnesses in America reflects South Africa back to Coetzee, and South Africa reflects America, in ways that hold both to account for their participation in the construction of nationalistic master myths of history, even as such dark reflections work to deconstruct such myths. Of this relationship, of the way one place evokes the other, Coetzee notes in his 1984 *New York Times* editorial, "How I Learned about America—and Africa—in Texas," that while he was working toward his PhD at the University of Texas in 1966,

> [o]ne Charles Whitman, a student (a fellow student? were they all fellow students? all 23,000 of them?) took the elevator to the top of the clock tower and commenced shooting people on the quadrangles below. He killed a fair number, then someone killed him. I hid under my desk for the duration. In Cape Town a Greek assassinated Hendrik Frensch Verwoerd, architect of Grand Apartheid.

Coetzee's linkage of these two events posits a relationship between acts of violence perpetuated on two different continents at the same historical moment, and the question of this relationship underlies an undergraduate course that I teach at Western Carolina University, Cultural Studies and Non-Western Literature. The connection that Coetzee's work evokes between America and South Africa (and the author's complex relationship with both) is a central focus in a semester-long analysis of discourse in the construction of our understanding of place as the product of narrative, both at home and abroad. In this essay, I will focus my pedagogical analysis on the discourse of America generated by *Dusklands* while situating that discourse in the context of "America" as it is depicted more broadly in Coetzee's oeuvre.

For my students, an examination of America within Coetzee's oeuvre provides a point of access to the writing of an author from a place, South Africa, with which they often have little if any direct knowledge, and the America that they see depicted by Coetzee is at once as familiar and as alien—and as imaginary—as is their initial understanding of the various imaginary Africas that we encounter first. We examine America and Africa via a direct analysis of the discourse that generates the image of how these places look from the perspective of the characters in Coetzee's fiction and fictionalized autobiographies, particularly Eugene Dawn and Jacobus Coetzee in *Dusklands*, Mrs. Curren in *Age of Iron*, John in *Youth*, and JC in *Diary of a Bad Year*. We also engage with America comparatively via a discussion of allegory and degrees of difference between the places depicted in Coetzee's fiction and points of reference in the media that generate our understanding of the place in which we live, the multiplicity that is America. We look again, for example, at the two parts of *Dusklands*, one situated in America in the 1970s and the other in South Africa in the 1760s; at the conflict between Empire and the barbarians in *Waiting for the Barbarians* and in the 2007 documentary *The Ghosts of Abu Ghraib*, which documents torture undertaken by United States armed forces on prisoners of the war on terror; and, most recently, at the ways that seemingly "doing nothing" functions as an act of resistance in both *Life & Times of Michael K* and the Occupy movements that occurred throughout the United States, a point made most apparent in a police officer's pepper spraying of a line of passive students at the University of California, Davis, in November of 2011.

In the case of *Waiting for the Barbarians*, a work devoid of a specific historical context or location, I note, as Patrick Lenta does, that "it has frequently been asserted that *Waiting for the Barbarians* was written in response to repressive state violence in apartheid South Africa, especially acts of torture perpetrated by the South African security forces on those deemed enemies of the apartheid state," but "the novel offers allegorical terms for thinking about the *relationship* between torture, power and law beyond the South African context" (72; my emphasis). As I have already noted, the concept of relationality is important in examining the American contexts present in Coetzee's fiction, but in looking at works in terms of relationships that allow for students to compare events in the United States with those depicted in the fictional world of Coetzee's novels, I am ever conscious of not conflating or drawing too close a connection between apartheid and postapartheid South Africa and events that have or are taking place in the United States or elsewhere. While *Waiting for the Barbarians* posits a set of circumstances that finds historical precedent in, for example, apartheid-era South Africa, the Holocaust, and Abu Ghraib prison in Iraq, to claim that all three events are synonymous—or that Coetzee's novel could be about any or all of these circumstances—would be unjust. Nonetheless, reading these events in relation to one another allows students to make connections between such disparate circumstances—and this is exactly what I feel Coetzee does in "The Vietnam Project" and "The Narrative of Jacobus Coetzee," the two parts of *Dusklands*. As Grant Hamilton notes, "*Dusklands* is a novel of *relations*": "while [Eugene] Dawn talks of the universal attempt of the West to determine itself in contrast to the Vietnamese Other . . . , Jacobus Coetzee reflects on his punitive raid on a Hottentot village as an act of self-determination" (300; my emphasis).

I teach at Western Carolina University (WCU), one of the sixteen campuses of the University of North Carolina system. WCU is a regional comprehensive university with just over ten thousand students located in the rural mountains of the western part of North Carolina; the people I teach are often of modest backgrounds, and many are first-generation college students. The student population is predominantly white, made up of people who, for the most part, have never traveled out of the United States. In this context—and, indeed, in any context in which I have taught Coetzee's writing and the writing of other African authors—I begin with a discussion of "Africa" as an entity that we (people in the United States, the students in my class, those of us that exist in locations other than Africa, as well as those who live on that continent) come to know predominantly through the various representations of Africa generated within our mainstream media. Considering Africa—and we talk quite a bit about the way that "Africa" is a monolithic construction in much of what we see—for my class, then, becomes a task of discourse analysis. To quote Paul Bové in the chapter "Discourse" in *Critical Terms for Literary Study*, discourses "produce knowledge about humans and their society," and an analysis of discourse aims to "describe the surface linkages between power, knowledge, institutions, intellectuals, the control of populations, and the modern state" as these intersect in systems of thought, and as represented in texts (55–56). As a class, we consider that we come to an understanding of Africa through popular media, and we work to parse and analyze the various images of Africa that the popular media constructs for us as well as the motivations that underlie the generation of those images.

We start, perhaps unsurprisingly, with Joseph Conrad's *Heart of Darkness* and Chinua Achebe's discourse analysis of that work, "An Image of Africa: Racism in Conrad's *Heart of Darkness*," in which Achebe asserts that *Heart of Darkness* "projects the image of Africa as . . . the antithesis of Europe and therefore of civilization, a place where man's vaunted intelligence and refinement are finally mocked by triumphant bestiality" (3). Through a sustained analysis of the text, Achebe posits that Conrad's depiction generates an image of a homogenous darkness (the Congo is never named, never distinguished from the rest of the Dark Continent, the blank space on the map that entices a young Marlow) peopled with Africans who are incapable of speech, presented primarily as masses of "limbs or rolling eyes" (5). And then we read Achebe's *Things Fall Apart* for another take on Africa, this time with more specificity, as Achebe's novel chronicles the life and times of Okonkwo, member of the Igbo clan of Nigeria in the 1880s. But lest this progression lead my students to the conclusion that Achebe's is the authentic representation, the "true" depiction of Africa, I introduce them to Flora Nwapa's *Efuru*, the first novel written in English by an African woman, and a novel written in direct response to what Nwapa felt was a misrepresentation of African women in Achebe's and other African male writers' narratives. As Nwapa claims in an interview with Marie Umeh, "I attempt to correct our menfolks when they started writing, when they wrote little or less about women, where their female characters are prostitutes and ne'er-do-wells. I started writing to tell them that this is not so" ("Poetics" 27).

The idea that I hope to impart via this progression is that all representations, whether written by Western or African authors, are partial representations, often shaped by specific political agendas: Conrad sought to expose the evils of Belgium's colonization of Congo and, in so doing, according to Achebe, made Africa a backdrop to one man's madness. Achebe sought to give voice and history to the African men rendered speechless by Conrad, and Nwapa sought to give voice to the women she felt were misrepresented by Achebe. From this vantage point, we then look at popular and contemporary cultural depictions of various imagined "Africas" that are generated by Western media. What, for example, does "Africa" look like in Disney's *The Lion King*? What does Sierra Leone look like in Edward Zwick's *Blood Diamond*—and how badly does Leonardo DiCaprio butcher his accent? Finally, what does South Africa look like in Clint Eastwood's *Invictus*? My motive in undertaking these analyses is to allow students to engage with the processes that shape representations and to make them aware that those processes are neither objective nor impartial; the goal is to bring to the fore the tacit mythology that informs our view of the world around us. After we process some of these images of Africa, I ask that we reverse the frame and consider the image of the West in general and "America" in particular that we see in non-Western works of literature. Enter, for example, Eugene Dawn of Coetzee's *Dusklands*, a character who implicitly references *Heart of Darkness* when he longs to have "lived two hundred years ago" so that he could "have had a continent to explore, to map, to open to colonization" (31–32).

Dawn is a mythographer researching, from the basement of the Harry S. Truman Library in Independence, Missouri, the efficacy of United States propaganda with regard to the Vietnam War. Coeztee traces the genesis of *Dusklands*, noting that in graduate school in Austin, he

> read the makeshift grammars put together by missionaries, went further back in time to the earliest linguistic records of the Hottentots, word lists compiled by 17th-century seafarers, and then followed the fortunes of the Hottentots in a history written not by them but for them, from above, by travelers and missionaries, not excluding my remote ancestor Jacobus Coetzee, fl. 1760. Years later, in Buffalo . . . I was to venture my own contribution to the history of the Hottentots: A memoir went on growing till it had been absorbed into a first novel, *Dusklands*.   ("How I Learned")

David Attwell notes that in *Dusklands* Coetzee situates America and South Africa beside one another via a dual act of parody that reveals a theme with which he continues to engage throughout his oeuvre, the unreliability and mythological nature of historical narrative. In "The Vietnam Project," the parodied documents "are the work of what Chomsky in the context of Vietnam called 'the backroom boys,' the military bureaucrats and planners in corporations allied to the Defense Department," while in "The Narrative of Jacobus Coetzee," "the parodied documents are drawn from the archives of colonial expansion published by the Van Reibeeck Society in South Africa" (Attwell, "Labyrinth" 8). Attwell notes that in addition to parody, what ultimately underlies both depictions is likely a "sense of estrangement and possibly, complicity, that Coetzee begins to feel as a white South African with an Afrikaner pedigree studying in Texas during the escalation of the Vietnam war" (9). My reading posits, in essence, that Coetzee's distance from his home country and his status as outsider in the United States allowed him a kind of detached perception that enabled a depiction of both locales as writerly constructions produced in the service of nation building.

Coetzee's statements in his *New York Times* editorial relate to his conception of history "written not by" marginalized peoples but "for them," particularly as such history is fashioned in the service of the justification for such marginalization, but they apply to "The Vietnam Project" as well. "The Narrative of Jacobus Coetzee" demonstrates the highly subjective nature of representation in that it purports to be Coetzee's translation of both "the Dutch of Jacobus Coetzee's narrative and the Afrikaans of [his] father's [Dr. S. J. Coetzee's] Introduction" to a previous volume (*Dusklands* 55). The primary text consists of the translator's note followed by a first-person account of Jacobus's two journeys across the Great River into the land of the Great Namaqua. The purpose of the first trek is to hunt elephants, and the goal of the second is not only to kill the servants who abandon Jacobus on his previous journey but also to annihilate the Namaqua camp and all of its inhabitants. The chronicle of these sojourns is followed by S. J. Coetzee's afterword, which "ventures to present a more complete and therefore more just view of Jacobus Coetzee. It is a work of piety but also a work of history" (108), and this "document" includes no information about the second journey whatsoever. The afterword is followed by a deposition made by Jacobus in 1760, the only authentic historical document among the various others that Coetzee presents as real. The act of reading these supposed historical documents — rearranged (Coetzee claims that the afterword in this text constitutes the introduction in his father's) and contradictory — serves to alienate the reader from any recognizable distinction between truth and lie, history and fiction. Furthermore, the multiplicity of subjectivities that inhabit these various documents — J. M. Coetzee, S. J. Coetzee, Jacobus Coetzee, and Rijk Tulbagh (who transcribes the deposition that constitutes the appendix) — engage in a dialogue with one another that ultimately debunks the enabling myth that allows for colonial domination.

Furthermore, Coetzee situates Eugene Dawn's American narrative, ostensibly written in 1972–73, prior to "The Narrative of Jacobus Coetzee," ostensibly written in 1760, thereby removing these two separate pieces of the text from any sense of linear chronology, and in so doing, he reveals the impossibility of accepting his representation of any locale discussed therein—Vietnam, America, or South Africa—as the truth. In fact, Dawn notes that prior to beginning his work on the Vietnam Project, he is offered a familiarization tour of Vietnam, which he refuses. Instead, "the truth of my Vietnam formulations already begins to shimmer . . . through the neat ranks of print. When these are transposed into print their authority will be binding" (15). The "truth," then, is what is subjectively codified: the "truth of *my* Vietnam," the political "master-myth of history" (26) approved for presentation as authoritative text. By the time we arrive at Dawn's narrative, my students have already done a considerable amount of work deconstructing the discourse about Africa that is generated by numerous works. What then, I ask, of the representation of "America" that Coetzee gives us in "The Vietnam Project"?[2] America is the land of suburban conformity represented by Dawn's wife, Marilyn, who, Dawn claims, "has a false conception of America. She cannot believe that America is big enough to contain its deviants. But America is bigger than all of us." Dawn feels that "in the true myth of America" (and how can there be a "true myth," after all?), he is not the deviant but the embodiment of what is real. He claims that Coetzee, his commanding officer, and "all those who no longer feel the authentic American destiny crackling within them and stiffening their marrow" are the true deviants. In *Dusklands*, America is monolithic and gigantic, a self-perpetuating myth that will "dissolve [Dawn] in the tides of its blood" (9) both in spite and because of the narrative he constructs with regard to America's treatment of the Vietnamese during the war. Dawn's attempt to write a narrative different from the one prescribed for him by Coetzee (and we might rightly ask which Coetzee) causes him to suffer a breakdown and stab his son. At the end of "The Vietnam Project," Dawn, restrained and under supervision, notes "in my cell in the heart of America . . . I ponder and ponder. I have high hopes of finding whose fault I am" (49).

Teresa Dovey reads *Dusklands* as a novel concerned with repetition: "[I]n *Dusklands* repetition is adopted as a strategy . . . of subversion which, while the novel participates in the discursive field of historiography, allows it at the same time to deconstruct . . . the concept of history itself" (17). In the context of Coetzee's deconstruction of historical narrative, my class and I ponder "whose fault" Eugene Dawn is, and we come to various and often divergent conclusions. As a fictional creation, Dawn is, quite literally, Coetzee's "fault," but as a character charged with chronicling the efficacy of America's propaganda campaign in Vietnam, he is also the product of a military bureaucracy aimed at generating a narrative to justify an ill-conceived war; he may be in possession of a particular truth, but he is alternately responsible for the myth that obscures it. He is the fault of America as Coetzee depicts it, a place, like South Africa, where dissent has, historically, proved intolerable. We hold the image of America that Coetzee gives us next to our own conceptions of this place, and in so doing, we are better able to recognize the myths about ourselves that we may have traditionally taken to be fact. And in that moment, I hope, we acquire a sense of humility requisite for considering the narratives presented to us, often written not by but for the rest of the world.

NOTES

[1] Despite much negative treatment of America in his work, Coetzee has nonetheless placed his papers in the Henry Ransom Humanities Research Center at the University of Texas, Austin (a decision that prompts Craig McKenzie to ask, "Why could Coetzee's papers not have found a home where they belong—in the matrix that gave them birth? And where people can pronounce his name?"), and has thereby situated his work, if not his physical presence, in the academic realm of the United States.

[2] I often pose this question after showing a brief clip from Ridley Scott's 1997 film *G.I. Jane*, in which Master Chief John James Urgayle (Viggo Mortensen) can be seen reading from a copy of *Dusklands*.

Teaching *Disgrace* at the University of Cape Town

Carrol Clarkson

It is 7 April 2007, and I am in lecture theater 2 of the Kramer Building on middle campus at the University of Cape Town (UCT). The topic of the lecture is Byron's poem "Lara"—but what is unusual for me on this occasion is that I am a student in the class, and the professor today is John Malkovich, playing the part of David Lurie during the filming of J. M. Coetzee's novel *Disgrace*. The atmosphere is rather tense, and Malkovich, powdered very white under the harsh lighting, seems disengaged, even bored, saying the same lines over and over again, "A mad heart. What is a mad heart?," and then skipping over a paragraph of Lurie's inner reflections in the novel to say his next words, "Never mind" (33). The whole situation is disappointing. "Where is the flash of revelation in this room?" I ask myself, as Lurie does in one of his other lectures, on Wordsworth (21). We break for lunch.

It is after we return to the set, however, that there is indeed something to be learned—not so much about Byron's poem or about Coetzee's novel but about Malkovich's art and by extension about the art of teaching. I had not realized before the lunch break that all the cameras were focused on the students in the lecture room: Malkovich had simply been saying his lines to fill in the spaces while the students were being filmed. During lunch, the cameras were switched so that the same scene could be filmed in the afternoon but with the focus on Malkovich. This time he was acting rather than just creating temporal gaps for his words. The difference between the morning and the afternoon sessions was a revelation. Once Malkovich started acting, it was as if he had recalibrated the setting in which we all found ourselves: we became the students in his class, could pick up the tension generated by the intrusive presence of Melanie's boyfriend, could sense in Lurie's body language intimations of his unspoken and disturbing reflections written in the novel—in relation to Melanie: "Despite himself, his heart goes out to her. Poor little bird, he thinks, whom I have held against my breast!" and in relation to the students in general: "He has long ceased to be surprised at the range of ignorance of his students. Post-Christian, posthistorical, postliterate, they might as well have been hatched from eggs yesterday" (32).

Reflecting on Malkovich's Byron lecture, I began to clarify something that I had been dimly aware of for a long time: whenever I have been moved by art—whether it is a work of literature, a painting, a sculpture, a performance of a piece of music, a play—I have been shunted out of my own world and into a different one in which I participate absolutely. This thought is hardly original but has become relevant to my teaching practice in a specific way: the teaching-learning event has the potential to realize the performative effects one usually associates with the creative arts. To occupy the place of the writer, artist, speaker, is to make subtle if complex displacements, through your teaching, by creating a setting in which your addressees respond.

If the performance or the operation of a work—and here I include the lecture, the tutorial, the seminar session—is to affect those who encounter it, it must bring about changes in thinking, in perspective, in an altered sense of what is important in its addressees. This idea is related to what Derek Attridge has called "the singularity of literature," which is "not a property but an event" (*Singularity* 64). Further,

> singularity is *constituted* by what we might call "contextual" operations; it is not some inviolable core at the heart of all accessible meaning, but is the product of a set of contexts bearing down upon a here and now—contexts which include the language, the literary tradition, generic properties, and cultural norms, and which construct the reading of a poem by constructing both poem and reader. (114)

Taking the lessons from Malkovich and Attridge together, I like to think of the singularity of teaching, of the responsiveness and responsibilities of the lecturer, of the lecture as performative event. For the duration of the lecture, the students and I inhabit another world. To hold on to that other world, I must be intensely responsive to them. Their receptiveness, in turn, is the medium in which the ideas can have life; if I lose the attention of the students, justice will not be done to the thoughts I want to express. A complex interpersonal relationship subtends what I choose to say—and the students and I are the only ones, in this lecture event, who can create and sustain that singular relationship. This lecture will never be replicated exactly, and in those forty-five minutes we travel a great distance from ourselves.

It is difficult, teaching *Disgrace* at UCT, the location that Coetzee fictionalizes in his novel, to create this sense that we are inhabiting a different and special world. The release of the film makes it even more difficult: several of the scenes were shot on campus—one in the corridor right outside my office in the Arts Block; another on the stairs across the way from the theater in the Beattie Building, where I give the lectures on *Disgrace*—and Antoinette Engel, who plays the part of Melanie Isaacs, was a third-year student in my classes at the time of the filming. The novel itself is filled with names, places, events, and situations all too familiar to UCT students, to the point of uncanniness.[1] For undergraduate students, the temptation is great indeed to read *Disgrace* as referring straightforwardly to the real world. Yet I teach the novel in a course in postmodernism. So a big challenge I face is to include, in that teaching, a consideration of self-reflexive questions about language and fiction. In this essay, I speak about one of my third-year lectures on *Disgrace* in which I try to create some sense of a world inhabited by the writer in South Africa. Discussion about the novel begins by thinking of the implications of writing about a particular place and its sociohistorical context, but questions of writing about place gradually give way to questions about the place of writing and about the authority and responsibilities of the one who writes.

I establish two points of departure: Coetzee's interview with Tony Morphet in 1983 and the young John's discussion in *Youth* about William Burchell and other nineteenth-century travel writers in the Cape. Morphet comments on the setting of *Life & Times of Michael K*: "The location of the story is very highly specified. Cape Town—Stellenbosch—Prince Albert—somewhere between 1985 [and] 1990." He goes on to suggest that the use of familiar place-names brings Michael K "very close to us" (by "us" he means a South African readership). He asks whether Coetzee is "looking for a more direct and immediate conversation with South African readers." Coetzee responds:

> The geography is, I fear, less trustworthy than you imagine—not because I deliberately set about altering the reality of Sea Point or Prince Albert but because I don't have much interest in, or can't seriously engage myself with, the kind of realism that takes pride in copying the "real" world.
>
> ("Two Interviews" 455)

This reply raises a difficult literary-philosophical question: Can we assume an everyday mode of reference in fiction's use of language? I encourage students to think about the preoccupations with language and representation that they have encountered in their other lectures on postmodernism. How might these preoccupations apply to a reading of *Disgrace*? What are the implications, for example, of the fact that so many of Coetzee's protagonists are writers or intellectuals themselves? What oscillations between author-character distance and proximity obtain in his relentless use of third-person, present-tense narration? Is there a postcolonial aspect to the self-reflexive attention Lurie pays to the contingencies of his own language and cultural heritage?

I direct the students to passages in *White Writing* and *Youth*. The young John of *Youth* is deeply moved by thoughts of South Africa when he reads the travel writings of John Barrow and William Burchell:

> It gives him an eerie feeling to sit in London reading about streets — Waalstraat, Buitengracht, Buitencingel — along which he alone, of all the people around him with their heads buried in their books, has walked. But even more than by accounts of old Cape Town is he captivated by stories of ventures into the interior . . . Zwartberg, Leeuwrivier, Dwyka: it is his country, the country of his heart, that he is reading about.   (137)

Yet even as these real places are being described, what matters is not the geography of the place but the history of the writer who is obliged to represent that place in the language — and hence in the context of a cultural inheritance — of the British colonizers. This is one of Coetzee's preoccupations: the writer whose native tongue is English bears the "burden of finding a home in Africa for a consciousness formed in and by a language whose history lies on another continent" (*White Writing* 173). Coetzee recognizes this burden in the writings of Burchell, a nineteenth-century English botanist and explorer (36–44). In *Youth*, the young John cites Burchell as a source of literary inspiration:

> The challenge [John] faces is a purely literary one: to write a book whose horizon of knowledge will be that of Burchell's time, the 1820s, yet whose response to the world around it will be alive in a way that [Burchell's], despite his energy and intelligence and curiosity and sang-froid, could not be because he was an Englishman in a foreign country, his mind half occupied with Pembrokeshire and the sisters he had left behind.   (138)

To demonstrate this distance in a graphic way to the students, I use a combination of writing, maps, and landscape paintings and photographs. I project a simple outline map of England onto a green chalkboard (England's "green and pleasant land" [Blake 514]), then onto a white board, overlaying a transparency of a nineteenth-century British landscape painting: John Constable's *The Hay Wain* (1820–21). I stress the dappled light, the reflections off the water, the verdure.

What happens when an artist coming from a European cultural background is asked to paint or write about the arid regions of South Africa — in a way that does justice to the landscape? What are the limitations of working in an inherited European cultural frame of reference?

In my lecture there is not much time for discussion, but I always ask students to take their notes in the form of questions and to leave blank spaces. Often they will work out responses to these questions among themselves and come to me in small groups for further discussion at another time. To present a lecture in the form of provocative questions rather than in the form of a body of a priori knowledge has the effect of encouraging students to engage with the material in a more thoughtful way. After such a lecture, student responses in exams and essays tend to be more varied and intellectually adventurous.

Removing Constable's painting and the map of England from the overhead projector, I quickly draw an outline of Southern Africa on a white board and project onto it David Goldblatt's photograph *Sheep Farm at Oubip* (32–33). The photograph, especially after the Constable painting, gives the impression of an infinite landscape bleached out and flattened by merciless light: empty sky; arid, stony earth; small clumps of dry grass and blackish bushes, without a place to rest one's gaze. I read a passage from Olive Schreiner's 1883 preface to *The Story of an African Farm*: "Sadly . . . [the writer] must squeeze the color from his brush, and dip it into the grey pigments around him. He must paint what lies before him" (24). What challenge does this landscape offer to the aesthetic imagination of the writer used to the artistic tradition of Constable or the literary traditions of the Romantic poets loved by David Lurie? For, "[t]hose brilliant phases and shapes which the imagination sees in far-off lands are not for [the writer] to portray" (Schreiner 24). Coetzee speaks of "a century of writing and overwriting (drab bushes, stunted trees, heat-stunned flats, shrilling of cicadas and so forth) . . . the Karoo threaten[s] only the tedium of reproduction, reproduction of a phraseology in which the Karoo has been done to death" (*Doubling* 142).

These quotations bring about a shift in the conversation. The emphasis turns from the landscape itself to the difficulty the writer has in representing it. This self-reflexiveness is something we already find in Burchell. I show the students one of his engravings: *A View of Cape Town, Table Bay and Tygerberg* (1: 24–25). The landscape is in muted tones, but this time the focal point is the artist: Burchell has included a tiny self-portrait in this picture. He is sitting at an easel under an umbrella, dressed in the brightest blue frock coat, painting the scene before him.

Now I move the board with the map of South Africa up and out of the way, and onto a clean white board I project Constable's *Salisbury Cathedral*—and return to Coetzee's discussions about Burchell, the picturesque, and the South African landscape in *White Writing* (especially passages relating to the risk of speaking about Africa in negative relation to Europe [36–44, 163–66]). I show the students Burchell's colored engraving *A Natural Stone Obelisk in the Country of the Bushmen*. In Burchell's almost monochrome pale gray-brown picture, we have stones, rocky outcrops, a vast cloudless sky, which in relation to Constable's painting amounts to an absence of trees, soft green vegetation, the sense of ever-shifting light. I bring the board with the map of South Africa back down, so that Burchell's painting is projected onto it.

This engraving was completed in 1823, the same year as Constable's *Salisbury Cathedral*, and the similarity in the composition (the spire of the cathedral in Constable's painting, the pile of stones in Burchell's image) makes me wonder whether Burchell had Constable's picture in mind when he completed his. To demonstrate the similarity, I place the transparency of Constable's picture on top of Burchell's and project them at the same time. Burchell's engraving is so muted that it is barely discernible through Constable's painting: the African landscape all but disappears. What happens, I ask the students, when you try to describe an African setting, but in English and in an English literary tradition? In *Youth*, John speaks about his "first experiment in prose," a story set in South Africa:

> Though the story he has written is minor (no doubt about that), it is not bad. Nevertheless, he sees no point in trying to publish it. The English will not understand it. For the beach in the story they will summon up an English idea of a beach, a few pebbles lapped by wavelets. They will not see a dazzling space of sand at the foot of rocky cliffs pounded by breakers, with gulls and cormorants screaming overhead as they battle the wind.   (62)

In the fictional worlds of Coetzee, characters express the doubt that European languages and cultures can offer any legitimate medium of response to Africa. Insistently in *Disgrace*, the sociopolitical aftermath of colonialism is indexed in the anachronistic disjuncture between a European heritage and the Africa it attempts to address or represent in that inherited language. When Petrus uses the word "benefactor," Lurie reflects:

> A distasteful word, it seems to him, double-edged, souring the moment. Yet can Petrus be blamed? The language he draws on with such aplomb is, if he only knew it, tired, friable, eaten from the inside as if by termites. Only the monosyllables can still be relied on, and not even all of them.
>
> What is to be done? Nothing that he, the one-time teacher of communications, can see. Nothing short of starting all over again with the ABC. By the time the big words come back reconstructed, purified, fit to be trusted once more, he will be long dead.   (129)

Yet if English is, according to Lurie, "an unfit medium for the truth of South Africa," unable to speak in an authentic way about the continent to which it is foreign, the language itself seems subject to the natural igneous processes that formed that continent in the first place:

> Stretches of English code whole sentences long have thickened, lost their articulations, their articulateness, their articulatedness. Like a dinosaur settling in the mud, the language has stiffened. Pressed into the mould of English, Petrus's story would come out arthritic, bygone.   (117)

Lurie's near-obsessive interest in being articulate himself results in his unearthing of a number of European resonances in each English word he so carefully turns over. To evoke the histories and etymological connections of these words while saying them in Africa is to place the speaker in a double bind. On the one hand, the testing of language is generated by a sincere desire to speak the truth, to find the right word. On the other hand, the etymological forays are a conscious reminder of an imperial elsewhere, of a linguistic continental drift, which draws attention to a colonial history. It does not seem possible to write about a South African landscape in English and obliterate all thought of colonialism in the same gesture.

If Lurie has thoughts about modes of communication other than English that perhaps do not evoke a colonial history so explicitly, Coetzee chooses to write in English, precisely because it does. "[W]hat I like about English," Coetzee says in an interview with Jean Sévry,

> and what I certainly don't find in Afrikaans, what does not exist in Afrikaans, is a historical layer in the language that enables you to work with historical contrasts and oppositions in prose . . . there is a genetic diversity about the language, which after all is not only a Germanic language with very heavy romance overlays, but is also a language which is very receptive to imported neologisms so that macaronic effects are possible—you can work with contrasts in the etymological basis of words.   (2)

Spelling out etymologies, testing the valence of English spoken in Africa, mentioning place-names no longer in use—these are just some of the ways in which Coetzee calls attention to the historical forces operative in his fiction. In leading readers to ask questions about the historically situated language that at the same time generates the fictional narrative, his writing expresses unsettling tensions of culture and history. One of the important aesthetic and philosophical consequences is that for Coetzee, the extent to which an author plays up these internal contrasts in language becomes a "measure of a writer's seriousness." From the perspective of the writer, it is "a matter of awakening the countervoices in oneself and embarking upon speech with them" (*Doubling* 65).[2] The ethics of countervoice in Coetzee becomes the topic of my next lecture.

My introductory lecture on *Disgrace* stresses the idea that writing about place becomes an interrogation about the place of writing. In Coetzee this interrogation is never simply an inward-looking art for art's sake. From *Dusklands* onward, the calling into question of the place of writing has intimately to do with the positioning of a colonial subject, with the testing of the authority of the one who writes, with representations of landscape that attempt to mark sites of human significance. In Coetzee the question of landscape involves the history of those who attempt to represent it. Coetzee's preoccupations, then, are postcolonial as much as they are postmodern—and *Disgrace* is a great teacherly text for demonstrating these preoccupations.

NOTES

This essay focuses on my teaching practice; the ideas on Coetzee find fuller expression in my book, *J. M. Coetzee: Countervoices*.

[1] As Ian Glenn and others have pointed out, David Lurie is the name of a well-known photographer in Cape Town, and the senior secretary of UCT's drama department is Melanie Isaacs.

[2] Countervoice is a core theme of my book on Coetzee.

Pedagogies of Discomfort: Teaching Coetzee's *The Lives of Animals*

Wendy Woodward

At the back of an undergraduate lecture theater, a student stands up and pointedly packs up his books. "Animals are not *moral!*" he sneers as he walks out. Later, another student tells me of his grief and impotent anger when a neighbor killed his dog without reprisal in his rural Eastern Cape village. At a postgraduate seminar, a student comments belligerently, "I have seen my uncle kill rabbits and chickens, and I was quite happy to eat them afterwards." His classmate turns to him, astonished: "So would you eat *humans*?" After the inevitable affirmative answer, we try to move on with the discussion but are interrupted by confessions of failed vegetarianism on the part of two female students.

The University of the Western Cape (UWC) in Bellville, in the northern suburbs of Cape Town, where I teach, was founded in 1960 as an apartheid institution, a second-rate bush college for colored students who were not allowed into historically white universities.[1] UWC challenged this construction, however, becoming known as "the home of the left" in the 1980s for its part in the anti-apartheid struggle. After the democratic elections of 1994, the university escaped the process of merging, which many tertiary institutions in South Africa were forced to do, probably because of its struggle history. But UWC is a lot more than its past. Today it is a productive research institution ranking in the top seven universities of South Africa. Students enrolled at UWC are African and colored, and most are the first in their family to attend a tertiary institution. Although I have taught in the English Department at UWC for more than two decades, including animal ethics in my syllabus followed Coetzee's *The Lives of Animals*, which was published in 1999.

Strong emotions permeate and sometimes even legislate the discussions of the book, which is incorporated into my second-year module Reading the Environment, my postgraduate course The Animal Subject, and my postgraduate creative writing class. The discomfort is not always that of the students, however. I worry about the relevance of notions of animal subjectivity and a vegetarian philosophy in relation to what Jennifer Wenzel terms "the urgencies of the spectral question posed in South Africa (and so many other places) 'how to eat *enough*?'" ("Meat Country" 129; italics mine). On an undergraduate level especially, where some students come to class hungry, is the text just too foreign in its preoccupations? *The Lives of Animals* provides a stringent critique of animal suffering brought about, predominantly, by the instrumentalizing of animals for food. In its ethical acknowledgment of the subjectivities of animals it transcends notions of animal rights. Yet even animal rights discourses are foreclosed in local political debate. Lindiwe Mazibuko, then a Democratic Alliance (DA) spokesperson, now parliamentary leader for the opposition DA, argues, "Only once we can promise food security and make it accessible to everyone so that they can eat on a daily basis, only then can we discuss the debate on organic versus free range versus factory farming" (qtd. in Kendal, Le Riche, and Yu 30). The imperative of human over animal rights recalls a prevalent criticism of feminism during the antiapartheid struggle, that democratic rights for all should take chronological precedence over women's rights. Deferring rights for animals, or even any acknowledgment of them, ignores the interconnections of human and animal suffering in postapartheid South Africa.

In *The Lives of Animals*, discomfort is a central emotion. Although the feelings of Elizabeth Costello range far beyond discomfort, to a kind of wounded despair, her audiences repeatedly experience dis-ease, as does her son, John. Her claim that she is "philosophical rather than polemical" is belied by her representations of animal suffering: the laboratory or the zoo is "hell"; daily, in the abattoir there is a "fresh holocaust," yet "our moral being is untouched. We do not feel tainted" (22, 30, 35). As Elisa Aaltola suggests, the text "accuses and polemicises" (131); at the same time, as Anton Leist and Peter Singer maintain, it does not promote "clear positive ethics," for "Coetzee lays all the options before the readers and suggests that they make their own choices" ("Introduction" 11). It is unusual for a text at the university level to appeal to the heart rather than to reason. Moreover, it challenges, even taunts its readers in its engagement with the tension between empathy and reason. (A philosophy student on another campus where I was giving a seminar refused to engage with *Lives* because, in his view, ethics is irrational.)

My initially naive intention as a teacher was to convince students that animals have the right to lives free from suffering. I always stress the literary-aesthetic aspects of acknowledging animal subjectivity—the sympathetic imagination, the idea that animals can have a point of view—but I also hoped, without being overtly polemical (I thought), to encourage some self-reflexivity in students about using animals as resources, to change students' accustomed relation to animals—the relation of eater to eaten, in the vein of David Lurie's riposte to Bev Shaw in *Disgrace*: "Do I like animals? I eat them so I suppose I must like them, some parts of them" (81). On a philosophical level, I wanted to stress Costello's challenge to conventional anthropocentric dualist thinking and draw attention to homologies of speciesism and racism—issues that the students found less difficult to entertain, perhaps partly because the personal is not so directly enlisted.

Iris Marion Young questions how, as "social moral agents," we think of our responsibility in relation to structural social injustice (75). Structural injustice does not connect in a causal way to one person who can be deemed guilty and hence is answerable legally. Instead, a "social connection model of responsibility . . . finds that all those who contribute by their actions to structural processes with some unjust outcomes share responsibility for the injustice" (96). The instrumentalizing and killing of animals for food, research, or clothing, although Young does not mention them as an example, could be defined as a structural social injustice. Taught in this context, the student reading *The Lives of Animals* is faced with being socially connected to and implicated in a system that Costello describes as "an enterprise of degradation, cruelty and killing which rivals anything that the Third Reich was capable of, indeed dwarfs it" (21).

According to Young's model, responsibility for structural social injustice should lead not to backward-looking guilt or faultfinding but to a proactive activism. Students from meat-eating cultures generally will not become vegetarians or animal rights activists (although there have been notable exceptions), and some either defensively or angrily reject the implication of the text that the reader should accept responsibility. They feel not addressed but harangued by Costello, yet the controversial comparison of the "willed ignorance" (20) of the Germans during the Holocaust and the suffering in the death camps with the willed ignorance of human beings about animal suffering does not elicit a vociferous response. The use of the metaphor of slavery does (59).

The emotional response of students to *Lives* can also be attributed to their being confronted by a "threshold concept," which according to Jan H. F. Meyer and Ray Land is "akin to a portal, opening up a new and inaccessible way of thinking about something." Significantly, "the transition to understanding can prove troublesome" (qtd. in Sibbett and Thompson 227). Caryl Sibbett and William Thompson develop this notion further in their consideration of "nettlesome knowledge," which they delineate as

> elements of knowledge that are deemed taboo in that they are defended against, repressed or ignored, because if they were grasped they might "sting" and this evokes a feared intense emotional and *embodied* response. . . . [N]ettlesome knowledge can make us uncomfortable and so it can be stigmatised.   (229)

Such knowledge "contradict[s] the learner's own cherished beliefs or assumptions" (227), just as the inescapability of the knowledge of animal suffering on a vast scale and the imperative for animal ethics contradict the sentimental belief that the animals we eat live a happy life and die a painless death. The African tradition of animal sacrifice to propitiate ancestors may give the lie to such denialist thinking, but it still instrumentalizes animals—even as privileged spiritual conduits. In this regard, Costello censures the invention of gods who grant "permission [to human beings] to eat [animal] flesh" (41).

Many such assumptions or beliefs are held up for scrutiny in Coetzee's text. I like to begin my lectures in the second-year Reading the Environment module with the statement that we are all animals, which is difficult enough for listeners to accept who consider evolutionary theory just another idea. Costello's rejoinder to Dean Arendt, who believes that animals are unaware and "live in a vacuum of consciousness," aims at the heart of the self-justifying denial of rights for animals. Her caustic comment that she "mind[s] what tends to come next. They have no consciousness therefore . . . we are free to use them for our own ends? Therefore we are free to kill them?" is provocative (44). The student who claimed that seeing animals slaughtered meant nothing to him had already taken Arendt's point of view.

Costello represents "our captive herds" as "slave populations. Their work is to breed for us. Even their sex becomes a form of labor" (59). The comparison of animals with slaves has occasioned much disquiet, because it has been interpreted by some students as devaluing the suffering of slaves and even eliding human consciousness with animal consciousness, an integral tenet of the discourse justifying slavery. I use Marjorie Spiegel's *The Dreaded Comparison: Human and Animal Slavery* to sharpen up hasty misreadings of Costello's argument.

That animals have a point of view is a less threatening concept, particularly as other texts I bring to the discussion illustrate it dramatically and even beguilingly. Still, understanding that the other has a different way of looking at the world is a profound concept. In Reading the Environment, students are introduced to the poems "Goat," by Jo Shapcott, and "Seen from Above," by Wisława Szymborska. The speaker in "Goat" embodies the animal in a surreal shape-shifting moment: "I lived for the push / of goat muscle and goat bone, the smell of goat fur, / goat breath and goat sex." The poem ends with the goat surmising that she or he "must have swallowed an office block" because of "grinding enormous indigestion"; the building has "at the far end, I know, a tiny human figure" that deftly and amusingly turns anthropocentricism on its head. The poem, along with *Lives* as a theoretical framework, makes a wonderful teaching resource. Szymborska's "Seen from Above" pictures "[a] dead beetle . . . on a dirt road" and then philosophizes about the import of the insect's death, which is "unlamented." The poem ends:

> it seems that nothing important happened here.
> Important supposedly only applies to us.
> Only to our life, only to our death,
> a death which enjoys a forced right of way.

The poems do not hector but are diverting, even as their ethical import is unavoidable.

Microcosmos, a beautifully filmed documentary about the lives of insects in a French meadow, has already been shown in the course, so that students are more open about regarding insects as living creatures. Also we are not so directly implicated in the death of insects. We do not eat them or farm them, although we may kill them with pesticides. *The Lives of Animals* never seeks to entertain the reader, of course, but rather to "shock us *into* thinking" as Aaltola puts it (134). Even Njabulo S. Ndebele's essay "The Year of the Dog: A Journey of the Imagination," which pictures a crowd stoning a dog to death, and "We Killed Mangy-Dog," by Luis Bernardo Honwana, a harrowingly violent short story that conflates sexism, racism, speciesism as well as attitudes to the differently abled, do not implicate the reader so directly as *Lives*.

Students cannot take too much reality about animal suffering and their attendant culpability, yet when *Lives* is deployed more as a theoretical frame for the ethics of animal representation in order to open up a reading of poems or short stories, the threshold concepts it foregrounds are more easily accepted and absorbed. Students' response confirms Leist and Singer's suggestion that "[e]thics, and applied ethics especially, is helped by the literary imagination, if it confronts the conflicting forces visible in different philosophical positions as well as in our everyday culture" ("Introduction" 13). In my postgraduate module The Animal Subject, the discussion of *Lives* precedes close reading of novels, so that the threshold concepts of Coetzee's text thread organically through novels like Justin Cartwright's *White Lightning*, Yann Martel's *Life of Pi*, and Paul Auster's *Timbuktu*. Students taking this course are also less likely to be intensely opposed to those concepts, but they tend to be convinced more by the representation of a specific, personalized cross-species relationship, the kind Barbara Smuts describes in her response to *Lives*, in *Lives,* than by Costello's theorizing. The startling immediacy of sharing the being of another (34) when that being is a wild baboon or domestic dog (although Smuts eschews such labels) supersedes Costello's poetic analysis.

If the idea of the sympathetic imagination generates fruitful discussion about language and anthropomorphism in the context of literary texts, films, and photographs, having to actually write a poem that involves empathy for animals and "think[ing]" oneself "into the being of another" (35), as Costello claims that she is able to do, proves a difficult assignment for my honors creative writing class. Designed to foster inspiration and expressiveness, this course familiarizes students with different poetic forms and themes, which they then try out themselves. We read Ted Hughes, Shapcott, and Ruth Miller, but when the time comes to write from the point of view of an animal or insect, the class balks. As Ido Geiger suggests, "thinking your way into the being of another is not attaining knowledge and a stable moral stance. It is a relation to another that exists only in its transitivity" (157–58). The assignment not only brings the students face to face with the limits of empathy and language in representing animal points of view but also raises the political question of speaking for the other, always a fraught issue in South African debates. After lengthy, emotional discussion, the students conclude that literary endeavor would cease without imaginative ventriloquism.

Another threshold concept embedded in *Lives* is that animals are souls. "To be alive is to be a living soul," says Costello; "An animal—and we are all animals—is an embodied soul" (33). In Reading the Environment, this statement has not caused undue dis-ease despite its contradiction of the belief that souls are an exclusive human attribute and of the conventional image of an anthropocentric afterlife in both Christianity and Islam—perhaps because domestic pets are so humanized that their having souls is not incredible, perhaps because students who hold to African traditional thinking regard cattle as having spiritual provenance and direct links to the ancestors. In The Animal Subject, the concept of an animal soul is borne out in the novels either explicitly or implicitly, through the baboon Piet in *White Lightning*, the tiger Richard Parker in *Life of Pi*, the dog focalizer Mr. Bones in *Timbuktu*.

The threshold concept informing all the courses I teach that include *The Lives of Animals* as a central text is that human and nonhuman animals cannot be represented, whether biologically or ethically, as entirely other. Patrick D. Murphy's term "anothers" (88) can be read as flattening difference between human and nonhuman; more useful is Val Plumwood's suggestion of "continuities and differences" between human and nonhuman (217). Undergraduates who begin to think differently about animals sometimes deny such differences, going to the extreme of negating any split between self and other in a conceptual dead end, which Mary Midgley calls "undue humanizing" (128); animals are not acknowledged for who they are but only for how they are perceived to mirror human emotions and behaviors.

Attempting to do justice to Costello's ethical position has sometimes made me feel that I am cast in her role of discomforting her audience. After years of teaching the text in various ways, however, I have come to appreciate why threshold concepts are resisted as well as how productive a pedagogy of discomfort can be, for shifting perceptions and for highlighting just what these perceptions are (invisible when they have always been taken for granted and accepted as a kind of common sense). Megan Boler and Michalinos Zembylas define a pedagogy of discomfort as one that "reshape[s] and expand[s] terms of discourse and practices in education, enabling different thoughts and feelings to be experienced, enlarging the space of discourses and practices" (132). By its very nature, it moves both teacher and learner out of their comfort zones (131). Zembylas acknowledges that anger can subvert "power relations" (111), which suggests that students' anger in relation to *The Lives of Animals* is directed at the lecturer as well as at the text. In retrospect, I was naive not to have anticipated that students would be angry with me or disconcerted by the subject matter; defensive outbursts came as a shock at the time. My restraint in response to this anger turned out to be a good strategy: Zembylas warns against what he calls "the domestication of anger," because "[e]motions and affects are the very site of the capacity to effect change" (112, 110).

That Costello's ideas extended conventional "space[s] of discourse and practices" was illustrated repeatedly by personal narratives about animals, which the courses had now legitimated. The story of the murdered dog was an extreme one, but other emotional anecdotes recurred during or after class discussion. A recent postgraduate discussion of *Lives* was almost occluded by female students who took the space to voice their shame about their failed attempts at becoming vegetarians and the near impossibility of keeping to such a regimen in families where meat eating was the norm. Narratives whirled around the text in a kind of vortex—stories of relationships with beloved cats and dogs, anxieties about walking small dogs when gangsters' pit bulls loomed—so much so that *Lives*, despite my efforts, seemed relegated to an ineffectual secondary status in comparison with personal experience.

Ironically it was Costello's ideas that gave students this space to tell their stories. To denigrate their responses as sentimental or as strategies to avoid reading a difficult text would have been to miss what Zembylas calls "a politics of emotion." He maintains that

> creating spaces for embracing affect in educational settings is an act of political and ethical practice that recovers a sense of witnessing. . . . Witnessing is a call to action—action hopefully as a result of learning to see differently. This does not [ensure] any change; however, it represents an important step toward that direction. (112)

(It is interesting, if dismaying, that not one of the pedagogical texts I refer to in this essay incorporates social justice for nonhuman animals.)

Discussions of difference and prejudice recur, but the primary dualistic thinking of human versus nonhuman animals is not included. Coetzee's Elizabeth Costello, with her discomforting lectures that so eloquently and starkly witness animal suffering, is a desperately needed teacher. The discomfort that I as a lecturer might feel and the discomfort and occasional anger of my students only confirm the ethical significance of her testimony.

NOTE

[1] *Colored* was an apartheid classification of people of mixed race. Rejected by anti-apartheid activists in the 1970s and 1980s, the term has become more accepted since 1994.

Open to Interpretation: Politics and Allegory in Coetzee's *Waiting for the Barbarians*

Robert Spencer

Waiting for the Barbarians has never been one of those novels that one can teach simply by guiding students' discussions of several key scenes or by asking a few questions about literary form. It has never been an easy novel to teach at all. Students' attention invariably moves at some point beyond the handful of basic but essential questions about the relation between civilization and barbarism, between the novel's allegorical mode and its first-person narration. Some of my most gratifying experiences in the classroom over the past few years have been the product of impromptu discussions of this novel's wider and very varied dimensions. *Waiting* describes the complicities, ordeals, and tentative moral awakening of its narrator. The Magistrate, which is the only name by which we know him, administers a small fort and agricultural settlement on the frontier between an Empire, unidentified, and its barbarian enemies. He is aware of the link between language and violence and between torture and the suspension of the law, and he reflects on the nature and scope of empathy. In this essay I focus on the novel's allegorical treatment of the violence of the Empire and on how attention to allegory encourages those extemporaneous conversations about colonial violence. These discussions can and should be prompted not by informing students about historical or contemporary situations that resemble the world depicted by the novel or by blunt questions about current affairs but by close, literary-critical attention in the classroom to the work's allegorical quality and narrative form.

An important part of the novel's effect is that its protagonist ultimately fails to achieve or even imagine a state of communication and equality with the barbarians. As Coetzee himself has said, *Waiting for the Barbarians* is "a field of *contestation*": a "*disconfirmation*" of the absolute divisions (between civilization and barbarism) with which the Empire maintains itself rather than a confirmation or anticipation of a world in which those divisions have been overcome (*Doubling* 143). Close readings of key scenes will bring most students to an appreciation of the novel's principal lesson that the responsibility for violence lies not just with those who inflict it but with all those who reside in unjust societies that necessitate violence or that espouse (or even just fail to repudiate) an ideology that sanctions violence. The Magistrate "is not . . . the indulgent pleasure-loving opposite of the cold rigid colonel. [He] was the lie that Empire tells itself when times are easy. [Colonel Joll is] the truth that Empire tells when harsh winds blow" (148). But is there "any principle" behind the Magistrate's opposition to Joll and his methods (85)? How effective is the novel at answering the Magistrate's crucial question about whether it is possible to escape the Empire's delusions of omniscience and intransience (146)? How can we surpass his "confused and futile gestures of expiation" and apply his lessons about self-consciousness, introspection, reparation, and equality to "the world of tranquil certainties *we* were born into" (148, 157; my emphasis)?

Our responsibility is to amplify those questions, which are about power and about its operations and alternatives. We should invite students' responses as well as help them identify the contexts in which those questions can be asked—in relation, for example, to contemporary debates about torture and to what Louis Tremaine has shown is the novel's preoccupation with what Coetzee calls "the lives of animals" (*Lives*). One stimulating effect the novel has on our students and one of the ways in which teaching it can fulfill the purpose of a literary education is its ability to provoke interpretative reflection on the world outside, on violence, law, and justice.

From David Attwell's identification of detailed parallels between the Empire and P. W. Botha's South Africa in the late 1970s (*J. M. Coetzee*) to Philip Glass's operatic version of the novel that premiered at the Erfurt Theater in Germany in 2005 to recent critical attempts to liken the atrocities perpetrated by the sinister Third Bureau under "emergency powers" (Coetzee, *Waiting* 1) to the similarly lethal and lawless war on terror (P. Lenta; Spencer, *Cosmopolitan Criticism* 104–37), *Waiting for the Barbarians* has proved to be an unusually versatile allegory. It is a novel that, to paraphrase the Colombian novelist Gabriel García Márquez, does not end on the last page (56).

Such novels provide students with an opportunity to ponder the wider relation between literature and power. *Waiting* allows them to think through for themselves the complex ways that a novel that narrates a colonial bureaucrat's exemplary process of moral and political introspection, that contests dominant versions of truth, and that subtly encourages readers to draw parallels between the narrator's situation and their own both unmasks and denounces the specific situation of colonial power that it dramatizes at the same time that it points to similar situations in readers' and students' lives.

To teach the novel, it is essential to sketch contextual information so that students can read it as being, on one level, an allegory of the South African situation in the 1970s. It was at the time of the novel's composition that apartheid South Africa came under concerted challenge from inside and outside its borders. A militant labor movement began to destabilize an already depressed economy, and an intense politicization of the black majority culminated in the Soweto Uprising of 1976. The country's rulers intensified their campaign of violence, surveillance, and torture against their internal opponents. In 1977, Steve Biko, a Black Consciousness activist, was tortured to death in police custody. Colonel Joll's patently fictitious report of the death of the barbarian prisoner who is tortured in the granary at the start of the novel (6) recalls the excuses given by the police officers who killed Biko. (My students are always intrigued to discover the origins of the name of the Manchester Students' Union: the Steve Biko Building.) In the 1970s, South Africa's rulers became convinced that the country was being besieged by enemies; just as Joll's expeditionary force ventures across the Empire's thousand-mile border and the Magistrate reports rumors "that the northern barbarians have joined forces with the western barbarians" (135). The last few colonial regimes in Africa were being overthrown, but the South African army continued to fight its protracted and convoluted border war with SWAPO forces in Namibia, Angolan revolutionaries, and the armed wing of the ANC.

That the Empire has no name and that the cold winter winds in the novel blow from the north (40), not, as in South Africa, from the south, suggest that what we are reading is a fable, a story about empires in general rather than just about apartheid South Africa. Therefore, in exploring the novel's versatile allegorical dimension, one should consider the novel's distinctive method of narration. What kind of narrative voice is the Magistrate's? Students will usually be able to list its characteristics: proud, conceited, self-delusional, partial (in both senses of that word), as well as ironically self-conscious with a capacity for protracted (albeit inconclusive) introspection. The Magistrate's halting and imperfect appreciation of his complicity is given immediacy and force by the use of the present tense. Use of the first person conveys a position of power and privilege but also self-awareness. The narrative voice, claiming none of the detachment or objectivity of an omniscient narrator, advertises its fallibility and alerts readers not to trust too much the Magistrate's narrative or accept the ideological assumptions (about the gulf between civilization and barbarism) that initially underpin it. Students quickly see that the Magistrate casually employs the dehumanizing rhetoric of colonial power yet becomes increasingly aware of the limits of his knowledge and conscience. They also appreciate that telling a story through a fallible narrator engenders a critical or at least interpretative stance in readers. I point out to students that all Coetzee's work has consistently problematic (though not exactly untrustworthy) narrators and is intensely introspective and self-critical, like the work of other white South African writers: Breyten Breytenbach, André Brink, and Nadine Gordimer (Lazarus, "Modernism" 139).

From *Dusklands* (1974) to *Disgrace* (1999), Coetzee's novels address apartheid but not by describing directly injustice and how people stand up to it. Coetzee is as much interested in the practice of representation as in the realities being represented. What is the effect of narrating in this way? Addressing these matters from the inside, as it were, can help students think in a more sophisticated way about the role that language and representation play in institutions of power. In what the Magistrate calls an "exemplary spectacle" in the town square (114), Joll's men write the word "ENEMY" on the backs of shackled barbarian prisoners and then beat them until sweat and blood have washed the words away (113–18). The Magistrate interrupts this horror, remonstrating with Joll and protesting that such cruelties must not be inflicted on fellow men. This is a valuable scene to discuss, not just because it provides an opportunity for students to consider Coetzee's ideas (set out in his 1986 essay "Into the Dark Chamber: The Writer and the South African State") about the ethics of representing torture but also because it focuses attention on how violence must use language to divide civilization from its enemies, those who are human and have rights from those who are denied both the status of humanity and the rights it confers. It is the form of the narrative as much as the novel's content that calls students' attention to the reliance of power on representation. Moreover, since the narrator here is so uncertain, so self-conscious, and eventually so penitent, it is also form that emphasizes the vulnerability and transience of colonial power.

Students can now be asked about the process of introspection and contrition ("a change in [his] moral being" [46–47]) that the Magistrate undergoes. A complacent life "sustained by the toil of others" (17), one taken up with idle pastimes, legal tasks, and desultory womanizing, is first plagued by doubt, then renounced in favor of outraged dissent. Finally he is overpowered by the spirit- and body-breaking experience of torture. In his doubt, guilt, increasingly disorderly and convoluted narrative, neglect of official duties, and disquieting infatuation with the barbarian girl who has been tortured by the secret police, he stages an exemplary process of self-questioning. Yet it is not just the Magistrate who must chew over troubling questions about "penance and reparation" (88). Torture, as I have argued elsewhere (Spencer, *Cosmopolitan Criticism* 104–37), is one of the novel's salient themes, and it is not uncommon for students to draw comparisons between the misdeeds of Coetzee's Empire and those committed at Abu Ghraib, and even comparisons between the Magistrate's dilemmas and complicities and their own. The book prompts us to ask again, *Quis custodiet ipsos custodes?* Who guards the guards? *Waiting for the Barbarians* gets students to ponder the relevance of Juvenal's question. Who are the barbarians? The Magistrate learns that they are in fact "people we call barbarians" (54) and realizes that "we are the enemy" and Colonel Joll and his torturers are the "new barbarians" (85).

Students soon understand that this is an allegory with more than one answer or solution. Derek Attridge is useful here, despite his reservations about the allegorical approach to Coetzee. Attridge argues that the allegory is to be found not outside the text, in a particular situation to which the text points, but in the shocking, challenging, and ultimately transforming process of reading the novel (*J. M. Coetzee* 32–48). Students should be asked to read the passages in which the potential of allegory becomes an explicit concern of the novel. One can also pursue, with a group, the implications that allegorical interpretation has for our practice as readers.

The Magistrate rummages through the ruined settlement near the fort and compulsively rearranges the wooden slips he excavated there (on which are painted characters in an indecipherable script from some extinct barbarian language), in the hope that these "calligraphic riddles" will reveal their significance and illuminate his plight in "a picture whose outline would leap at me if I struck on the right arrangement" (79, 17). He learns little by little that the slips' original meaning—if they ever had one—is now lost. Therefore painstaking and imaginative interpretation is needed if the slips are to divulge some sense. "The fact that the slips do not hold a single and unambiguous meaning does not mean that they are without meaning," as Susan VanZanten Gallagher observes, "just as Coetzee's multifaceted allegory can reveal truth" (124). When Colonel Joll asks the Magistrate, during interrogation, to translate the poplar slips, he is thwarted by the Magistrate's allegorical method of reading. Joll assumes that the slips contain a single meaning (e.g., a coded message between barbarian fighters), but the Magistrate offers interpretations that are parodic and minatory. The slips "form an allegory," he says, "each single slip can be read in many ways." He also reads the slips as a history of "the old Empire" (122), reminding readers perhaps of the impermanence of the new Empire. The novel, like the outskirts of the settlement, is littered with figurative reminders "of folk who thought they would find safety behind high walls" (16). "[A]llegorical sets" of slips "can be found buried all over the desert," and the "sighs and cries" of the dead are everywhere; these "reminders of the dead" can be made out "if you listen carefully, with a sensitive ear" and, crucially, they "are open to many interpretations" (123). The novel too has multiple meanings and significances; it educates readers in the way it wishes to be read, and therefore this scene, in which the Magistrate, previously so commanding an author of his circumstances, is learning how to read, merits lengthy and detailed attention.

I usually end my classes by discussing the Magistrate's dream. In the dream, which recurs throughout the novel with subtle variations and additions, a figure in a hood (who is gradually revealed to be the girl with whom the Magistrate was briefly besotted) and some children in the town square are using snow to construct a model of the fort. Though the meaning of these dreams escapes him, they call for interpretation. Many students will view them as images of communication and solidarity. For Sam Durrant the dreams "are the site of a transmission of pain, of an identification with the suffering of the other" ("Bearing Witness" 444). Close reading, possibly in group work, can explore the significance of the snow that has erased the boundaries between people and things, revealing a commonality in adversity; of the "bare flagpole" that appears to denote a suspension or transcendence of loyalties (9); of the prominent role played by children in the dreams (the novel is dedicated to Coetzee's children); of the Magistrate's manipulative offer of a coin to the girl and her solicitous proffering of bread after the Magistrate has been assaulted; of the fact that he is on the margin of the unfolding drama of the dream; and of the way in which the novel's final scene resembles the dream world, as the children begin to construct figures to people a model settlement, suggesting the possibly that his fantasies of renewal and reconciliation are realizable (or at least conceivable) in the wake of the soldiers' flight.

That the novel encourages readers to draw parallels between the events of the novel and their own situations presents a pedagogical problem. The text has obvious political implications, but not all students will share its views, and one must be careful not to exploit one's clout as teacher in the classroom by seeking to sway students to a particular position. *Waiting for the Barbarians* was criticized, by Gordimer most prominently, for "den[ying] the energy of the will to resist evil"; Coetzee, according to Gordimer, "hold[s] himself clear of events and their daily, grubby, tragic consequences" ("Idea" 3). Students should be made aware that many scholars in the field of postcolonial studies have heeded the call of Edward Said (among others) for the study of literary representations of colonial violence to be conducted with reference to ongoing realities of conflict and struggle ("Opponents"). But is there not a contradiction between, on the one hand, the Saidian claim that literature is meaningful only when it is read in relation to the worldly contexts in which it is produced and read (and therefore when it is involved politically) and, on the other hand, the conviction that Said expresses elsewhere—and that most of us share—that teaching literature and arguing about politics are like oil and water?

> I don't advocate, and I'm very much against, the teaching of literature as a form of politics. I think there's a distinction between pamphlets and novels. I don't think the classroom should become a place to advocate political ideas. I've never taught political ideas in a classroom. I believe that what I'm there to teach is the interpretation and reading of literary texts.
> (Said, *Pen* 77–78)

The two positions can be reconciled. We ought to understand the role of the teacher of literature to be not the making of tendentious political statements or the measuring of them or their authors against some political criterion but rather the encouragement of faculties of attentiveness, curiosity, and interpretative skill that can be put to use in other spheres. Lack of commitment to a movement or involvement in a cause is hardly a problem in the classroom, because politics is not the yardstick with which we want our students to measure novels. A novel's oblique relation to its author's political beliefs should not perturb us: the politics of the book are not to be found between its pages. We are concerned not with what students believe but with how they think: let it be knowledgeably, sensitively, and critically. As Nicholas Harrison has observed, our role as teachers of literature "is curatorial and lies in presenting and circulating works of whose value one is convinced" (13). For me, *Waiting for the Barbarians* is such a work. Its value is that it allows students to imitate the Magistrate and turn their gazes inward (39), a process incompatible with prescriptive teaching. I encourage students to develop the skills of a sensitive reader: analytic attentiveness to details and contradictions; a capacity for painstaking reflection on language; a critical as well as self-critical examination of ideologies and preconceptions; and, ultimately, in the words of Richard Poirier, one of Said's intellectual mentors, a willingness to let literature teach us "about what words do to us and how, in turn, we might try to do something to them which will perhaps modify the order of things on which they depend for their meaning" (134).

Who's Appropriating Whose Voice in Coetzee's *Life & Times of Michael K?*

Patricia Merivale

Teaching J. M. Coetzee's *Life & Times of Michael K*—arguably Coetzee's best book, clearly one of his most attractive, and apparently one of his most accessible—culminates for me where historical, political, postcolonial, philosophical, and theoretical concerns meet narrative structure: they meet at the appropriation of voice—that is, the writer's or character's imposing a story, and thus an interpretation, on the colonized other, by speaking for him or her.

With an author like Coetzee, to discover what the story is telling, a reader needs to work out how the story is told. We notice at once *Michael K's* division into three parts, of strikingly unequal length and differing narrative voices. I suggest, counterintuitively, that the same amount of class time be devoted to each of the three parts. Part 1 (124 pages) and part 3 (14 pages) together make up most of the book, and both are told by a third-person omniscient narrator—but is it the same narrator?—on behalf of the titular hero, Michael K. Part 2 (38 pages) is the first-person narrative of the not wholly sympathetic medical officer. When your students first read part 1, do they see a relatively unproblematic and quite moving story of Michael K's journey of heroic endurance in the face of bereavement, hunger, political oppression, and misunderstanding? Of course they do! If they read closely, they may find some inconsistencies between the character portrayed and what free indirect discourse suggests is going on in his mind (ask them), but these are unlikely to affect their sympathy for or analysis of him. Parts 2 and 3 will be more puzzling, as not quite hooking up with part 1, but—as most critics of the book seem to have decided—they do not necessarily undermine Michael's privileged position established in part 1.

Most readers are happy with this arrangement, at the price of finding part 2 redundant at best and an aesthetic mistake at worst, and even part 3 is not easy to account for. After the first reading, reread backward: part 1 looks rather different seen through a reading of part 2, while part 3 may make the rereading of parts 1 and 2 more cautious.

Read how? Textual close reading and intertextual comparative reading are strategies endorsed by Coetzee himself. In his essay "Homage" (to his modernist predecessors), he advocates what he calls "slow" (i.e., careful, attentive, close) reading. To skip over words and details, "non sequiturs or oddities," when reading William Faulkner and other modernists, is to miss clues and thus, as in reading "the classic detective story," to miss resolutions of "the enigma the story has posed" (6).

Perhaps, with our pedagogical rather than our critical hats on, we can take Coetzee at his word and suggest some things that reading "intently and intensively" ("Interview" [Begam] 429) might tell us about *Michael K.* Coetzee asserts, inverting Ezra Pound's dictum, that "[p]rose should be at least as well written as poetry," if it is to convey adequately "the voice of the mind, the voice in the mind" while finding "a form for the movements of the mind" ("Homage" 6). Most Coetzee critics seem more committed to the "movements" than to the "form." Teachers of Coetzee should attempt to redress the balance, perhaps by following Michael Cheney's blogged example: "I realized that I was marking up my teaching copy of *Michael K, as if I were marking up a poem* . . . lots of circled words, [and] 'cf.'s referring me to words and phrases in other parts of the book . . . an overall tone-structure, a scaffold of utterance" (my emphasis). The beginnings of that scaffold are supplied by "marking up" the teaspoons that open and close the book—the teaspoon from which Michael is fed at birth (3), and the one with which he "would" measure out the water to keep himself alive at the end (184; cf. 110: ". . . the clash of a spoon . . . the splash of water" signals the interruption of his brief idyll on the farm, in the middle of his journey from watery birth to watery death). The marginal cf.'s of the slow reader mark key parallels, whose repeated variants—of escape from pursuit, say, or returning whence one came (Michael's two very different returns to Cape Town, for instance)—tie the parts together textually, even as narrative pace intensifies with the speeding up of ever shorter versions.

Then we move out from close reading to close comparative reading, as Coetzee both invites and exemplifies in "Homage." But my favorite formulation of the importance of intertextuality in his writing and our teaching of it remains Stephen Watson's "the initial difficulties of his novels vanish when one happens to have read the same books that he has" ("Colonialism" [Huggan and Watson] 25),[1] including, I might add, several that Coetzee has written himself.

The "initial difficult[y]," for our immediate purposes, is the medical officer's narrative, incommensurate as it is with Michael's own story. Here Coetzee's other, closely related 1980s novels, *Waiting for the Barbarians*, *Age of Iron*, and *Foe*, provide useful analogues: they are told by, and openly constitute the stories of, uneasily complacent, nervously self-deceiving white liberal narrators who encounter indecipherable and virtually silent others. Michael K seems far more accessible to us, more likable than these other others, and indeed noble rather than unknowable.

Questions about the real nature and identity of these others have been long since acknowledged futile in accounting for these novels, largely because we realize that we can see the others—the barbarian girl, Vercueil, and Friday—only through the screens of their respective first-person narrators, the Magistrate, Mrs. Curren, and Susan Barton, "whose attempts to appropriate Friday through her hermeneutic understanding of him" (Iddiols 186) rival the medical officer's appropriations of Michael K while being much more obvious.

In *Michael K*, the single first-person narrator, the medical officer, who distinctly resembles these other Coetzeean narrators, is sidelined by most critics, and probably by almost all readers, in favor of questions about the real nature and significance of Michael K, the intractably unknowable other. But K only seems more knowable than Friday et alia, I suggest, because the narrator has obliquely appropriated so much more of his story: we get Michael K, in part 1 and perhaps also at the end of part 3, as the medical officer wishes and, for his own psychopolitical purposes, needs to see him; although disguised, this picture is not inconsistent with his openly first-person narration of part 2.

In Coetzee's book the anticipations of parts 2 and 3 thicken in the last thirty pages of part 1: Michael's return to the farm, his capture, the imposition on him of the designation of "insurgent" (or, in our terms, "terrorist"), and his being taken to the rehabilitation camp, formerly the Cape Town race course, where he is shoved, in real narrative time, into the orbit of the medical officer. The medical officer, now in his own voice (part 2), imposes his even more fundamentally confining story on Michael; he is all the more manipulative for being clever, benevolent, and seriously dedicated to establishing, by any means necessary, Michael's real story, for Michael's own good.

Imagery suggestive of that key postcolonial impropriety, "appropriation of voice," here the imposing of a narrative on the man who refuses to supply his own, punctuates Coetzee's whole book. "When K shook his head the man signed the paper himself" is an early example (31); others saturate the parallel concluding sections of each part. "See if he's got a tongue," orders an officer (cf. the apparent tonguelessness of Friday in Coetzee's *Foe*; the multivalent significances of that tonguelessness are developed by Yoshida and by Mathuray). "Tell me your story," says the soldier (122) and fills Michael's silence with his own story of Michael's aid to the guerrillas—ample grounds for taking Michael to the rehabilitation camp of part 2. There the stupid and violent facts of his captors' story are transposed into the register of the camp: Michaels (the name slightly wrong, of course) "is an arsonist . . . an escapee from a labour camp . . . running a flourishing garden on an abandoned farm and feeding the local guerrilla population when he was captured." "If this Michaels was running a flourishing garden, why was he starving to death?" asks the medical officer rhetorically (131).

The medical officer's darkly comic and explicitly fictional revision sardonically shows up those dim-witted soldiers: *Make up something for the report,*" the medical officer says (141), thus clearing the way for imposing another story, one that can validate his own longed-for escape (a kind of salvation) from "captivity" with the help of his idealized version of Michael, both "escape artist" (166) and savior: "I have chosen you to show me the way" (163).

The key trope of their shared captivity is that, allegorically, everybody in prison (the entire state is a prison), whether prisoner or guard, is a prisoner. "I had . . . given myself up as a prisoner to this war," says the medical officer (157). Part 2 ends with his imagined version, first of his own slightly more practical escape with his colleague, the camp administrator, and then of his unlikely pursuit of the fleeing Michael, which is meant to segue into his entirely unlikely—indeed hallucinatory—escape with Michael. Michael has sussed out the territory and knows, the medical officer supposes, where to go in order to cultivate a garden outside of history and outside "all the camps at the same time" (182).

In part 1, Michael flees the heavy-handed comradeship of the farm owner's grandson, who clumsily envisions a peaceful life sharing his farm with Michael, the trespassing vagrant who has planted a few pumpkins and melons there. For this boy "had tried to turn him into a body-servant," thus imposing on Michael a caricatured role from an Afrikaner pastoral (65).[2] Michael seems to feel instinctively that the medical officer has a similar if far subtler servitude in mind for him, from which it is even more necessary to flee. The medical officer, seeking a utopian escape from history into the nonhistorical, projects his yearning onto Michael K, blending the sentimental possibilities of the noble savage with his more sophisticated version of the pastoral.

The medical officer's interpretation of Michael K in these messianic terms may be largely responsible for some high-flown critical readings of Michael K. Has Coetzee in any other book given so much ammunition to those who might wish to read him sentimentally? And many have read the novel sentimentally. Words and phrases like "inspirational" in reviews and blogs, "a spirit of ecological endurance" (D. Wright 439),[3] and Michael K's "combining . . . the figures of Christ and Kafka's K . . . in his thirty-third year, rising from the dead" (Brink, "Writing" 193–94) seem to have provoked Coetzee, usually so unwilling to interpret or comment on his books, into remarks like "the narrator of Part I may not know as much as he thinks he does about Michael K, may not know very much at all" (Penner 94; qtd. in Head, "Gardening" 99), "I was taking a risk by putting K at the centre of the book . . . you must not forget the doctor in the second part of the book. He is by no means a person of limited consciousness" ("Two Interviews" 455), and "It is important that K should not emerge from the book as an angel" (457). Michela Canepari-Labib quotes Coetzee's last statement, yet she speaks on the next page of a "new Adam," an "Eden," a "semi-idyllic image of the farm," with no apparent sense of irony or contradiction (275, 276).

Critical overprivileging of Michael, concurrent with the underprivileging of the medical officer, leads to the dubious judgment by several critics that part 2 is an aesthetic failure. Cynthia Ozick finds the book's flaw in the "self-indulgent diary of the prison doctor . . . [which] is superfluous . . . redundant. The sister-melons and the brother-pumpkins have already had their eloquent say . . ." (32–33). To the objection that many admirers of Michael K will rightly raise, that he is wonderfully believable, not obviously condescended to, and not without a certain self-irony, I can only suggest that Coetzee has created, in the medical officer, a fairly good novelist, and that the sentimental readers among the bloggers, the critics, our students, and ourselves are not entirely wrong.

At this stage, the class might find useful some selections from largely modernist key intertexts: Franz Kafka's parables of "The Burrow" and "A Hunger Artist" (Merivale 160–62) help shape Michael K, but for the problems that the medical officer's narrative presents, Herman Melville's "Bartleby the Scrivener" and Samuel Beckett's *Molloy* (Yeoh, "J. M. Coetzee and Samuel Beckett: Nothingness") are especially valuable palimpsests: source texts dimly visible beneath or through the text we are reading.

Gilbert Yeoh has written two articles on Coetzee's Beckettian intertexts: on *Waiting for the Barbarians* and *Age of Iron* ("J. M. Coetzee and Samuel Beckett: Ethics"), and on Michael K as a deliberate reworking of Beckett's *Molloy* ("J. M. Coetzee and Samuel Beckett: Nothingness"). Yeoh sees the medical officer, a sophisticated, prickly, unlikable, self-deceiving Moran-like pursuer, trying to catch up with, to define, and particularly to report on (and thereby appropriate) the more natural and likable Molloy analogue, Michael K. The two pursued, Molloy and Michael, are unwashed, malingering vagrants, unwilling to conform to such social norms as the grateful acceptance of charity; they are continually evading the camps and especially those confining and, worse, imposed definitions of themselves that come with the camps. In the closely parallel, almost isomorphic, conclusions to parts 2 (especially the last seven pages) and 3 (the last thirty lines of the book), Michael and the medical officer reach the almost identity of that Beckettian pseudo-couple, Moran the pursuer and Molloy the pursued, as they almost merge.

The parallels between Beckett's and Coetzee's narrative structures are further strengthened if one sees the pursuer as writing the story of the man he seeks to, or happens to, almost become—one of the many possible synchronous and shimmering readings of *Michael K* and *Molloy*. Yeoh, in a fine piece of both close and comparative reading, notes detailed resemblances between Molloy and Michael K: Michael has "a different packet of seeds for each pocket" (Coetzee, *Life* 182; Yeoh, "J. M. Coetzee and Samuel Beckett: Nothingness" 121), like Molloy's stones; Molloy's signature bicycles, tucked away in *Michael K* (I add, "Three strange men on two bicycles" [Coetzee, *Life* 93—these cyclists, superfluous to the plot, seem a gratuitous tip of the hat to Beckett]), along with Michael K's cunningly adapted wheelbarrow and the "stranger and stranger conveyances" of the other refugees (21). There are broader parallels as well: their rejection of charity, their uneasy dealings with the police, their confused and incomplete names and identities.

Yeoh cogently defines parallel narrative structures in *Age of Iron* and *Waiting for the Barbarians*, seeing their narrators as unreliable appropriators of voice and thereby authors of "self-consoling narratives of *false empathy and identification . . . with the victims of colonialism and apartheid*" ("J. M. Coetzee and Samuel Beckett: Ethics" 337, 340; my emphasis). Their self-deceiving confessional exonerations turn out to be projections onto the others of needs of their own: "even [their] most sincere act of self-examination cannot transcend [their] blind spot of self-interest" (335). I find Yeoh's "J. M. Coetzee and Samuel Beckett: Ethics, Truth-Telling, and Self-Deception" a better guide to *Michael K* than "J. M. Coetzee and Samuel Beckett: Nothingness, Minimalism, and Indeterminacy," for it is precisely self-deception and self-interest that the medical officer shares with the Magistrate and Mrs. Curren.

If my notion of the medical officer as the actual hidden narrator and crypto-novelist of part 1 and perhaps part 3 of *Michael K* stretches readerly imagination too far, the reader might consider a powerful but less inconveniently tangible metaphor. Arnim Mennecke develops a fruitful reading of Michael K's story as the medical officer's mental construct, a projection of his quasi-authorial consciousness. Mennecke's book deserves to be better known.[4]

Both Beckett's Moran and the medical officer can be seen as narrators of elegiac romance, autobiography masquerading as biography and inevitably featuring a subset of the unreliable narrator: each tells the story of his (arguably) dead hero in order to tell the story of himself. Consider, as part of the small library needed to read *Michael K*, "Bartleby the Scrivener," perhaps the earliest elegiac romance.[5] Melville's well-meaning, self-deceiving lawyer-narrator discovers the hard way the difficulty of being charitable. Bartleby, whom he employs as a human photocopy machine, lives on ginger nuts, like a prototype of Kafka's hunger artist or of Michael K, with his diet of pumpkins. The lawyer asks him to "be reasonable": to do his work and to account for himself. Bartleby, repeatedly, declares that he "would prefer not to" (this phrase, with slight variations, recurs thirty times in the course of the story). The lawyer's supposition that, by being less than absolutely horrible to Bartleby, he "can cheaply purchase a delicious self-approval" (15), fits the medical officer rather well. Again, as with *Michael K*, critics take the lawyer-narrator more or less at his own valuation; they have crowded in to analyze (as a Christ figure, among other things) Bartleby, who resists both their interpretations and the lawyer's charity.

The medical officer begins the last section of part 2 with an elaborate letter to Michael (149–52)—as undeliverable by its writer as it is unreadable by its recipient-nonrecipient—neatly blending Bartleby's Dead Letter Office (41) with Kafka's parable of the imperial message ("Imperial Message"). Two pages later, Michael's escape from the camp forces the medical officer, I conjecture, to construct Michael's story himself. I quote the last lines of part 2 and recommend an especially slow and careful reading of this part's last eight pages:

> . . . shouting my last words to you as you plunged far ahead into the deepest wattle thickets, running more strongly now than one would ever expect from someone who did not eat—"Am I right?" I would shout. "Have I understood you? If I am right, hold up your right hand; if I am wrong, hold up your left!" (167)

The short concluding section, again in free indirect discourse, suggests, in its grubby and sordidly uncomfortable realism, a sensibility rather different from that of the medical officer, as if, one is tempted to say, a superior author, with an eye for the actual, decides to look in for a moment. Hania Nashef, seeing "Coetzee and not Michael" (36) as the narrator of part 3, shrewdly points to the Michael K described in pages 171–80 as being distinctly closer to the real Michael of a novel than to the pastoral Michael of part 1. The three pages from "Now I am back, he thought" to the end of the book (181–84) are another matter.

Note the haunting encounters, in all sections of the book, with little old men hardly distinguishable from one another. One of them is putatively Michael himself, aged thirty-two, on his arrival in the camp, as seen by the medical officer (129); another is an anonymous, seemingly purely decorative "old man . . . riding a [distinctly Beckettian] bicycle" (156). The medical officer considers following this old man to the Cape Town beach. It is as if he has been shadowing the same old man all along, to make him serve as his guide to the free zone, the liminal, perhaps terminal, beach, the place outside history.

The last page of part 3 is seemingly Michael's version, likewise in the subjunctive, of an escape from Cape Town with "a little old man" who is looking for "a guide who knew the roads" (183), in a mirror image of the medical officer's exclamatory musings (161–67) about Michael at the end of part 2.

Michael K encounters, or dreams up from earlier scenes (or the medical officer dreams him dreaming up), this little old man, who is, textually speaking, the medical officer. He imagines that the two will leave the city together, he guiding the medical officer, much as the medical officer postulated at the end of part 2, back to the farm, to dip a bent teaspoon into the shattered well, thus bringing up a spoonful of water: "and in that way, [Michael] *would* say, one can live" (184; my emphasis).

But of course one cannot: death rather than rebirth is adumbrated in this closing of yet another textual circle, back to the opening scene of Michael's birth, after which, because of his harelip, his first nourishment came to him only in teaspoons. In a kind of textual joint hallucination, the two men are, like Molloy, "to come back to die here with our heads upon our mothers' laps" (*Life* 124).

Most readers, including Nadine Gordimer,[6] reach, not always approvingly, for a Voltairean ending to the book, in which Michael/Candide sets out yet again to cultivate his garden. Sam Durrant goes further: "Michael K's minimalist demonstration of how 'one can live' is perhaps the most unequivocally affirmative of Coetzee's endings" (*Postcolonial Narrative* 50).[7] Yeoh tends to see in Coetzee's endings a Beckettian assertion of narrative control, as in Moran's writing the last words of *Molloy*: "It is midnight. The rain is beating on the windows. It was not midnight. It was not raining" (Yeoh, "J. M. Coetzee and Samuel Beckett: Nothingness" xx; Beckett 171). But this scene also suggests an ironic Ernest Hemingway ending, like the last words of *The Sun Also Rises*: "Isn't it pretty to think so?"—to think, that is, that one could live from teaspoons of water (251). The last scene is thus a death scene, as is both implied and elided by the book's title: the life cannot usually be told until after the death, though Coetzee preferred to leave that point uncertain ("Two Interviews" 454).

The Voltairean cultivation of gardens, the pastoral ideal punctuating the text throughout, is held firmly in the grip of its own utopian impossibility, with its ironic echo of the Afrikaner pastoral: "how terribly transitory that garden life of K's is: he can't hope to keep the garden because, finally, the whole surface of South Africa has been surveyed and mapped and disposed of" (Kossew, *Pen*

144).[8] For teaching *Michael K*, the one indispensable critical work (though there are many useful ones) is Gordimer's review of it, "The Idea of Gardening." Gordimer famously complained of the lack of historicity and political activism in the passive quietism of K's gardening, essentially accusing Coetzee of appropriation of voice. Numerous other critics, particularly South African critics in the 1980s, did so too—but few with so large an audience or with such good credentials, both literary and political. Any class studying the book must come to terms with her views and thus with Coetzee's novel as a fact in the world as well as an artifact.

Having earlier declared that "the novel is after bigger game" than (Gordimer's) "critical realism" ("Speaking" 24), Coetzee, with his characteristic ironic evasiveness, said of her famous review, "One writes the books one wants to write" (*Doubling* 207), or, appealingly but apocryphally, "Mrs. Gordimer is entitled to her opinion."

Michael K, albeit obliquely, indeed manifests wholesale appropriation of voice: critics have commented that everybody is trying to tell Michael's story for him, in the teeth of his reluctance to tell it for himself. Coetzee's narrative sleight of hand here distracted even so savvy a critic as Derek Wright, who spotted "the doctor's later fantasy of K" in part 2, into finding "'faking' a non-white perspective . . . by an Afrikaner author" to be "problematic" (442–43).

It is not Coetzee but the medical officer, the ethically challenged white liberal, who has appropriated Michael K's voice throughout the book. Coetzee has undertaken the subtler task of writing the novel of, by, and about the medical officer, a champion among appropriators of voice. Did Gordimer fail to take this interpretation of the book into account? Discuss!

NOTES

[1] Note Nadine Gordimer's brisk disagreement: "[A]ll writers have read a great many books" (Preface x).

[2] The Afrikaner pastoral is a genre that Coetzee discusses in acrid detail in *White Writing*.

[3] On Derek Wright, *Michael K*, and the ecological, see Barilla.

[4] See Mennecke 129–73 ("als Phantasie des Lagerarztes" [152], "zentrale[s] Bewusstsein" [131]).

[5] Coetzee wrote his MA thesis on Ford Madox Ford, whose *The Good Soldier* is an exemplary elegiac romance. See Bruffee.

[6] On Gordimer and Coetzee as readers of each other and of Kafka, see Merivale 153–55, 165.

[7] For a quick skewering of that bubble, see Janes 117.

[8] Kossew quotes Coetzee from his 1983 interview in "Two Interviews."

Biopolitical Coetzee; or, "The Will to Be Against"

Keith Leslie Johnson

One of the most evocative passages, though it is brief, in Michael Hardt and Antonio Negri's *Empire* draws a parallel among Herman Melville's Bartleby, the political philosopher Étienne de La Boétie, and J. M. Coetzee's Michael K. What unites these three is their absolute refusal of authority, what Hardt and Negri call their "will to be against" (210). That they enact this will with varying levels of consciousness is immaterial; they have in their passivity engendered a kind of ethic of abstention. Though Coetzee is mentioned but this once in *Empire*, we have here the kernel of a much fuller engagement with his work, one that provides real dividends in the classroom.

My seminar-style course called Genealogies of Resistance examines how political resistance has been figured in nineteenth- and twentieth-century fiction, from "Bartleby, the Scrivener" (the fictional ur-text, as it were, of biopolitics), Fyodor Dostoevsky's *Demons*, Henry James's *The Princess Casamassima*, Joseph Conrad's *The Nigger of the* Narcissus, and Jaroslav Hašek's *The Good Soldier Švejk* to Coetzee. The working thesis of the course is that political resistance, which initially takes the form of anarchic violence, gradually divests itself until all that is left is malingering (Conrad's James Wait), Quixotean fantasy (Hašek's Švejk), and radical passivity (Coetzee's Michael K).

Coetzee's work assumes a startling and unique specificity in the biopolitical framework I describe in this essay. Students can better grasp how Coetzee engages with political reality if they do not reduce his works to those *petites histoires* to which they are sometimes prone: literature as merely the encoded or allegorized form of some actual event or other. Conversely, a biopolitical approach can help them stay focused on the more or less immediate, human context of the novels without leaping straightway to existential concerns. Walter Benjamin wrote that there are "two ways to miss the point" of Kafka's works: "One is to interpret them naturally; the other is to interpret them from a supernatural perspective" ("Franz Kafka" 806). The same could be said of Coetzee. For our purposes, the natural perspective is to read historically, the supernatural to read existentially. If these are the Scylla and Charybdis of interpreting Coetzee, then perhaps biopolitics can help us and our students better navigate the channel between.

The Ethical Coetzee

The term by which scholars have most often, and successfully, navigated Coetzee's work is *ethics* — it is in fact the central hermeneutical term in the criticism. But ethics, especially when heard in its poststructuralist key, can often seem to students airy or even recondite. Biopolitics, on the other hand, subsumes ethical issues in a way grounded, intuitively and historically, in experience. It is important, nonetheless, for both students and teachers to have a sense of what ethical approaches to Coetzee's novels are about, and so it is worthwhile here to rehearse and evaluate them. In fact, such a rehearsal can be useful in the classroom, where it has the happy result not only of guiding students beyond their subjective responses to Coetzee but also of engaging them with the largely unfamiliar idiom of Coetzee's academic reception.

If students occasionally regard an assigned author as an emperor with no clothes, then critics are like the terra-cotta army guarding his empty tomb. For most undergraduates, who often have trouble differentiating between authors, never mind articulating why a particular author is considered important, critics can appear as an anonymous but imposing bunch. Unfortunately, most academic prose does little to dispel this impression. I have found that if I expose students, early and often, to the strongest secondary works, not only does the author in question become more vivid, but so do the critics.

If you are assigning Coetzee in an upper-division course, adding one or more of the following secondary texts to your syllabus can enhance discussion. But students should be prepared regarding the ethical paradigms that prevail in the criticism. A handout or brief lecture can dispel misconceptions about what literary scholars today mean by *ethics*. If students themselves have a working definition of the word, it will likely be something on the order of "a behavioral code determining what is appropriate or inappropriate in a given situation." But there is a world of difference between ethics as courtesy and the ethics of Coetzee.

Michael Marais's "'Little Enough, Less Than Little: Nothing': Ethics, Engagement, and Change in the Fiction of J. M. Coetzee" is a fluent introduction not only to Coetzee, whose works from *Dusklands* to *Disgrace* are briefly surveyed, but to the ethics of radical alterity as well. Marais shuttles among Emmanuel Lévinas, Maurice Blanchot, and Coetzee, the circuit becoming increasingly clear, if not always the destination. The essay seeks to demonstrate that "Coetzee's refusal to treat history as an a priori system is directly related to the strong concern with an otherness outside history" (159), and the best part of it from a pedagogical perspective is that Marais explains why we should care. He loosely frames the essay as a rejoinder to those who slight Coetzee for not directly engaging with apartheid. He subtly points up the impossibility of a direct engagement and the (ethical) ineffectuality of an explicit one. As he puts it in a more recent essay, "for Coetzee, the literary work's capacity to engage with its context is not simply a given, . . . the work must wrest itself from the very domain in which it is ineluctably located" ("From the Standpoint" 230). In other words, there must be some sort of ironic, dialectical distance if a work is going to engage ethically with history, else we risk reducing history to a stage on which our fictions strut and fret, which is to neglect, if not negate, its traumas. Trauma as such cannot be depicted; the unrepresentability of it is partly what makes it traumatic. A literary work, in this view, must engage with history indirectly, implicitly, or, to use the Lévinasian term, otherwise (Lévinas, *Otherwise* 3).

Important nuances notwithstanding, most ethical engagements with Coetzee resemble Marais's (or Marais's resembles them). Such reading draws us into questions that can productively shape individual class sessions and, indeed, whole courses: What sorts of relations exist among literature, history, and ethics? Does literature have ethical responsibilities to history? How can literature bear witness to historical trauma without portraying it? This last question is posed by Derek Attridge in a sophisticated but initially puzzling form: that of allegory. His "Against Allegory: *Waiting for the Barbarians, Life & Times of Michael K*, and the Question of Literary Reading" suggests that all interpretations that "encourage the reader to look for meanings beyond the literal, in a realm of significance that the novels may be said to imply without ever directly naming" (63), are in effect allegorical. When it comes to Coetzee, the poles of allegory unsurprisingly resemble the poles of misprision Benjamin identified apropos of Kafka:[1] on the one hand, the "historical situation of [South Africa] and the suffering of the majority of its people" (Attridge, "Against Allegory" 64); on the other hand, the "truths—frequently the dark truths—of the human condition" (63). Against allegorizing historical and existential readings, Attridge proposes not negating but supplementing them with what he calls literal reading, which "is grounded in the experience of reading as an *event* . . . something that comes into being only in the process of understanding and responding that I, as an individual reader in a specific time and place, conditioned by a specific history, go through" (67).

The upshot of Attridge's argument is that before we start the game of substitutions that defines conventional interpretation—fictional event A standing in for historical event X, fictional character B standing in for real-life politician Y—we ought to attend to literature phenomenologically and ethically, as an encounter with otherness. Attridge means that the literary event is not so much a model of the ethical encounter (that would be just another allegory) as a modality of it. To approach literature this way is a form of doing justice to it, responding to "whatever it is about it that challenges our preferences and preconceptions, that stretches our powers of thought and feeling, that resists the encompassing grasp of our interpretive techniques" (Attridge, "Ethical Modernism" 655). Coetzee's work is of particular importance for Attridge not only for its staging of ethical encounters but also for the formal innovations that themselves yield ethical encounters by thwarting our usual ways of knowing, by presenting us with the other (670).

Getting students to understand this argument can be difficult. But however abstruse Lévinas might be, however pharisaical, at least there is a human other in the ethical encounter, right? If the basic elements of the ethical in his work can be conceived, if students can acknowledge that the other must elicit obligation, then it is possible to extend that obligation to include animals, plants, and even literature. Some students may not go the whole distance, but arguments like Attridge's will help engender the dialectical awareness that makes them better readers. They will become more attuned to the ways the text is address-ing them, challenging their assumptions and expectations.

Dialectic does not stop after its first iteration, and there is nothing wrong with meditating on the myriad connections literature forges with the so-called real world. After all, for critics like Gayatri Spivak, all this business of ethics and his-tory comes full circle in the process of *Bildung*. The essay of hers I have in mind is "Ethics and Politics in Tagore, Coetzee, and Certain Scenes of Teaching." For all the radicality of their claims, Marais's and Attridge's essays are, formally speaking, standard fare; Spivak's is anything but, combining academic exposition with biographical, anecdotal, and near-apothegmatic forms. The lyrical, Mon-taignean structure of her essay may confuse or empower students, depending on their general level of preparation and on the way that the instructor sets up the text. The essay works well as a follow-up to the other two, in part because Spivak seems to be responding, *avant la lettre*, to Attridge—she addresses "not only fiction as event but also fiction as task" (18)—but also because she returns to recognizable situations (i.e., education, nation building), where the stakes of literature, ethics, and history become especially visible.

The Biopolitical Coetzee

There remains an essential tension in ethical approaches when they are coordi-nated with history and politics. Students become aware of it, even if they can't always articulate what niggles; Marais, Attridge, and Spivak are all aware of it: it is the wholly natural tension between an antinormative discourse and a nor-mative one. Coetzee's novels self-consciously thematize it. Coetzee notes, "the political versus the ethical . . . [is] played out again and again" (*Doubling* 338). How can we help students get beyond the impasse that can result from tarrying too long in the ethical? Biopolitics offers a solution.

One of the virtues of biopolitics in the classroom is that, despite being a rich and sophisticated theoretical discourse, it is fairly easy to summarize. Its mod-ern version is generally traced back to the work of Carl Schmitt, a German jurist whose writings on sovereignty are still central. His elegant, epigrammatic defi-nition of the sovereign—"he who decides on the exception" (5)—is immedi-ately comprehensible to anyone who has ever set foot on an elementary school playground. It is not who gets to make the rules so much as who gets to suspend them at will. This definition implies a legal order that the sovereign is at once a part of and above. It gets students thinking in interesting ways about *Waiting for the Barbarians*, where the question of sovereignty, of who is in charge, is particularly volatile. For example, how does the Magistrate exercise sovereignty and when? The answer, students find, involves an interesting paradox. He is not a sovereign as such but one who acts in the name of the sovereign (i.e., the nameless Empire), as an avatar. He does exercise something like sovereignty when he initiates a sexual rapport with the barbarian girl, a rapport that gradually deepens despite her ethical inscrutability. Curiously, this deciding on the exception (to the moral and political norms of the Empire) is precisely what puts him at odds with the sovereignty of the Empire and leads to his deposition. This simple example helps detach the notion of sovereignty from that of power. Coetzee's novel is certainly a critique of power as politicoeconomic exploitation, but its subtlest points seem directed more at the crossroads where institutional power meets the subject position of the sovereign.

The question of sovereignty is always volatilized by its opposite, abjection. In the ethical model we are all abject: beholden to the other by an obligation that can never be expunged. It is in fact the very weakness of the other, the nakedness and vulnerability of the other, that disempowers and obliges us: "The face [of the other] is exposed, menaced, as if inviting us to an act of violence. At the same time, the face is what forbids us to kill" (Lévinas, *Ethics* 86). Students in my experience have found this notion compelling, even moving. Yet it is here, at the moment of violence, that biopolitics departs from (even while assuming) ethics. Lévinas states the obvious: "Murder . . . is a banal fact: one can kill the Other; the ethical exigency is not ontological necessity" (*Ethics* 87). Even if we are all abject from his sublime ethical perspective, at the end of the day some of us sleep in silk sheets while others, like the deposed Magistrate, curl up on a flea-infested sack. Biopolitics picks up where ethical exigency leaves off; it offers a concrete vocabulary for the all too ontological violence that ensues under conditions of abjection.

From Schmitt's definition of sovereign power—or in Michel Foucault's pithy, menacing formulation "the right to *take* life or *let* live" (*History* 136)—I sketch out the basic concepts of biopolitics: biopower, or the "numerous and diverse techniques for achieving the subjugation of bodies and the control of populations" that were "indispensable . . . in the development of capitalism" (140–41); life considered solely in its biological, as opposed to political and ethical, dimension; *homo sacer* as an instance of that bare life—a paradoxical, criminal designation that disqualifies one from civil rights (i.e., placing one, like the sovereign, both inside and outside the law); the state of exception, whereby constitutional law is suspended in times of emergency, the exception eventually becoming the new status quo; the camp, or Giorgio Agamben's name for life lived under conditions of exception (*Homo Sacer* 166–80); and so forth. Theoretical texts that provide the backbone of this explication are Benjamin's "Critique of Violence"; lecture 11 of Foucault's *"Society Must Be Defended"* as well as lectures 4 and 5 of his *Abnormal*; Agamben's *Homo Sacer: Sovereign Power and Bare Life* as well as chapter 1 of his *State of Exception*; chapter 1 of Roberto Esposito's *Bíos: Biopolitics and Philosophy*; and chapter 1 of Eric Santner's *On Creaturely Life: Rilke, Benjamin, Sebald*. Students need not read all these texts; the basic ideas are simply transmitted: biopower, bare life, *homo sacer*, the state of exception, the camp, the creaturely life. They all appear in Coetzee's work.

Life & Times of Michael K contains many scenes that stunningly express Agamben's notion of exception: the political suspension of law in times of emergency, a suspension that becomes the new paradigm of government. Captured at a roadblock without travel permits, Michael K is forced into a labor gang repairing damaged railroad tracks. His complaints are met with impatience by his fellows: "This isn't jail. This isn't a life sentence. This is just labour gang. It's peanuts" (43). Later, when he contemplates escape from the camp at Jakkalsdrif, his desire to leave is met with similar incredulity, by both interns and guards. "This isn't a prison," an intern informs Michael K. "Didn't you hear the policeman tell you it isn't a prison? This is Jakkalsdrif. This is a camp. Don't you know what a camp is? A camp is for people without jobs. . . . [W]hy should people with nowhere to go run away from the nice life we've got here?" (78). The guard echoes this advice (85).

What do we make of the complicity of opinion here? What does it mean when both guards and detainees accept the conditions of incarceration? Is this what Agamben means by bare life, life reduced to its animal essence, to eating, sleeping, laboring? "The essence of the camp," according to Agamben, "consists in the materialization of the state of exception and in the subsequent creation of a space in which bare life and the juridical rule enter into a threshold of indistinction" (*Homo Sacer* 174). He concludes, rather chillingly, that "the birth of the camp in our time appears as an event that decisively signals the political space of modernity itself" (74). I dwell on these passages in Agamben to point out that the intern and the guard are right: there is little point in escaping from Jakkalsdrif if the whole country has become a camp. Agamben helps students see the full, horrifying implications of Coetzee's novel.

But does not Michael K escape in the end? Concluding discussion of the novel with this question takes us back to the idea of resistance. Resistance is a more fruitful way of thinking about the novel than, say, desire. It is a temptation, when thinking or talking about an enigmatic figure like Michael K, to psychologize him. The novel itself thematizes this temptation: part 2 is narrated by a medical officer trying to do just that—figure out Michael K. It is instructive to direct students' attention to that section of the novel in order to pose a series of questions: Why does the medical officer fail in his attempts to understand Michael K? What assumptions is he making in his inquiry? What meaning does his failure have for us, the readers? And so forth. Such questions often deflect students' need to search for what we might call, following Ludwig Wittgenstein, the "real artichoke": "In order to find [it], we divested it of its leaves" (164). The artichoke *is* nothing but its leaves, and so too, if you will accept the pun, is Michael K.

Once the Magistrate is branded an enemy, from the point of view of sovereign power he ceases to be human, a being with desires, with an interiority. A scene in *Waiting for the Barbarians* that can be useful when making this point is when he observes the public beating of Colonel Joll's prisoners. The beating is both an act of inscription—the word "ENEMY" is written in charcoal on each naked back—and erasure: "The game . . . is to beat them till their backs are washed clean [by their own blood]" (103). The inscription on the flesh has its correlate on the walls of the village: "WE STAY" (128). WE STAY is in effect the name of the Empire, ENEMY the name of everything else. Walter Benn Michaels perceptively notes that

> if, according to Hardt and Negri's *Empire*, the rise of Empire is the end of national conflict, the "enemy" now, whoever he is, can no longer be ideological or national. The enemy must now be understood as a kind of criminal, as someone who represents a threat not to a political system but to the law. This is the enemy as terrorist.   (171)

All kinds of pedagogical possibilities open up with this realization. In the biopolitical framework I have indicated, both *Waiting for the Barbarians* and *Life & Times of Michael K* can provide a bracing conclusion to a conventional course or module on postcolonialism, a conclusion that draws its concerns out to their broadest political scope and indicates their essential humanity. Pairing Michael K and the Magistrate is not in itself a novelty, but it assumes a slightly different valence in this context. The differences between the two protagonists quickly become legible as a matter of degree rather than kind: both are ultimately trapped in a state of creaturely abjection in the face of sovereign power. If we get students to see this parallel, we have accomplished three things: we have indicated in a more sophisticated way how imperialism creates and then relates to its subjects, regardless of social stratum; we have provided a concrete example of the continuity of Coetzee's thought; and we have empowered students with interpretive tools that help them gain purchase not only on the primary texts but on the secondary texts as well.

NOTE

[1] Lévinas defends the Pharisee in *Difficult Freedom* as one who, by virtue of unflinching legalism, refuses to domesticate or narrativize God, as one who, against the romanticizing tendencies of Hasidism, maintains the absolute exteriority of God (29).

Reconciling Whiteness: *Disgrace* as Postcolonial Text at a Historically Black University

Kay Heath

For many undergraduates studying postcolonial Africa, novels about resistance to a white-dominant, imperialistic perspective are eye-opening. In a postcolonial literature class at Virginia State (VSU), a historically black university, most students are African American, a majority young women in their late teens or early twenties. As we read novels of former British colonies, they easily relate to Africans' struggle for identity and find especially compelling the protagonist of Chimamanda Ngozi Adichie's *Purple Hibiscus*, a young Igbo girl. The problems of David Lurie and Melanie Isaacs in J. M. Coetzee's *Disgrace* are less familiar—confusing and, for some, even repellant. Though Melanie is a young woman of color, Coetzee portrays her through the consciousness of a white, postapartheid male, and she seems alien to my students, while David is a mystery. Students submit weekly online reading journals, and their entries are peppered with questions about David and Melanie's relationship, about the attack on David and his daughter, Lucy, and about whether the novel achieves any resolution.

These issues, I would assume, frequently are raised by undergraduates reading *Disgrace*, but at a historically black university they carry a special resonance. My students have a diversity of experience with and opinions about race and possess varying degrees of knowledge regarding its history and construction in different periods and cultures. But they (and I) share the general conviction that racism remains a major problem, both in the United States and around the world—an idea that might not be accepted in the small town adjacent to our campus where Confederate flags decorate porches and pickup trucks. In addition, my students often have a keen interest in Africa based on identification with the continent as part of their family history. Like most Americans, though, they tend to look at Africa monolithically, through the stereotypes of television and movies, and the racial landscape of South Africa is enigmatic to them, corresponding to what they know of United States racial history in some ways but not in others. In addition, many have never considered the existence of white Africans or their position in a postcolony. As a result, my students initially find Coetzee's novel to be a strange, rather closed text, and their struggles to come to terms with its central characters illustrate several challenges inherent in teaching it. I put *Disgrace* in dialogue with other texts, not only providing a context for its issues but also opening space for agreement and disagreement and ultimately for an open-ended reading of the novel.

Adichie's *Purple Hibiscus*, which precedes *Disgrace* on my course syllabus, is an excellent and engaging introduction to issues of identity in another postcolonial nation, Nigeria, among the Igbo people. Because our departmental curriculum reflects VSU's mission as a historically black university, my students have studied more African American literature than students generally have at a predominantly white institution. African countries and their literatures, however, are less familiar to my students, though in high school many have read Chinua Achebe's account of Igbo culture dismantled by the British in *Things Fall Apart*. This background, along with Adichie's engaging style, makes the class immediately comfortable with *Purple Hibiscus*.

From its first words, "Things started to fall apart at home when . . . ," the novel returns to issues raised by Achebe but reframed from the perspective of his grandchildren's generation. Adichie often is considered Achebe's direct literary heir. Adichie grew up in a house once lived in by the famous author, and she frequently mentions him in interviews as one of her earliest influences (Murray). His endorsement decorates the cover of *Purple Hibiscus*, and many critics have asked the question posed by the Nigerian *Daily Sun*: "Is Chimamanda the new Achebe?" (Akubuiro).

Most of my students immediately identify with and have sympathy for the struggles of Kambili, the fifteen-year-old protagonist of *Purple Hibiscus*. They take a passionate interest in her attempts to fashion an identity that incorporates competing cultural narratives as she integrates the indigenous and forbidden spirituality of her Igbo grandfather into the British Catholicism rigidly imposed by her hypocritical, abusive father. Visiting her Aunty Ifeoma, a professor of African studies at the University of Nigeria, she learns how to blend traditional Igbo and Western ways into a life symbolized by the purple hibiscus, a hybrid strain created at the university from the native red hibiscus. We briefly discuss the history of the Igbo people, who were colonized by the British in the nineteenth century, persecuted by the Hausa-Fulani and Yoruba majority in the twentieth, and declared a short-lived independence in the Nigerian-Biafran War of 1967 to 1970. Though my students struggle with the Igbo words Adichie incorporates in the text, they are fascinated by details of Igboland and culture, as Kambili rolls *fufu* between her fingers to dip in her soup or watches the masked *mmuo* dancers her father has declared "devilish folklore" (85).

The class easily recognizes Kambili's situation as representative of wider cultural issues in the postcolony. She searches for the decolonized mind to which Ngũgĩ wa Thiong'o alludes in the title of his well-known book, transcending her father's shame at his Igbo roots, hybridizing old and new.[1] Almost unanimously, my students love this novel, telling me, "It's the best book I've ever read," and even, "I'm buying it for my mother for Christmas!"

Students' initial reactions to *Disgrace* contrast sharply with those to *Purple Hibiscus*, and they approach cautiously with many questions. Knowing that Coetzee's novel is their first exposure to South African literature, I come to class prepared to provide an overview of apartheid and share anew with them shock at the gross inequalities between white and black populations in jobs, wages, land, housing, education, and health care, injustices systematically enforced into the 1990s. Apartheid reminds them of United States slavery's legacy in Jim Crow laws, which they consider part of their own history but a distant one, a history studied in school and passed down in stories told by grandparents. Though readily identifying and passionately discussing its lingering aftereffects, they still consider such egregious discrimination another generation's story and are amazed to learn that apartheid was upheld in South Africa within their lifetime.

To understand *Disgrace*, students need an awareness of the work and goals of the Truth and Reconciliation Commission (TRC). The novel not only appeared immediately after the close of the TRC hearings but also raises provocative questions about the power of storytelling to heal personal and national wounds. To illustrate the work of the TRC, we read accounts of testimony from both victims and perpetrators in Antjie Krog's *Country of My Skull*, and we watch reenactments of the hearings from *In My Country*, a movie based on her book. Krog's graphic accounts of atrocities appall the class: "I stared at her . . . my most beautiful friend . . . her hair flaming and her chest like a furnace . . . she died a day later" (38); "I saw him dragging my child. Sonnyboy was already dead. . . . It's an everlasting pain. It will stop never in my heart" (40). After hearing from victims, students consider what Krog refers to as the "second narrative" (74), the confessions of perpetrators. We look at an excerpt from an anonymous letter Desmond Tutu read before the commission: "Then I cry over what has happened. . . . I look inside myself to understand . . . how it is possible that often I also just looked on. Then I wonder how it is possible to live with this inner guilt and shame" (qtd. in Krog 62). *White guilt* is a term new to several students. Can we hear this guilt as genuine remorse, I ask, or only as regret for being exposed?

At the heart of our discussion is reconciliation, basic to the goals of the TRC and part of its name. I read Tutu's plea quoted by Krog: "We should all be deeply humbled by what we've heard, but we've got to finish quickly and really turn our backs on this awful past and say: 'Life is for living'" (42). I ask, Is such reconciliation justifiable or even possible? We read the testimony of another victim, Mr. Sikwepere: ". . . I feel what has been making me sick all the time is the fact that I couldn't tell my story. But now I—it feels like I got my sight back by coming here and telling you my story" (qtd. in Krog 43). Can storytelling, especially when the storyteller is given a public hearing, begin the healing process? We discuss the South African term *ubuntu* as Tutu defines it: "a proper self-assurance that comes from [a person's] knowing that he or she belongs in a greater whole and is diminished when others are humiliated or diminished, when others are tortured or oppressed" (Tutu 31). Are *ubuntu* and justice related or opposed principles? Students are deeply divided on the issue of reconciliation in South Africa: some believe that justice is not served without punishment, that the perpetrators are getting away with murder; others feel that forgiveness is the only way forward to a healthy society. This complex question serves as background that informs our reading.

As our discussion of *Disgrace* begins, I quote from students' journals posted online before class, entries revealing their initial negative responses to the novel. Offended by the behavior of David toward women and his affair with a student, they call him weird, disgusting, messed up, crazy, disturbed, a sex addict, a stalker, and, the most common descriptor of all, a pervert. We discuss age bias, how one age cohort may marginalize another and the extent to which, in Western culture, we believe that the only worthy sex takes place between the young, the beautiful, the physically able. Students are surprised to discover that ageist stereotypes inform their thinking: one student notes that much of the class was disgusted with the thought that people over forty even have sex.

Students also are bothered by the incestuous and pedophilic overtones in David and Melanie's relationship. We find evidence for this reading: not only does David have sex with Melanie in his daughter's bed and speaks to her "as a cajoling parent, not a lover" (20) but he sometimes looks at her as a child, thinking, "Her hips are as slim as a twelve-year-old's" (19), and, *"No more than a child! What am I doing?"* (20). If "he is aware that he is abusing his position of authority as Melanie's teacher," as Sue Kossew argues ("Politics" 159), does his guilt make him more or less culpable in our eyes? In order to relate this behavior to wider issues, I turn our focus to dynamics of power with regard to race, age, and professional position.

One problem inherent in teaching *Disgrace* is Coetzee's subtle racial descriptions, which are difficult to decipher even for students quite sensitive to issues of race. On their first reading, most of the class does not register a racial difference between David and Melanie. We closely read descriptions of both Melanie and Soraya, putting them in the context of apartheid racial categories as well as of other power inequities. Soraya, twelve years younger than David, is Middle Eastern, with a "honey brown body, unmarked by the sun" and "long black hair and dark liquid eyes" (1), chosen by him from an escort agency catalog under the heading "exotic" (7). Melanie is thirty years younger than David. Though Coetzee describes her merely as having "close-cropped black hair" and "wide, almost Chinese cheekbones, large, dark eyes" (11), David enjoys thinking of her as "Meláni: the dark one" (18). I read to the class Derek Attridge's comment about "the many details suggesting that the Issacs family are, according to apartheid race classifications, 'colored'" (*J. M. Coetzee* 173n15). Students comment on a pattern that emerges: David chooses younger women over whom he has some sort of control, many of them from groups oppressed by apartheid. One student writes that she has a new perspective after realizing Soraya is Middle Eastern and Melanie is of mixed race; now she sees David at the beginning of the novel as a man trying to retain white privilege and control over people of color.

The class is confused by Melanie. Why does she acquiesce to David's overtures when they are not welcome but later approaches him and willingly continues their sexual relationship? I ask whether she has been coerced, if she can make an autonomous choice when put in this situation by a person in power over her. We look at passages that describe her passive sexual response, and I bring up David's use of a charged term: "Not rape, not quite that, but undesired nevertheless, undesired to the core" (25). We discuss whether "rape" is an apt word. Some students say she is being harassed, stalked, and exploited. Others counter that she is not powerless and has brought the situation on herself. She is old enough to know how to say no to a man, they argue, and should not be considered a victim. The class remains divided.

As critics have noted, the attack on Lucy and David marks a turning point in the novel as well as a change in David's perspective. I summarize the critical debate about the scene: some accuse Coetzee of reinforcing the worst racist stereotypes by portraying black men as rapists who prey on whites, while others interpret the attack as a provocative representation of the postapartheid power shift (Attridge, *J. M. Coetzee* 170 and "J. M. Coetzee's *Disgrace*" 317). In addition, the parallel between Lucy's rape and what David chooses to think of as his "not quite" rape of Melanie frequently has been discussed as an indictment of white culture for similar but even more pervasive crimes (Attridge, *J. M. Coetzee* 171; Cooper 25; Boehmer, "Not Saying" 344; P. McDonald 327).

When I ask the class how they interpret the attack, one student comments about the complexity of white guilt, making a case for both sides of the argument between David and his daughter. Because of her guilt about apartheid and sense of the injustice done to people of color, Lucy does not want her attackers apprehended. But, the student continues, she can also understand David's urging that the assailants be punished. If they are not, the crime spree may continue. How can the cycle of violence be broken? I bring up Tutu's concept of retributive versus restorative justice and ask whether justice and forgiveness are dichotomous terms. The class links David with retributive and Lucy with restorative justice, but students diverge in their interpretations of how each responds to the assault.

While some are critical of Lucy, others are sympathetic to her plight and accuse their peers of being harsh. One student is surprised that our postcolonial literature class, which is filled with women, should have so little compassion for a rape victim. She and several others argue that Lucy, by refusing to pros-ecute her attackers and accepting the pregnancy, is trying to live the principle of *ubuntu*. They point out that her plan has several advantages. Not only is she now enabled to become a mother, although a lesbian, but also as one of Petrus's wives in name and social position she will give her child a place in an accepted family structure under male protection in a world that seems dangerous to women. Others in the class assert that this is a marriage of convenience, a fraud. Lucy no longer owns her property and is incorporated into a sexist system that denies her independence, even though the land eventually may go to her child. For these students, Lucy's life is overshadowed by patriarchy and retribution that overwhelm her attempts at reconciliation. Her plan only perpetuates the cycle of abuse.

In regard to David, the class agrees that the attack changes him, but students differ about whether he has gone beyond old-order thinking, whether, as one puts it, he has "learned a lesson." We closely read several scenes between David and Bev, identifying his changed attitude. Now he is in the position of being se-duced by someone he does not desire; he is a passive, distanced partner merely going along with the woman's wishes.

I turn our focus on Coetzee's use of animals to portray David's changing self-image. We consider how David looks away from the goat's blowfly-infested tes-ticles, its choices either sterility or death. David represses parallels with his own situation, "the problem of sex" for an aging man (1), and, in a larger sense, his position as a disempowered white male in postapartheid South Africa. We read the scene in which he equates himself with a golden retriever punished for howling after females in heat. He concludes that the dog "might have preferred being shot" to becoming sexless, echoing his response to the university inquiry board: instead of being "reformed," and therefore "castrated," he would "prefer simply to be put against a wall and shot" (66). Sterility or death—the alterna-tives facing the golden retriever and the goat—are, he now implies, the only options left for him.

But David's deepening compassion for beleaguered animals suggests a fun-damental change of heart. He weeps for the doomed clinic dogs and "saves the honour of corpses" by disposing of them himself (146). We discuss parallels between the disabled dog Driepoot, whom he befriends and "gives up" in the book's last line, with his vision of himself in terms of the waning sexuality, power, and privilege of an aging, postapartheid white man. I offer a variety of critical opinions: does David find repentance and grace through abjection (Cooper 35; Boehmer, "Not Saying" 349), achieve enlightenment as an asexual grandfather (Segall 45), or avoid responsibility for his failings (Diala 58)? Or does Coetzee resist such conclusions (Attridge, *J. M. Coetzee* 177)? Some students maintain that the ending is ambiguous, but others argue that by killing Driepoot, David acts out his despairing anger, refusing reconciliation. Most believe he is stuck in patriarchal, old-order thinking (an interpretation contrary to my own, which falls somewhere between Attridge's and Cooper's but which I do not emphasize). They find it difficult to believe that David will countenance Lucy's marriage to Petrus, arguing that he cannot accept a black man into his family.

In our final discussion, I read Tutu's claim, "You can only be human in a humane society. If you live with hatred and revenge in your heart, you dehumanize not only yourself, but your community" (qtd. in Krog 143). I ask whether *Disgrace*'s ending offers any hope for reconciliation. One student observes that Lucy's child is a cultural hybrid, like Adichie's purple hibiscus, and suggests that David, by accepting Lucy's pregnancy, moves past retaliation toward *ubuntu*. Others are suspicious of his imagined grandfatherhood, asserting that he has not changed and cannot love a mixed-race child.

Though my students are fascinated by the cultural hybridity Adichie suggests and admire the concept of *ubuntu*, they disagree whether reconciliation is possible in the postapartheid South Africa of Coetzee's novel. We leave that thought-provoking question unresolved, like the undetermined ending of an Igbo dilemma tale. As we have discovered, no one answer serves the complexity and possibility offered by Coetzee's *Disgrace*.

NOTE

[1] While Ngũgĩ does not use the term "decolonized mind" specifically in his book, it provides the structuring theme of *Decolonising the Mind: The Politics of Language in African Literature*.

Teaching Coetzee's *The Lives of Animals* in the First-Year Composition Classroom

Shannon Payne

In the composition classroom, the complex rhetorical situation (relations among characters, topic, and audience) in J. M. Coetzee's *The Lives of Animals* challenges students to read carefully and critically but, even more important, to consider an argument that claims there is no definitive right or wrong. "The Philosophers and the Animals" and "The Poets and the Animals" use every part of the text (setting, perspective, lectures, a letter) to deliver social critique and philosophical argument, but in the end there is no firm ethical ground on which to stand. The text destabilizes first-year students' tendency to want clear either-or categories, and it thwarts their need or desire to work within the constraints of the three-body-paragraph essay. When students respond to Coetzee's text, unlike other articles and essays we read in first-year composition, they cannot approximate the style or density of the prose. They engage *The Lives of Animals* primarily as an exercise in critical reading, which gradually becomes a study in the many choices an author makes to assemble a text. When students confront Coetzee's text as writers, they revisit their experience as readers in order to shape, for their own reading audience, a dialogue with the text that analyzes its content and form together. They analyze provocative claims to reveal the strategic purposes behind them. By underlining slippery details, they note how and when characters become sympathetic—or not.

The form and content of Coetzee's writing can be daunting for first-year readers and writers, and so I pair *Lives* with Michael Pollan's "An Animal's Place," which is a first-person study of the moral and practical considerations of an omnivorous diet. Pollan's article originally appeared in the *New York Times Magazine*, but perhaps because of his current fame as the author of *The Omnivore's Dilemma: A Natural History of Four Meals*, it is now available as the sole content of several Web sites with a simple Internet search. Pollan, a journalist, begins his article as he sits down to a steak dinner while reading Peter Singer's *Animal Liberation*, a centerpiece to the animal rights movement since 1975. Students appreciate almost everything about Pollan's piece: its moderate viewpoint, its clear language and accessibility, and its humor and permissive tone. In class discussion, they refer easily to it, citing specific lines of text, questioning concepts and philosophical threads. Coetzee's piece is more difficult, and students at first refer to its ideas and characters in sweeping, dismissive terms. The characters seem too intense, the politics too overt, and students struggle to make it through the first reading.

I assign "The Philosophers and the Animals" separately from "The Poets and the Animals" and explain why each must be read thoroughly and twice. There is a difference between just reading for class, I suggest, and reading to understand the links between concepts and the order of events. When I ask students to give examples of the benefits of rereading, they primarily mention film: repeated viewings profoundly change the way they see and understand movies of all kinds. *The Usual Suspects* is one of their examples, as its surprise ending forces them to reverse-engineer their experience of watching in an attempt to locate when, and by whom, they were duped. I ask them to ground their rereadings of Coetzee's text in analysis, using a set of questions taken from our course text, a custom edition of the *Penguin Handbook*. The list of questions includes the following: How is the piece of writing organized? What does the writer assume the readers know and believe? Where is the evidence? Does the evidence support the thesis and main claims? Can you think of contradictory evidence? Does the writer acknowledge opposing views? Does the writer deal fairly with opposing views?

On the first day of discussion, we list major characters and establish their relationships to one another. After we have responded to the handbook's questions, we turn to another list of questions the handbook offers to address more subtle details of rhetorical analysis. How does the writer represent himself or herself in the text? How does the author establish a credible ethos? How is the main idea supported? Does the writer use humor or satire? How is the style related to the purpose of the piece? When these questions are difficult to answer (and they are all difficult in *The Lives of Animals*), we talk about the difference between author and character and about the multiple filters with which any character or idea may be seen in this text.

Students invariably find Pollan's article more streamlined, focused, and purposeful than Coetzee's book. Pollan, in this first-person narrative, struggles through the major ethical questions that agrobusiness presents everyday consumers. My students are easy with his line of questioning and comfortable as members of his audience. He does the work and remains moderate (reasonable) throughout. He explains that some animal rightists believe that "[t]o exclude the chimp from moral consideration simply because he's not human is no different from excluding the slave simply because he's not white" but posits himself that the chimp is excluded from moral consideration "because he's a chimp!" Clear and simple: students love it. They are more shy but no less supportive of Pollan when he presents the argument that scientific progress has made heterosexual sexual intercourse among humans unnecessary—just as an omnivorous diet is no longer a necessity—and concludes by analogy that "[w]hatever else it is, our meat eating is something very deep indeed."

In contrast, Elizabeth Costello is a study of extremes. She is invariably too formal, too personal, too committed, or too aloof. The only qualm students feel as Pollan's readers is that their work is too easy. They fear the sting of being duped and wonder if there is more to the story. When pressed, they raise objections about the scope and cost of the coordinated ethical and economic solution Pollan imagines: small farms, organics rather than nonorganics, and higher prices. They want to be fair but wonder if his solution is too simple or out of reach. Turning back to Costello, they find her sympathetic, at least to the extent that, like Pollan, she presents an earnest and trustworthy face. When she is discredited, the reason is not her doing but the criticism of her appearance by the narrator and other characters. From the moment she is introduced, "her shoulders stoop; her flesh has grown flabby" (15). From this introduction, students notice that they are being set up to mistrust or at the very least discount this old woman.

The arguments in each lecture are difficult, and to understand the linkages between characters and philosophical positions we connect relevant figures (Immanuel Kant, Jeremy Bentham, Peter Singer, et al.) with ideological positions and characters in web diagrams on the chalkboard. This exercise is helpful for two reasons: first, it clarifies content; second, it becomes an important tool to substantiate connections among the three works. The most obvious connection made between Coetzee and Pollan is Pollan's explicit reference to Costello when he acknowledges her inflammatory position on animal rights, the speciesist perspective:

> Will history someday judge us as harshly as it judges the Germans who went about their ordinary lives in the shadow of Treblinka? Precisely that question was recently posed by J. M. Coetzee, the South African novelist, in a lecture delivered at Princeton; he answered it in the affirmative. If animal rightists are right, "a crime of stupefying proportions" (in Coetzee's words) is going on all around us every day, just beneath our notice.
> ("Animal's Place")

Students begin to see the exact point at which they disagree with or take offense at a statement, the moments in which they wish to raise a question or suggest an alternative position. The web diagrams show them the significant overlaps between Costello and Pollan as well as the clear points of dissent. Part of the final assignment requires them to observe how and why the essays intersect, but more than that, they must create a dialogue that is rooted in an issue or idea that resonates in all three texts. Once they have isolated that issue or idea, they must explain to their audience how and why rhetoric shapes its content. The assignment is this:

> Perform critical analysis and rhetorical analysis to discuss the complexities of an issue or idea in *The Lives of Animals* and "An Animal's Place." Assume that while your reading audience has read both Coetzee's and Pollan's works, they have not read them as companion pieces and so have not reaped the benefits of comparative analysis or juxtaposition. Show your reader why each piece (in form and content) usefully brings the two others into the fullness of their complexity.

My goal is to give students no possible avenue to trot out a summary paper or reproduce a three-body-paragraph essay. Once they realize how involved the narrative perspective may be in an essay (Coetzee's *Lives* is a masterful example), they gain new respect for reading. Reading becomes its own intellectual feat, an active engagement rather than a passive activity. Moreover, even though Pollan interchanges character and author in his quote above, a rhetorical analysis of Coetzee's essays breaks the habit of reading character as interchangeable with author, of reading narrative description as truth. As participants in a conversation among the three pieces, students learn that they cannot stage a direct attack on an author but must couch it in terms of ideas.

Because the ideas in these texts are often new to the students and complex, our in-class discussions largely determine the focus and direction of student papers. Students are reluctant to stray from connections they have established among the pieces and have related to positions they hold or questions they wish to ask. Most of what they must do in this assignment as writers is new to them: critical analysis, rhetorical analysis, and taking stock of their own reading audience. The combination of these tasks can be overwhelming, so we address them individually in separate drafts. Peer editors underline quotations from Coetzee and Pollan to determine where and how usefully these texts are employed. To direct their critical analysis, students ask one another, What is this paper about, and why does it matter? They come away from this workshop with the understanding that simpler is better and that a good strategy in the dialogue may be to state how each text makes them think. They realize that the three-body-paragraph essay they learned in high school constrains them even as it organizes them. It resists nuance in their representation of the literary and philosophical components of these texts.

Students look back to Coetzee's characters and to Pollan and see that a writer or speaker can make a point but not cover it in any depth. In a sentence or two, students can note the point, briefly explain its relevance, then move on to their central concern. For example, if a student's focus is on the disagreement between Abraham Stern and Costello regarding the Holocaust as an analogue to the practice of factory farming, the student may find it relevant to mention the characters' ages. Both Stern and Costello use their age and experience to buttress their moral authority. Costello, for example, says, "I say what I mean. I am an old woman. I do not have the time any longer to say things I do not mean" (18). In the first drafts, a student may be distracted by the density of Coetzee's works and attempt to imitate it by attaching a discussion of reason and religion to that of age. Asking and answering questions like, What is this about, and how is it important?, helps students simplify their arguments. They learn that an author must make choices: there is not room in a single essay for every good thought a student has had on the subject.

The inconsistency of Costello is a challenge for students. She opens her divisive lecture, "I want to find a way of speaking to fellow human beings that will be cool rather than heated, philosophical rather than polemical, that will bring enlightenment rather than seeking to divide us into the righteous and the sinners, the saved and the damned, the sheep and the goats" (22). Yet she does not pursue a philosophical or enlightening point. Her ideas and language are polarizing. Composition students are frustrated by this statement, because it gives no precise way to chart a compare-and-contrast course. Pollan, they want to say, is philosophical and enlightening. He should win or at least be more in the right. One of the best lessons from Coetzee's text is that dialogue is soft-edged, that when we, as writers, present a position or experience (our own or someone else's), it may not be made of certainties. Our ideas may be rigidly defined and painstakingly consistent, but our actions probably will not be. This is the territory of nuance. But how do you describe nuance? Students are fond of Costello's expressed desire to be philosophical and not polemical, and they are also taken by her response to President Garrard, who wrongly addresses her as "Mrs. Costello" and proclaims his "great respect" for her "way of life" as a vegetarian (43). Her reply is that her vegetarianism "comes out of a desire to save my soul," then admits, "I'm wearing leather shoes . . . I'm carrying a leather purse. I wouldn't have overmuch respect if I were you" (43). At first, students are glad to wash the nuance from the frame. They'd like to turn away from such moments or acknowledge them, respond with disapproval, and move on. But in a dialogue, consistency is not a virtue. Pollan too contributes inconsistency, as his steak dinner with *Animal Liberation* is more than a framing device. It is difficult to resist the urge to compare and contrast, to elevate and to damn, but there are alternatives when students function as writer-moderators.

Breaking the habit of oversimplifying involves a shift from vague or suggestive language to specific examples. The format of a dialogue in this assignment reinforces the importance of precise language, lest the writer misrepresent a voice or perspective. Precise language, though, can lead to a rigid structure, an assemblage of quotations rather than a dialogue. How do we get out of this trap? Some students, opting to play the role of moderator, acknowledge that the works being discussed are in tension. Coetzee's characters cannot resolve the ethical human-animal dilemma, while Pollan's piece solves it with "a new dietary category" that studiously avoids "nonindustrial animals" and therefore takes the high moral ground. If students do not challenge the high moral ground, they will lose the strategy of dialogue and side with moderates, like Pollan, who sees no harm in his philosophical approach and practical decisions. They will praise the reasonableness of "An Animal's Place" and find that Costello's argument lacks any real foundation. They might avoid a one-sided solution by revisiting Costello, who argues that "reason looks to me suspiciously like the being of human thought; worse than that, like the being of one tendency in human thought. Reason is the being of a certain spectrum of human thinking" (23). Pollan employs the wisdom of Benjamin Franklin: "The advantage of being a 'reasonable creature,' Franklin remarks, is that you can find a reason for whatever you want to do." Back and forth, they might go on forever. But most students choose to resolve philosophical argument with practical action. Most see animals as food and urge their readers to understand that there are ways to produce and consume that food responsibly. End of discussion.

My intention is to foster critical reading practices and rhetorical analysis, which typically produce position papers or essays that adopt the tone of an educational pamphlet. I stress revision and require final papers to demonstrate the following: thoughtful use of texts (the best possible quotations appear and are carefully contextualized so that readers know exactly how the writer reads the text and uses it to further the argument), an awareness of reading audience (the piece reads like a dialogue between three authors, and connections, transitions, and symmetries-asymmetries are made so that they require no further work by the reader), innovative contribution to the conversation (the writer's personal voice and ideas are instrumental in the direction and meaning of the essay), and engaged and sustained critical and rhetorical analyses (attention to examples that demonstrate how the texts are assembled and why their elements are significant). Students do their best to distinguish between characters and authors, between narrative description and the presentation of ideas. Some provide transitions from one idea to another; others juxtapose ideas to create tension and dialogue. That characters are often presented in contradictory terms (Pollan is both misleading and trustworthy; Costello is both coy and argumentative) I take as evidence of nuance rather than unstable thinking. Complex characters and difficult rhetorical situations challenge students but help them move away from the oversimplified terrain of either-or categories and the familiar but constraining format of the three-body-paragraph essay.

Teaching Coetzee's *Foe*
in an Undergraduate Theory Classroom

Emily S. Davis

While Coetzee's work has made its way into courses on the novel as well as a range of special-topics courses, I have found it particularly useful for teaching theory to undergraduates. When students encounter Coetzee in the theory classroom, they have an opportunity to engage directly with the intertextual nature of his writing, in relation both to earlier fiction and to generations of theoretical discourse. Working to map the genealogies in his fiction, students learn to appreciate his highly self-conscious appropriations even as they wrestle with concrete examples of challenging theoretical concepts. In this essay, I discuss how my undergraduate theory survey uses Coetzee's 1986 novel *Foe* as a primary text for a unit on structuralism and deconstruction, as well as how the novel lays the groundwork for students to appreciate the influence of poststructuralism on contemporary theoretical interventions in areas such as postcolonial studies. Although *Foe* is by no means the only text that can speak to a multitude of theoretical questions, Coetzee's sophisticated engagement with theory in this novel (as indeed in his larger oeuvre) makes theoretically informed reading of his work an especially instructive and satisfying experience for students.

My university's undergraduate literary theory course, like similar courses at many institutions, is designed to provide students with a broad overview of the theoretical approaches used by scholars in literary studies. My version of this course is organized into four units, each of which addresses two complementary critical discourses in relation to one novel. I pair feminist theory and psychoanalysis with Charlotte Brontë's *Jane Eyre*, materialism and cultural studies with Daniel Defoe's *Robinson Crusoe*, structuralism and deconstruction with Coetzee's *Foe*, and postcolonial theory and queer theory with Shyam Selvadurai's *Funny Boy*. I chose these particular texts not only because they offer rich possibilities for readings grounded in these theoretical approaches but also because they share many of the same thematic concerns, including the difficulty of establishing a voice as a minoritized subject and the reliance of repressive ideologies on binary constructions of race, gender, and class. In my course, we use Lois Tyson's *Critical Theory Today* as a textbook, but this framework would work equally well with another reader or with representative articles from major figures associated with different theoretical approaches.

For students new to theory, some of whom resist the idea of imposing theoretical readings on helpless and unsuspecting texts, it can be an eye-opening experience to encounter an author so keenly attuned to contemporary critical debates. Part of the appeal of Coetzee for scholars, of course, is precisely that he demonstrates such an awareness of the field of literary studies. When I introduce *Foe* in my class, I make a point of mentioning that Coetzee wrote a dissertation using structuralist methods to analyze Samuel Beckett's fiction and taught for many years in the English department at the University of Cape Town. Theoretical approaches form part of a larger constellation in his work of master narratives and what we might call master questions to which he expertly and obsessively returns. But my introduction ends on a cautionary note: like theory, especially deconstruction, his writing is slippery. He knows the game and is usually a step ahead of his reader. Reading *Foe* alongside theory teaches students to recognize that they cannot always fix meaning and that closure is not necessarily the goal of critical reading.

By the time my students begin Coetzee's novel, they have already worked through the chapters on structuralist and deconstructive criticism in Tyson's textbook, so we can consider two key structuralist premises during our first discussion of *Foe*. First, language is differential and relational, in that signs derive meaning from other signs and from the difference between them. Second, sign systems are culturally specific in that signifiers refer to signifieds agreed on by a particular linguistic community rather than to actual objects, actions, or concepts in the world. Once we have established that language is a shared system of signs, Roland Barthes's discussion of semiotics and popular culture (Tyson 216–19) leads us to think about the ways in which human rituals from the senior prom to one's favorite reality television program can also be characterized as sign systems. If, according to structuralism, everything from language to rites of passage participates in larger semiotic systems accessible to and shared by cultural groups, it only makes sense that literary narratives would contain patterns and figures common to those systems. Tzvetan Todorov's grammar of narrative provides us with an example of how structuralist critics bring these insights to literary analysis. For Todorov, characters are combined with certain actions to form propositions, which are strung together to form a sequence and ultimately a story (Tyson 226–27).

Foe, which is deeply indebted to poststructuralism, represents structuralism parodically instead of accepting its claims uncritically. Our classroom discussions of structuralism in the novel work through a series of moments in which characters articulate structuralist concepts that are undermined by the novel. The passage in which Susan Barton argues with Foe about the proper structure for her story provides our starting point for tracking the novel's dialogue with structuralism, because students can readily see how Foe attempts to squeeze her complex story into established narrative conventions. As he informs her, "We therefore have five parts in all: the loss of the daughter; the quest for the daughter in Brazil; abandonment of the quest, and the adventure of the island; assumption of the quest by the daughter; and reunion of the daughter with the mother. It is thus that we make up a book: loss, then quest, then recovery; beginning, then middle, then end" (117). The passage echoes Todorov's description of the components of narrative while hinting at the poststructuralist insight that narratives tend to exceed the formulas meant to describe them.

Most important for our discussion at this stage, the passage makes it clear to students that readers expect certain patterns from certain genres.

What exactly are the key elements of the castaway story or Robinsonade? At this point, we put common tropes on the board, using *Robinson Crusoe*, which students read in the previous unit, as one of many examples of the genre. I show a film clip from *Robinson Crusoe on Mars*, a Cold War example, and they typically bring up the film *Castaway* and the recent television series *Lost* as well. Having established a basic set of characteristics for the castaway genre, we consider how *Foe* matches or does not match this formula. As students quickly point out, *Foe* introduces the genre of the castaway story in part to question its efficacy within the text. For one thing, in Coetzee's novel it is available only to white men—not to Susan Barton or Friday. But even Coetzee's Cruso fails to do the things necessary for the typical Robinsonade. For example, he shows what would be for any faithful adaptation of the genre a scandalous disinterest in escaping from his island. His story, like Susan's, exceeds the narrative formula meant to describe it. After our discussion of how different characters unsuccessfully attempt to make Susan's or Cruso's story match the structure of the conventional castaway narrative, we begin to consider how the novel's commentary on language and storytelling challenges structuralism's belief in shared networks of meaning. In this way we transition into our discussion of deconstruction in the novel.

It is as a tool for teaching deconstruction that *Foe* really shines. Since the terminology of deconstruction tends to be overwhelming for students, we focus our attention on three main concepts: *différance*, Derrida's term for the ways in which language both defers meaning and is based on a system in which words mean because they differ from other words; the ideological nature of language; and the instability of binary oppositions. Incidents that call attention to the slippage between signifier and signified abound in *Foe*. Once Susan takes up residence in Foe's house, she writes him a letter from his own writing desk. In it she notes how different his desk, his chest of papers, and even the view from his window are from what she had imagined: "What I thought would be your writing-table is not a table but a bureau. The window overlooks not woods and pastures but your garden. . . . The chest is not a true chest but a dispatch box" (65). She highlights one of the central claims of deconstruction: there is always a gap between what we imagine and what we see, between objects and their meaning in language. This is our first example of *différance*.

Interestingly, Susan ends her letter by claiming, "Nevertheless, it is all close enough. Does it surprise you as much as it does me, this correspondence between things as they are and the pictures we have of them in our minds?" (65). This passage offers a wonderful opportunity to think through the differences between structuralism and deconstruction. For structuralist linguistics, the correspondence she identifies necessitates that the actual objects match her preconceived mental images of them, not vice versa, because we can understand the world only on the basis of what Tyson describes as the "conceptual framework" we bring to it (214). But what Susan sees does not match her conceptual framework. The correspondence between things and her images of them turns out to be no correspondence at all. The images are not the same, but rather "close enough." The gap between signifier and signified in this passage offers a student-friendly example of a text's drawing on concepts from deconstruction to point to the ambiguity of language and its dependence on a shared frame of reference to produce meaning.

This ambiguity crops up in numerous places in the novel, but I limit my discussion here to four other passages we work with closely in class. First, midway through the novel, a young woman appears, claiming to be Susan's long-lost daughter, also named Susan Barton. As Derek Attridge points out, the subplot of the lost daughter invokes Defoe's *Roxana*, yet another intertextual reference in a highly allusive work (*J. M. Coetzee* 78). For the purposes of my reading, it is the argument the woman uses to make her case as Susan's daughter that is of interest. When a skeptical Susan informs the woman that she must be confusing her with someone else, the young Susan Barton

> smiles again and shakes her head. "Behold the sign by which we may know our true mother," she says, and leans forward and places her hand beside mine. "See," she says, "we have the same hand. The same hand and the same eyes."
>
> I stare at the two hands side by side. My hand is long, hers short. Her fingers are the plump unformed fingers of a child. Her eyes are grey, mine brown. (76)

Again, the mental image does not match the actual objects, and declaring that they are equivalent fails to make them so. My students immediately identify this passage as another case in which structuralism's assumption of a stable system of codes in which signifiers refer to shared signifieds breaks down. Instead of fixing the meaning of the relationship between the two women within language and, by extension, within culture, this interaction only further alienates the older Susan.

Next we examine the passage in which Susan attempts to teach Friday the names of everyday objects, including a spoon. As she meditates on her attempt, she becomes less and less sure that she and Friday can share the common frame of reference necessary for language to generate meaning: "When I take the spoon from his hand (but is it truly a spoon to him, or a mere thing?—I do not know), and say *Spoon*, how can I be sure he does not think I am chattering to myself as a magpie or an ape does . . . ?" (57). In class, this passage tends to spark a lively discussion about how difficult it is to define any word unambiguously. When Susan says *spoon*, how can she know how her lesson is interpreted by Friday? How could one explain *spoon* without defining it against other eating utensils? Even if one could successfully convey the association between the word and the object, how would one communicate the idea that *spoon* is also a movement one makes while holding the object? Doesn't someone need to eat in a particular way for *spoon* to be meaningful?

These questions may not seem particularly deep, but they prepare the ground for our discussion of the ideological nature of language by underscoring the cultural referents and value judgments involved in Susan's attempts to make Friday speak. If deconstruction tells us that structuralism's belief in a stable system of signs is a myth, the stability of meaning is also challenged by cultural and racial difference. When, in a desperate attempt to find out how Friday lost his tongue, Susan shows him two sketches she has made—one in which a man dressed like Cruso kneels before a black man and looks as if he is preparing to cut out the black man's tongue, and another in which a man she understands as a Moorish slave trader prepares to cut out the black man's tongue—she quickly realizes that she has no idea how Friday might interpret the sketches. As she declares, "even as I spoke I began to doubt myself. For if Friday's gaze indeed became troubled, might that not be because I came striding out of the house, demanding that he look at pictures, something I've never done before?" (68). The pictures are open to multiple interpretations, she decides: "For, examining [the first image] anew, I recognized with chagrin that it might also be taken to show Cruso as a beneficent father putting a lump of fish into the mouth of child Friday" (68–69). The ambiguity she identifies in this moment has everything to do with the fact that she and Friday are positioned in certain ways in an imperial society. Even when she is not attempting to perpetuate the myth of the beneficent colonial father, the power of this myth is embedded in the very system of representation she is forced to use.

As students grapple with this conundrum, I refer them back to the passage in which Susan attempts to describe the spoon, as well as a broom, a spade, and a book, in order to consider language as a tool of empire. There she begins to doubt her motives for attempting to teach Friday her language:

> I tell myself I talk to Friday to educate him out of darkness and silence. But is that the truth? There are times when benevolence deserts me and I use words only as the shortest way to subject him to my will. At such times, I understand why Cruso preferred not to disturb his muteness. I understand, that is to say, why a man will choose to be a slaveowner.
> (60–61)

This passage points directly to the poststructuralist notion that, as Tyson puts it, "language is wholly ideological: it consists entirely of the numerous conflicting, dynamic ideologies . . . operating at any given point in any given culture" (253). When Susan questions her motivations for teaching Friday, we as readers see how she is shaped by the ideologies of her time, from the belief in white supremacy that justified the transatlantic slave trade to the notion of cultural superiority that supported English efforts to uplift the peoples they encountered as part of the imperial mission. Her teaching moments underscore Gauri

Viswanathan's claim that language was just as essential a tool for British imperialism as military might and indeed went hand in hand with economic and military domination.

Once *Foe* has brought us to this larger insight about the relation between language and ideology, our class can train a poststructuralist eye on the novels and critical approaches we covered earlier in the course by exploring how Coetzee's text exposes the instability of binary oppositions. Having already discussed in Marxist terms *Robinson Crusoe*'s narrative of capitalist accumulation and ownership, students can now grasp how *Foe* deconstructs Defoe's text by demonstrating how ideologies such as capitalism and imperialism manifest their contradictions under scrutiny. In this light, Cruso's refusal to accumulate possessions and inability to cultivate the island in *Foe* are designed to counter the earlier Crusoe's obsession with subordinating the island's animals and plants to a colonial plantation system. By pressing at binaries such as civilization/savagery and wealth/poverty, Coetzee's impotent imperialist Cruso undermines the earlier adventure narrative's function as an advertisement for the benefits of an emerging global capitalism.

Students can also see the influence of poststructuralism in the novel's treatment of gender. Referring to Simone de Beauvoir's argument that women are constructed as the inessential other against which men define themselves in the binary sexual system of western civilization (Tyson 96) provides us with a way to understand Susan Barton's repeated statements that she feels as if she lacks substance and has been reduced to a story she did not choose. In fact, when Foe tries to reshape her castaway experience into a mother-daughter tale, which he finds more appropriate, she protests, "I am not a story, Mr. Foe" (131). Echoing Virginia Woolf's *A Room of One's Own*, she astutely observes that living in a patriarchal society robs her of substance and denies her the material and intellectual tools she needs to write her own story. "To tell the truth in all its substance," she explains to Foe, "you must have quiet, and a comfortable chair away from all distraction, and a window to stare through . . . and at your fingertips the words with which to capture the vision before it fades. I have none of these, while you have all" (51–52). Her struggle throughout the novel to tell her story highlights the woman writer's inability to speak as author within the confines of a binary sex-gender system.

If Susan's story cannot be told because of her lack of access to authorial control as a woman, Friday's story constitutes the unspoken at the heart not only of *Foe* but of *Robinson Crusoe* as well. Indeed, as Charles W. Pollard notes, "The story of slavery is the aporia . . . of Western culture from the Enlightenment to the postmodern present" (163). In the unit on structuralist and poststructuralist theory, we discuss how the stories of Cruso and Susan as Western subjects depend on the silence of Friday, even as they attempt, in the words of Gayatri Spivak, to "give the native voice" (*Critique* 187). As we transition to the course's final unit on postcolonial theory and queer theory, our background in poststructuralist theory provides a fitting starting place for the questions about subaltern voice and agency that Spivak so famously describes. We wrestle in class with the ethical concerns her questions open up: Does Friday already speak in Coetzee's novel through his music, his dance, his drawings? If Friday does not speak, how do we understand our various attempts to interpret his actions? If he does speak, must he be forced to speak in our language in order for us to understand? What new modes of listening might his speech demand? Our conversation about the impossible position he occupies in *Foe* prepares us for a productive encounter with Selvadurai's *Funny Boy*. Reading *Funny Boy* after Coetzee's novel highlights the questions of subaltern voice and Western authorial modes raised by Susan's and Foe's failed attempts to make Friday's silence speak; it also makes clear the debt owed by both postcolonial theory and queer theory to poststructuralism. By the time students read this final novel, they are keenly aware of how a variety of repressive ideologies sustain themselves through binary oppositions as well as how deconstruction provides one set of tools to dismantle those oppositions.

In my literary theory course, *Foe* has proved to be a fruitful tool for helping students new to theory explicate the various concerns of theoretical discourses, especially deconstruction. Moreover, structuring a course in a way that makes some of the intertextual network cited by Coetzee's novel, both fictional and theoretical, available to students gives them a deeper appreciation of the richness of his work. But it is how the novel helps them articulate their own positions as critics that is most powerful to observe in the theory classroom. Watching Coetzee engage with and deconstruct some of the most widely known canonical texts and established ideas of Western modernity inspires students to turn a more sophisticated critical eye on other cultural texts. Since many of my students are training to teach at the secondary level, this enthusiasm for theoretically informed analysis of culture is the best lesson I can offer them.

Coetzee and Close Reading

Patrick Hayes

Close reading has a bad name. At worst it is associated with the conservative cultural agenda held by some of the leading exponents of New Criticism; at best it is linked to a more diffuse depoliticization of literature—a narrow and idealizing focus on the text that leads, perhaps in equal measure, to an abstract formalism and to a hypervaluation of literary discourse. So why should we revive this old idea in relation to Coetzee? Surely such a move will only add force to the accusation, made most famously by Nadine Gordimer ("Idea"), that his writing emerges out of, and contributes toward, an overfastidious, high-culturalist distrust of politics?

I should state at the outset that I have no interest in depoliticizing, or dehistoricizing, or otherwise disinterring the corpse of New Criticism. Indeed, one of the seminars I teach on Coetzee sets out to historicize his fiction as one aspect of the complex cross-currents of 1970s South African literary culture: I situate *Waiting for the Barbarians* alongside literary texts by Njabulo Ndebele, Mangane Serote, and Mafika Gwala, together with Steve Biko's political journalism and the South African Students' Organization (SASO) manifesto statements (now easily available for teaching purposes thanks to the excellent *Digital Innovation South Africa* Web site: www.disa.ukzn.ac.za/). In this essay I focus on the question of close reading because I have found Coetzee's work extremely useful and provocative in thinking about a distinctive educational need that many of today's approaches to teaching literature neglect.

In my experience, good students often decide to study literature at the university because they feel that the sheer cultural reach of our subject will help them pursue a range of intellectual interests. They are concerned with political issues, moral questions, and historical problems; they have read widely in these different areas, often inspired to do so by literary texts. But the very best students who take courses in English literature will also have a particular excitement about literature. They will be able to recall extended passages of poetry; they will reread texts again and again; they will sense, though not always be able to articulate how or why, that something unusual happens to those political, moral, historical questions when they appear in a literary text that cannot be reproduced without actually rereading (closely) the text itself. But despite the concern students have with both the literary and the political, literature courses at the university today tend to focus much more, and sometimes exclusively, on the political. In his seminal collection of essays *The Politics of Interpretation*—a collection that did much to inaugurate the present horizon of concern—W. J. T. Mitchell rightly insisted that "criticism and interpretation, the arts of explanation and understanding, have a deep and complex relation with politics, the structures of power and social value that organize human life" (1). But Mitchell's claim "that interpretation is politics by other means" (1), controversial in 1983, is surely not controversial now. The challenge confronting today's academy is no longer to politicize literature but instead to reach out to those students who have an interest in the special powers of literary experience without reverting to the unhelpful narrowness that the term "close reading" has come to imply.

Coetzee has long placed questions about the value of literature and what it means to read at the heart of his concerns as a writer, not least because of the special intensity with which these questions were posed in South Africa of the apartheid period. The second section of *Life & Times of Michael K* describes the attempts of a well-meaning reader to extract some kind of moral or political wisdom from a text that remains infuriatingly unreceptive to his needs. Each time the medical officer tries to conceptualize the figure of Michael K in a morally useful way—whether as an irrelevant fool or an atypical hero of resistance—he fails: even his final attempt to describe Michael's life as somehow "an allegory . . . of how scandalously, how outrageously a meaning can take up residence in a system without becoming a term in it" (106) is a concept from which Michael K himself is imagined to flee. Is the medical officer simply wrong to try to give a political or moral interpretation to Michael K? If so, what could conceivably be the value of an approach to reading that wholly rejects the will to interpret and thus refuses to extract any kind of political significance from the text?

These questions are posed even more sharply in a later novel, *The Master of Petersburg*, where Coetzee stages a confrontation between a fictionalized version of the novelist Fyodor Dostoevsky and a police inspector named Maximov over how to read a story written by Dostoevsky's stepson Pavel, who recently died in mysterious circumstances. The story is about a young man named Sergei who murders a brutish and rapacious landlord with an ax, and it ends with Sergei's referring to the ax as "the weapon of the Russian people, our means of defence and our means of revenge" (41). Maximov quite plausibly claims that the story expresses the ideology of a radical group known as the "People's Vengeance" (37) and thus implicates Pavel in a series of crimes against the state. Dostoevsky responds by insisting on a practice of close reading that abstracts the text from any kind of political meaning whatsoever. "You do not know how to read," he tells Maximov, claiming that his desire to assign an allegorical meaning to the text secretly derives from a fear of the text's emotional power, "as though the words might leap out from the page and strangle you" (46). True reading, Dostoevsky claims, is instead a form of close reading so deeply involved in the affective charge of the particular drama enacted on the page that it bypasses cognitive evaluation: "reading is being the arm and being the axe *and* being the skull; reading is giving yourself up, not holding yourself at a distance and jeering" (47).

Of course Dostoevsky's insistence on elevating close reading above political interpretation, and in more general terms the concrete above the abstract, might be self-serving: it exculpates Pavel's story (and by extension Dostoevsky) from police attention, and it helps Dostoevsky evade his submerged fear that his stepson's portrait of the rapacious landlord is in fact a portrait of Dostoevsky. But are we prepared to accept this rather one-dimensional way of interpreting the scene? If we as readers side with Maximov in distrusting Dostoevsky's motives at this point, to what extent do we become vulnerable to Dostoevsky's own accusation that the very cognitive assurance of our interpretation is itself deconstructable as a self-protective gesture of some kind? That is to say, is our willingness to translate the scene into a claim of knowledge about Dostoevsky's intentions in fact a way of generating for ourselves an illusion of power over the text—one that smooths out the opacity of Dostoevsky's desires and offers to control the potential of Coetzee's words to "leap out from the page"?

A further twist to these questions is the thought raised by Coetzee in his essay "Confession and Double Thoughts" that our willingness to enter into this line of skeptical questioning is laden with the potential for self-deception and indeed moral hazard: to move past naive trust is to risk either betrayal (what entitles or empowers us to doubt another's word?) or a special kind of evasiveness (where can this line of questioning ever end?). How can we navigate these competing, yet equally troubling, kinds of risk?

The insinuating acuity of the questions Coetzee poses about what is at stake in the act of reading is characteristic of his work, and my way of teaching his fiction emphasizes his impact on the long-standing debates around close reading. At my university there are two introductory courses that run in parallel, one an introduction to concepts in literary studies, the other a general course on twentieth-century fiction and poetry. I take advantage of these offerings by teaching two interrelated seminars: one entitled What Is Close Reading?, geared to the first course, then a seminar on Coetzee that develops the theoretical questions raised in a different way. It is useful to think about Coetzee not only as someone responding to the debates taking place among literary intellectuals in the recent past—debates staged in the encounter between Dostoevsky and Maximov—but also as someone whose writing suggests a way beyond the impasse those debates have reached.

In the What Is Close Reading? seminar, I bring up a recent chapter in this impasse. The seminar focuses on a handout made up of extracts from the *Politics of Interpretation*, especially from Mitchell's introduction, and Edward Said's critique of close reading "Opponents, Audiences, Constituencies, and Community." The seminar also features examples of the different kinds of close reading to which Said refers: extracts from John Crowe Ransom's *The New Criticism* and from Roland Barthes's *Writing Degree Zero*. I set the first two chapters of Timothy Clark's *Poetics of Singularity* as preparatory reading, along with the opening chapter of Derek Attridge's *The Singularity of Literature*. The purpose of the seminar is threefold: to define different concepts of close reading and examine what understanding of literary value is connected to each, to identify the criticisms leveled at close reading (which students will quickly see is something of a moving target), and to generate debate on the relative adequacy of the alternative notions of literary value at stake in each theorist.

I start the seminar with a discussion of Said's diagnosis, made in 1982, of what has gone wrong in English studies—namely, his attack on "the role voluntarily accepted by humanists whose notion of what they do is neutralised, specialized, and non-political in the extreme" (Mitchell 25) and his assessment that literary studies has betrayed its original aim of a broad address to "politics" from "culture." Both American New Criticism and what he calls "the French *nouvelle critique*" (and associates with Barthes) aimed to be "competitors for authority within mass culture, not other-worldly alternatives to it," yet both have degenerated into what he calls "private-clique consciousness": advocates of *"close reading* or of *écriture"* are now more concerned with "turning the creed into an intensely separatist orthodoxy than . . . forming a large community of readers" (Mitchell 11–12). Said's view is therefore that different traditions of close reading tend to be premised on a broad ambition to value literature as a distinctive way of addressing politics, but that their obsession with textual analysis leads them to decline into a depoliticized clique mentality—a proliferation of academic monographs read only by the initiated. The polemical diagnosis by Said is a good basis for asking about the ideas of literary value inscribed in the different forms of close reading he lumps together, not least because of his acknowledgment that they are not merely formalist in ambition.

Discussion of Ivor Winters and of Ransom can focus on the different ways in which these writers mark out the distinctive value of literary discourse; discussion can also consider the limitations of each approach. With Barthes, it is easy for the class to recognize the risks Said identifies in *nouvelle critique*. But *Writing Degree Zero* is more intriguing—especially Barthes's close reading of past- and present-tense narration, his connection of present-tense narration with important political and ethical impacts, and his insistence that a worthwhile literary criticism must attend to the disorienting quality of specifically literary effects if it is to be politically engaged. (One can raise the contextual question of how Barthes handles the politics of reading in relation to Sartre's *Qu'est-ce que la littérature?* (*What Is Literature?*), to which he is in part responding.) I conclude the seminar with the concept of singularity—not to define it in detail but to inspire independent thinking on the subject. Can we distinguish an approach that emphasizes literary singularity from the weaknesses of different types of close reading? What idea of literary value does singularity inscribe? Must a reading practice that emphasizes the singularizing pressures of the text inevitably degenerate into the overspecialized affair that Said criticizes? How can it be distinguished from the evasiveness a Maximov would detect in a Dostoevsky?

This work on close reading establishes an intellectual context for the Coetzee seminar: it opens up ways of thinking about Coetzee as someone self-consciously responding to the debate over the nature of literary value and thus creates a framework for critical reflection on what is involved in the often baffling experience of trying to interpret his writing. My next seminar has three parts: a focus on Coetzee as himself a close reader, especially in relation to what Said called *nouvelle critique*; Coetzee's statements on the debate over the relation between the literary and the political; and how Coetzee develops a self-consciously singularizing mode of political address in his writing.

I have found two of his early essays, in *Doubling the Point*, to be particularly useful because of their brevity and polemical force. "The First Sentence of Yvonne Burgess's *The Strike*" and "A Note on Writing" are an excellent introduction to what Coetzee thinks is at stake in the act of reading. Students can immediately connect his practice of close reading to Barthes in *Writing Degree Zero* (Coetzee makes specific references to Barthes), as both writers are convinced that both representation and interpretation make an important political impact on a formal level. Discussion can move on to how Coetzee's early fiction absorbs and works with these literary-critical ideas, and thinking about just the first couple of pages of *In the Heart of the Country* is useful here: the text can be read as a highly politicized form of close reading in itself—an ongoing criticism of different reading practices dominant within the novel. (There are a number of important and complex contexts operating here—most obviously the farm novel but also the debate over literature and identity generated by the Black Consciousness writers in South Africa—but this introduction aims only to whet appetites for further work.) To sharpen understanding of Coetzee on the politics of reading, I make available to students "The Novel Today," his rather irascible and defensive 1987 lecture. This essay requires a preface about politicized reading practices in South Africa of the 1980s—the People's Culture campaign of the United Democratic Front in particular—and the influence of Lukácsian ideas of literary responsibility. The point here is to spur thinking about the different concepts of literary value that Coetzee outlines: he distinguishes primarily between literature as a supplement to politics and literature as a rival to politics in a way that compares to the disagreement between Dostoevsky and Maximov in *The Master of Petersburg*. The class can start to identify these positions with the ideas on literary value discussed in the previous seminar. For instance, it is easy to identify Said and Mitchell with the concept of supplementarity—but what about Winters? It is easy to connect Ransom with rivalry, but does it also encompass Barthes? For an advanced or very able group I would tackle Coetzee's complex later essay "Erasmus: Madness and Rivalry," collected in *Giving Offense*: it retracts from his apparent commitment to rivalry and develops the idea of a nonposition. What might it mean to develop a mode of address that is "nonpositioned"? How is this different from "rivalry"?

The second half of the seminar engages with a literary text and with the question of how Coetzee is trying to position literary discourse. A number of different texts should work well here; easiest to use are the fictionalized lectures in cultural criticism that he developed in *Elizabeth Costello*. I open discussion with the seemingly simple question of how to interpret the lecture "The Problem of Evil" (Coetzee, "Elizabeth Costello"). What is Coetzee saying? Is he really trying to resurrect a counter-Enlightenment and quasi-theological account of evil ("She has begun to wonder whether writing what one desires, any more than reading what one desires, is itself a good thing" [*Elizabeth Costello* 160])?

Or is he showing the futility of such an attempt (*"Elizabeth Costello,"* her fellow writers complain, *"has turned into old Mother Grundy"* [168])? The only way to answer this question is through a close reading of the text, and in a seminar some interesting reading effects can take place. A particularly good passage to focus on features Elizabeth's darkest meditations on evil—on "Satan's century"; but they take place in the loo, and feature her being interrupted by a small child, who hears her muttering to herself and announces this fact to her mother (in Dutch) (178–81).[1] Reading the passage inevitably inspires disagreement on the status and seriousness of what Elizabeth says—her discourse makes a claim, but the comic interruptions, among other effects, keep placing a singularizing pressure on those claims. Debate on interpretation should lead to a consideration of the particular mode of narration used—which is of course the present tense that Barthes of *Writing Degree Zero* admires—and discussion can at last be returned to the terms of "The Novel Today." Is the text positioned as a "supplement" or as a "rival"? Or are these terms now inadequate?

Diary of a Bad Year offers a much fuller and more complex example of a singularizing intervention into politics. Close reading of this text could focus on the extraordinary passage near the end of part 1, where the different positions at stake (JC's archaic and resoundingly negative discourse on political modernity, the different but interrelated celebrations of modernity made by Anya and Alan) overlap and become mutually challenged. In the chapter titled "On Political Life in Australia" (115–20), where Anya's critique of JC's honor discourse starts to bite, just at the point when it is revealed that Alan is behaving in a thoroughly "dishonorable" fashion, we start to feel afresh something of the strength and reach of JC's views. The experience of reading this passage in a group creates a strong sense of how the text keeps unsettling the felt value of the different discourses it entertains: it insists, to borrow Clark's words, on becoming "not something one can simply think, but something that has to be *let think*, in its own way, within a space one tries to hold open" (9), and discussion can consider what might be involved in describing the value of this process.

It is equally possible, though I think more complex, to use *Disgrace* in this seminar. Discussion would first have to center around the subject of what "values" the figure of David Lurie embodies—what type of moral and political position he takes in the arguments in which he is continually embroiled, and to what extent the text upholds those values. Close reading could then focus on the scenes involving the dogs, especially those at the end of the text: here Lurie makes his most powerful and moving claims for what might be summarized as his Romantic individualism (claims that have led to his ejection from the university and to his daughter's sustained hostility), but the seriousness of these claims is continually offset by the bathetic presence of the animals, who, of course, have no cognizance of or relation to the metaphysical system on which they depend. (This is precisely what *The Lives of the Animals* experiments with—the increasing instability of Elizabeth's discourse as she tries to do justice to animal experience.) Close reading will focus on the complex movement between pathos and bathos, just as with Elizabeth's thoughts in the loo in "The Problem of Evil," which acts as a singularizing pressure on our judgment of Lurie. The text engages what Clark speaks of as the "the force of a possible discontinuity" in the act of interpreting (3), one whose value lies in its potential to open up new ways of negotiating the status of Lurie's ideas in the new South Africa.

I have found that another, more literary-historical way of approaching what are ultimately the same problems is by thinking about Coetzee in relation to Samuel Beckett and about how Coetzee tries to assimilate the self-consciously singularizing energies of Beckett's writing to the political questions that most concern him. I have run a seminar that begins with a general exploration of the concept of metafiction, focusing on Beckett's statements on literature and silence and then turning to a Beckett text: one of the late shorter texts (*Ping*; *Imagination Dead Imagine*) works well for a larger group. Contrasting Beckett to Coetzee's fiction (I have used *Foe* in the past) shows how Coetzee assimilates and politicizes the reading effects generated by Beckett. One student saw that the *ping* sound in Beckett's text, which seems to both disrupt and inspire the act of representation that is being staged, in some ways modulates into the figure of Friday in *Foe*, who both disrupts and inspires Susan and ultimately Foe himself.

The aim of these seminars is not to resolve but to raise afresh important questions about why and how we read and to entertain more sophisticated ways of understanding Coetzee's distinctive contribution to a long-standing and important debate. Teaching Coetzee in this way aims both to develop students' sense of what is at stake in reading literature and to generate an absorbing and singularly unpredictable discussion about the important political questions with which his texts engage.

NOTE

[1] In the midst of a passage of searching self-doubt comes the following: "There is a scratching at the door, a child's voice. 'Mammie, er zit een vrouw erin, ik kan haar schoenen zien!' ['Mummy, there's a woman sitting in there. I can see her shoes!'] Hurriedly she flushes the bowl, unlocks the door, emerges. 'Sorry,' she says, evading the eyes of mother and daughter" (181).

NOTES ON CONTRIBUTORS

David Attwell is professor of English at the University of York. He is author of *J. M. Coetzee: South Africa and the Politics of Writing* and editor of Coetzee's *Doubling the Point: Essays and Interviews*. With Derek Attridge he coedited *The Cambridge History of South African Literature*.

Rita Barnard is professor of English and comparative literature at the University of Pennsylvania and professor extraordinaire at Stellenbosch. She is author of *The Great Depression and the Culture of Abundance* and *Apartheid and Beyond: South African Writers and the Politics of Place*.

Michael Bell is professor emeritus in the Department of English and Comparative Literary Studies, University of Warwick. He is author of *D. H. Lawrence: Language and Being*; *Gabriel García Márquez: Solitude and Solidarity*; and *Open Secrets: Literature, Education, and Authority from J-J. Rousseau to J. M. Coetzee*.

Louise Bethlehem is senior lecturer in the Program in Cultural Studies and in the Department of English at the Hebrew University of Jerusalem. She is author of *Skin Tight: Apartheid Literary Culture and Its Aftermath* and has coedited six volumes in African and cultural studies.

Elleke Boehmer is professor of world literature in English at the University of Oxford. She is author of *Colonial and Postcolonial Literature*; *Empire, the National and the Postcolonial*; *Nelson Mandela*; and *Stories of Women*. She has coedited *J. M. Coetzee in Context and Theory*; *The Indian Postcolonial*; and *The Postcolonial Low Countries*. She has had published four novels and a collection of short stories.

Carrol Clarkson is professor of English at the University of Cape Town. She is author of *J. M. Coetzee: Countervoices* and *Drawing the Line: Toward an Aesthetics of Transitional Justice*. Her research interests are in the interstitial zones between literature, philosophy, and the visual arts.

Stephen Clingman is professor of English and director of the Interdisciplinary Studies Institute at the University of Massachusetts, Amherst. He is author of *The Novels of Nadine Gordimer: History from the Inside*; *Bram Fischer: Afrikaner Revolutionary*; and *The Grammar of Identity: Transnational Fiction and the Nature of the Boundary*.

Emily S. Davis is assistant professor of English at the University of Delaware. She is author of *Rethinking the Romance Genre: Global Intimacies in Contemporary Literary and Visual Culture* as well as essays about postapartheid South African fiction, global film, and genre.

Gerald Gaylard works in the English Department at the University of the Witwatersrand. His publications include *After Colonialism: African Postmodernism and Magical Realism* and *Marginal Spaces: Reading Ivan Vladislavić*.

Johan Geertsema teaches in the University Scholars Programme of the National University of Singapore. He is preparing a book that considers Coetzee's late work as a set of ironic confrontations with the sublime.

Martina Ghosh-Schellhorn is professor of transcultural anglophone studies at Saarland University. She is author of *Anthony Burgess: A Study in Character* and *Steep Stairs to Myself: Transitionality and Autobiography* and coeditor, with R. Marti, of *Playing by the Rules of the Game*.

Erik Grayson is assistant professor of American literature and culture at Wartburg College. He is completing a book on J. M. Coetzee based on his doctoral dissertation. His research interests are American literature, postcolonial literature, existentialism, and apocalyptic fiction.

Patrick Hayes is a fellow of Saint John's College, Oxford. He is author of *J. M. Coetzee and the Novel: Writing and Politics after Beckett* and a forthcoming study of Philip Roth.

Kay Heath is associate professor of English at Georgia Regents University. She is author of *Aging by the Book*.

Keith Leslie Johnson is associate professor of English at Augusta State University. He is author of essays on Walter Benjamin, Aldous Huxley, and Franz Kafka. For the essay on Kafka he won the KSA Emerging Scholar Prize.

Patricia Merivale is professor emeritus of English and comparative literature at the University of British Columbia. She is author of *Pan the Goat-God: His Myth in Modern Times* and coeditor, with S. E. Sweeney, of *Detecting Texts: The Metaphysical Detective Story from Poe to Postmodernism*.

Shannon Payne is chair of the English Department at the Academy of the Sacred Heart in New Orleans. She is working on a book on literatures by and about the United States homeless.

Jane Poyner is senior lecturer in postcolonial literature and theory in the Department of English at the University of Exeter. She is author of *J. M. Coetzee and the Paradox of Postcolonial Authorship* and editor of *J. M. Coetzee and the Idea of the Public Intellectual*.

Robert Spencer lectures in postcolonial literature and culture at the University of Manchester. He is author of *Cosmopolitan Criticism and Postcolonial Literature* and is currently working on a study of the potential longevity of modernist themes and forms in postcolonial writing.

Andrew van der Vlies teaches in the School of English and Drama at Queen Mary, University of London. He is author of *South African Textual Cultures* and *J. M. Coetzee's* Disgrace: *A Reader's Guide* and editor of *Print, Text, and Book Cultures in South Africa*.

Pieter Vermeulen is assistant professor in English literature at Stockholm University. He is author of *Romanticism after the Holocaust* and is working on a monograph on the paradoxical productivity of the idea of the end of the novel in contemporary fiction.

Wendy Woodward is senior professor in the English Department at the University of the Western Cape. She is author of *The Animal Gaze: Animal Subjectivities in Southern African Narratives*.

Laura Wright is associate professor of postcolonial literature and chair of the English Department at Western Carolina University. She is author of *Writing "Out of All the Camps": J. M. Coetzee's Narratives of Displacement* and *"Wilderness into Civilized Shapes": Reading the Postcolonial Environment*.

SURVEY RESPONDENTS

Michael Bell, *University of Warwick*
Louise Bethlehem, *Hebrew University of Jerusalem*
Stephen Clingman, *University of Massachusetts, Amherst*
Emily S. Davis, *University of Delaware*
Kai Easton, *SOAS, University of London*
Maureen N. Eke, *Central Michigan University*
Johan Geertsema, *National University of Singapore*
Elizabeth Swanson Goldberg, *Babson College*
Michael Harris, *Central College*
Patrick Hayes, *Oxford University*
Kay Heath, *Virginia State University*
Sonia Kane, *Hunter College, City University of New York*
Eric Leuschner, *Fort Hays State University*
Thomas J. Lynn, *Penn State University, Berks*
Patricia Merivale, *University of British Columbia, Vancouver*
Kwame Okoampa-Ahoofe, Jr., *Nassau Community College, State University of New York*
Shannon Payne, *University of Massachusetts, Amherst*
Aimee Pozorski, *Central Connecticut State University*
Laura Quinn, *Allegheny College*
Kim Rostan, *Marquette University*
Lorena Russell, *University of North Carolina, Asheville*
Lily Saint, *Baruch College, City University of New York*
Kalpana Rahita Seshadri, *Boston College*
Andrew van der Vlies, *University of Sheffield*
Pieter Vermeulen, *University of Leuven*
Chull Wang, *Chonbuk National University*
Laura Wright, *Western Carolina University*

WORKS CITED

Aaltola, Elisa. "Coetzee and Alternative Ethics." Leist and Singer, *J. M. Coetzee* 119–44.

Achebe, Chinua. "An Image of Africa: Racism in Conrad's *Heart of Darkness*." *Research in African Literatures* 9.1 (1978): 1–15. Print.

———. *Things Fall Apart*. London: Heinemann, 1958. Print.

Adichie, Chimamanda Ngozi. *Purple Hibiscus*. Chapel Hill: Algonquin, 2003. Print.

Agamben, Giorgio. *Homo Sacer: Sovereign Power and Bare Life*. Trans. Daniel Heller-Roazen. Stanford: Stanford UP, 1998. Print.

———. *State of Exception*. Trans. Kevin Attell. Chicago: U of Chicago P, 2005. Print.

———. "The Thing Itself." Trans. Juliana Schiesari. *Substance* 16.2 (1987): 18–28. Print.

Ahmed, Sarah. "Affective Economies." *Social Text* 22.2 (2004): 117–39. *Project Muse*. Web. 1 Oct. 2009.

Akubuiro, Henry. "Is Chimamanda the New Achebe?" *Sun: Voice of the Nation*. Sun News, 17 June 2007. Web. 26 Aug. 2011.

Alexander, Neville. *An Ordinary Country: Issues in the Transition from Apartheid to Democracy in South Africa*. Pietermaritzburg: U of Natal P, 2002. Print.

Amandla: A Revolution in Four-Part Harmony. Dir. Lee Hirsch. Artisan, 2002. DVD.

ANC Submission to the Human Rights Commission Hearings on Racism in the Media. African Natl. Congress, 5 Apr. 2000. Web. 5 May 2013.

Appiah, Kwame Anthony. "Is the Post in Post-modernism the Post in Postcolonial?" *Critical Inquiry* 17.2 (1991): 336–57. Print.

Aristotle. *Nichomachean Ethics*. Trans. Roger Crisp. Cambridge: Cambridge UP, 2000. Print.

Ashcroft, Bill, Gareth Griffiths, and Helen Tiffin. *The Empire Writes Back: Theory and Practice in Postcolonial Literatures*. London: Routledge, 1989. Print.

———, eds. *The Postcolonial Studies Reader*. London: Routledge, 1995. Print.

Attridge, Derek. "Against Allegory: *Waiting for the Barbarians*, *Life & Times of Michael K*, and the Question of Literary Reading." Poyner, *J. M. Coetzee and the Idea* 63–82.

———. "Age of Bronze, State of Grace: Music and Dogs in Coetzee's *Disgrace*." *Novel* 34.1 (2000): 98–121. Print.

———. "Ethical Modernism: Servants as Others in J. M. Coetzee's Early Fiction." *Poetics Today* 25.4 (2004): 653–71. Print.

———. *J. M. Coetzee and the Ethics of Reading: Literature in the Event*. Chicago: U of Chicago P, 2004. Print.

———. "J. M. Coetzee's *Boyhood*, Confession, and Truth." *Critical Survey* 11.2 (1999): 77–93. Print.

———. "J. M. Coetzee's *Disgrace*: Introduction." Attridge and McDonald 315–20.

———. "Oppressive Silence: J. M. Coetzee's *Foe* and the Politics of Canonization." Huggan and Watson 168–90.

———. *The Singularity of Literature*. London: Routledge, 2004. Print.

———. "Trusting the Other: Ethics and Politics in J. M. Coetzee's *Age of Iron*." *South Atlantic Quarterly* 93.1 (1994): 59–82. Print.

Attridge, Derek, and David Attwell, eds. *The Cambridge History of South African Literature*. Cambridge: Cambridge UP, 2012. Print.

Attridge, Derek, and Rosemary Jane Jolly, eds. *Writing South Africa: Literature, Apartheid, and Democracy, 1970–1995*. Cambridge: Cambridge UP, 1998. Print.

Attridge, Derek, and Peter D. McDonald, eds. *J. M. Coetzee's* Disgrace. Spec. issue of *Interventions* 4.3 (2002): 315–468. Print.

Attwell, David. "J. M. Coetzee and South Africa: Thoughts on the Social Life of Fiction." Bradshaw and Neill 163–76.

———. *J. M. Coetzee: South Africa and the Politics of Writing*. Berkeley: U of California P, 1993. Print.

———. "The Labyrinth of My History: J. M. Coetzee's *Dusklands*." *Novel: A Forum on Fiction* 25.1 (1991): 7–32. Print.

———. "The Life and Times of Elizabeth Costello: J. M. Coetzee and the Public Sphere." Poyner, *J. M. Coetzee and the Idea* 25–41.

———. "Race in *Disgrace*." Attridge and McDonald 331–41.

Auster, Paul. *Timbuktu*. New York: Henry Holt, 1999. Print.

Banville, John. "Endgame: *Disgrace* by J. M. Coetzee." *New York Review* 20 Jan. 2000: 23–25. Print.

Barilla, James. "A Mosaic of Landscapes: Ecological Restoration in the Work of Leopold, Coetzee, and Silko." *Coming into Contact: Explorations in Ecocritical Theory and Practice*. Ed. Annie Merrill Ingram et al. Athens: U of Georgia P, 2007. 128–40. Print.

Barnard, Rita. "Dream Topographies: J. M. Coetzee and the South African Pastoral." *The Writings of J. M. Coetzee*. Ed. Michael Valdez Moses. Spec. issue of *South Atlantic Quarterly* 93.1 (1994): 33–58. Print.

———. "'Imagining the Unimaginable': J. M. Coetzee, History, and Autobiography." Rev. of *Doubling the Point*, by J. M. Coetzee. *Postmodern Culture* 4.1 (1993): n. pag. *Project MUSE*. Web. 4 Dec. 2013.

———. "J. M. Coetzee's Country Ways." Attridge and McDonald 384–94.

———. "J. M. Coetzee's *Disgrace* and the South African Pastoral." *Contemporary Literature* 44.2 (2003): 199–224. Print.

Barnett, Clive. "Constructions of Apartheid in the International Reception of J. M. Coetzee." *Journal of South African Studies* 25.2 (1999): 287–301. Print.

Barthes, Roland. *A Lover's Discourse: Fragments*. Trans. Richard Howard. New York: Hill, 1997. Print.

———. *The Pleasure of the Text*. Trans. Richard Miller. New York: Hill, 1975. Print.

———. *Roland Barthes*. Trans. Richard Howard. New York: Hill, 1977. Print.

———. *Writing Degree Zero*. Trans. Annette Lavers and Colin Smith. London: Cape, 1967. Print.

Bartnik, Ryszard. "The Politics of Engagement in J. M. Coetzee's *Foe* and *In the Heart of the Country*." *A Universe of (Hi)Stories: Essays on J. M. Coetzee*. Ed. Liliana Sikorska. Frankfurt am Main: Lang, 2006. 45–58. Print.

Beard, Margot. "Lessons from the Dead Masters: Wordsworth and Byron in J. M. Coetzee's *Disgrace*." *English in Africa* 34.1 (2007): 59–77. Print.

Beckett, Samuel. *Molloy*. 1955. New York: Grove, 1995. Print.

Beinart, William. *Twentieth-Century South Africa*. 2nd ed. Oxford: Oxford UP, 2001. Print.

Bell, Michael. "What Is It Like to Be a Nonracist? Costello and Coetzee on the Lives of Animals and Men." Poyner, *J. M. Coetzee and the Idea* 172–92.

Benjamin, Walter. "Critique of Violence." Trans. Edmund Jephcott. *Selected Writings*. Vol. 1. Ed. Marcus Bullock and Michael W. Jennings. Cambridge: Harvard UP, 1996. 236–52. Print.

———. "Franz Kafka: On the Tenth Anniversary of His Death." Trans. Harry Zohn. *Selected Writings*. Vol. 2. Ed. Michael W. Jennings, Howard Eiland, and Gary Smith. Cambridge: Belknap–Harvard UP, 1999. 794–818. Print.

Bethlehem, Louise. "Aneconomy in an Economy of Melancholy: Embodiment and Gendered Identity in J. M. Coetzee's *Disgrace*." *African Identities* 1.2 (2003): 167–85. Print.

———. "'A Primary Need as Strong as Hunger': The Rhetoric of Urgency in South African Literary Culture under Apartheid." *Poetics Today* 22.2 (2001): 365–89. Print.

———. *Skin Tight: Apartheid Literary Culture and Its Aftermath*. Pretoria: U of South Africa P; Leiden: Koninklijke Brill, 2006. Print.

Blade Runner. Dir. Ridley Scott. Perf. Harrison Ford, Rutger Hauer, and Sean Young. Warner Bros., 1982. DVD.

Blake, William. "Milton." *The Complete Poems*. Ed. Alicia Ostriker. London: Penguin, 1977. 513–607. Print.

Blatchford, Matthew. "A Good Book—Burn It." *Mail and Guardian* [Johannesburg] 24 Oct. 2003: 38. Print.

Blood Diamond. Dir. Edward Zwick. Perf. Leonardo DiCaprio, Djimon Hounsou, and Jennifer Connelly. Warner Bros., 2006. DVD.

Bloom, Harold, ed. *Franz Kafka*. Philadelphia: Chelsea, 2003. Print.

Boehmer, Elleke. *Colonial and Postcolonial Literature: Migrant Metaphors*. 2nd rev. ed. Oxford: Oxford UP, 2004. Print.

———. "Endings and New Beginnings: South African Fiction in Transition." Attridge and Jolly 43–56.

———. "Not Saying Sorry, Not Speaking Pain: Gender Implications in *Disgrace*." Attridge and McDonald 342–51.

———. "Sorry, Sorrier, Sorriest: The Gendering of Contrition in J. M. Coetzee's *Disgrace*." Poyner, *J. M. Coetzee and the Idea* 135–47.

———. *Stories of Women: Gender and Narrative in the Postcolonial Nation*. Manchester: Manchester UP, 2005. Print.

———. "Transfiguring: Colonial Body into Postcolonial Narrative." *Novel* 26.3 (1993): 268–77. Print.

Boehmer, Elleke, Katy Iddiols, and Robert Eaglestone, eds. *J. M. Coetzee in Context and Theory*. London: Continuum, 2009. Print.

Boler, Megan, and Michalinos Zembylas. "Discomforting Truths: The Emotional Terrain of Understanding Difference." *Pedagogies of Difference: Rethinking Education for Social Change*. Ed. Peter Pericles Trifonas. New York: Routledge, 2003. 110–36. Print.

Bové, Paul. "Discourse." *Critical Terms for Literary Study*. Ed. Frank Lentricchia and Thomas McLaughlin. Chicago: U of Chicago P, 1995. 50–65. Print.

Bradshaw, Graham, and Michael Neill, eds. *J. M. Coetzee's Austerities*. Farnham: Ashgate, 2010. Print.

Breytenbach, Breyten. "Andersheid as Andersmaak, of te wel die Afrikaner as Afrikaan (Berig aan Frederck Van Zyl Slabbert)." *Fragmente* 4 (1999): 26–44. Print.

Briganti, Chiara. "A Bored Spinster with a Locked Diary: The Politics of Hysteria in *In the Heart of the Country*." *Research in African Literatures* 25.4 (1994): 33–49. *EBSCO Host*. Web. 4 Aug. 2011.

Brink, André. *Cape of Storms: The First Life of Adamastor*. New York: Simon, 1993. Print.

———. "A Myth of Origin." Vladislavić, *T'kama-Adamastor* 41–47.

———. *Reinventing a Continent: Writing and Politics in South Africa, 1982–1998*. Cambridge: Zoland, 2000. Print.

———. "Writing against Big Brother: Notes on Apocalyptic Fiction in South Africa." *World Literature Today* 58 (1984): 189–94. Print.

Brontë, Charlotte. *Jane Eyre*. New York: Norton, 2001. Print.

Bruffee, Kenneth. *Elegiac Romance*. Ithaca: Cornell UP, 1983. Print.

Burchell, William. *Travels in the Interior of Southern Africa*. 2 vols. Cape Town: Struik, 1967. Print.

Butler, Judith. *Bodies That Matter: On the Discursive Limits of "Sex."* New York: Routledge, 1993. Print.

———. *Gender Trouble: Feminism and the Subversion of Identity*. New York: Routledge, 1990. Print.

Butler, Marilyn. *Romantics, Rebels, and Reactionaries: English Literature and Its Background, 1760–1830*. New York: Oxford UP, 1982. Print.

Byron, George Gordon. *Lord Byron's Works V1: Containing* The Bride of Abydos, The Corsair, Lara, Parisina, *Etc.* 1821. Whitefish: Kessinger, 2010. Print.

Camões, Luíz Vaz de. *The Lusiads*. 1572. Trans. L. White. Oxford: Oxford UP, 1997. Print.

Campbell, Roy. "Rounding the Cape." *Adamastor: Poems*. London: Faber, 1930. 38. Print.

Canepari-Labib, Michela. *Old Myths—Modern Empires: Power, Language, and Identity in J. M. Coetzee's Work*. Bern: Lang, 2005. Print.

Carey, Peter. *Theft: A Love Story*. New York: Vintage, 2007. Print.

———. *True History of the Kelly Gang*. London: Faber, 2000. Print.

Carter, Paul. *Living in a New Country*. London: Faber, 1992. Print.

———. *The Road to Botany Bay*. London: Faber, 1987. Print.

Cartwright, Justin. *White Lightning*. London: Hodder, 2002. Print.

Castaway. Dir. Robert Zemeckis. Perf. Tom Hanks. Twentieth Century–Fox, 2000. DVD.

Caughie, Pamela L. *Passing and Pedagogy: The Dynamics of Responsibility.* Urbana: U of Illinois P, 1999. Print.

Cavafy, C. P. "Waiting for the Barbarians." Trans. Edmund Keeley and Philip Sherrard. *Collected Poems*. Ed. George Savidis. Rev. ed. Princeton: Princeton UP, 1992. 18–19. Print.

Chapman, Michael. *Southern African Literatures.* London: Longman, 1996. Print.

Chapman, Michael, Colin Gardner, and Es'kia Mphahlele, eds. *Perspectives on South African English Literature.* Johannesburg: Donker, 1992. Print.

Cheney, Michael. "Review of *Life & Times of Michael K.*" *J. M. Coetzee Watch #12. Matilda*. Perry Middlemiss, 22 Oct. 2008. Web. 21 Aug. 2009.

Christensen, Jerome. *Romanticism at the End of History*. Baltimore: Johns Hopkins UP, 2000. Print.

Clark, Timothy. *The Poetics of Singularity: The Counter-culturalist Turn in Heidegger, Derrida, Blanchot and the Later Gadamer*. Edinburgh: Edinburgh UP, 2005. Print.

Clarkson, Carrol. *J. M. Coetzee: Countervoices*. Houndmills: Palgrave, 2009. Print.

Clendinnen, Inga. "A Federer Game: J. M. Coetzee's *Summertime*." *Monthly* 49 (2009): n. pag. Web. 16 Mar. 2012.

Clingman, Stephen. *The Grammar of Identity: Transnational Fiction and the Nature of the Boundary*. Oxford: Oxford UP, 2009. Print.

Coetzee, J. M. *Age of Iron.* London: Penguin, 1991. Print.

———. "Age of Iron." MS Material. 1987–90. Harry Ransom Humanities Research Center, U of Texas, Austin.

———. "Blood, Taint, Flaw, Degeneration: The Novels of Sarah Gertrude Millin." Coetzee, *White Writing* 136–62.

———. *Boyhood: A Memoir*. London: Vintage, 1998. Print.

———. *The Childhood of Jesus*. London: Harvill, 2013. Print.

———. "Confession and Double Thoughts: Tolstoy, Rousseau, Dostoevsky." Coetzee, *Doubling* 251–93.

———. "Critic and Citizen: A Response." *Pretexts* 9.1 (2000): 109–11. Print.

———. *Diary of a Bad Year*. New York: Penguin, 2007. Print.

———. *Disgrace*. New York: Penguin, 1999. Print.

———. *Doubling the Point: Essays and Interviews*. Ed. David Attwell. Cambridge: Harvard UP, 1992. Print.

———. *Dusklands*. New York: Penguin, 1985. Print.

———. *Elizabeth Costello*. New York: Penguin, 2003. Print.

———. "Elizabeth Costello and the Problem of Evil." *Salmagundi* 137–38 (2003): 48–64. Print.

———. *Foe*. New York: Penguin, 1987. Print.

———. *Giving Offense: Essays on Censorship*. Chicago: Chicago UP, 1996. Print.

———. "Homage." *Threepenny Review* 53.1 (1993): 5–7. Print.

———. "How I Learned about America—and Africa—in Texas." *The New York Times*. New York Times, 15 Apr. 1984. Web. 10 Jan. 2012.

———. Interview. By Jane Poyner. Poyner, *J. M. Coetzee and the Idea* 21–24.

———. "An Interview with J. M. Coetzee." By Richard Begam. *Contemporary Literature* 33.3 (1992): 419–31. Print.

———. "An Interview with J. M. Coetzee." By Jean Sévry. *Commonwealth: Essays and Studies* 9.1 (1986): 1–7. Print.

———. *In the Heart of the Country*. 1977. New York: Penguin, 1982. Print.

———. "Into the Dark Chamber: The Writer and the South African State." *New York Times* 12 Jan. 1986, Late City Final ed., sec. 7: 13. Print.

———. *Life & Times of Michael K*. New York: Penguin, 1985. Print.

———. *The Lives of Animals*. Ed. Amy Gutmann. Princeton: Princeton UP, 1999. Print.

———. "The Making of Samuel Beckett." *New York Review of Books* 30 Apr. 2009: n. pag. *The New York Review of Books*. Web. 20 Aug. 2013.

———. *The Master of Petersburg*. New York: Penguin, 1995. Print.

———. "Nobel Lecture: He and His Man." *Nobelprize.org*. Nobel Media AB, n.d. Web. 9 Dec. 2013.

———. "The Novel Today." *Upstream* 6 (1998): 2–5. Print.

———. *Scenes from Provincial Life*. London: Harvill, 2011. Print.

———. *Slow Man*. New York: Penguin, 2005. Print.

———. "Speaking: J. M. Coetzee." Interview by Stephen Watson. *Speak: Critical Arts Journal* 1.3 (1978): 21–24. Print.

———. *Summertime*. New York: Penguin, 2009. Print.

———. "Two Interviews with J. M. Coetzee, 1983 and 1987." By Tony Morphet. *Triquarterly* 69 (1987): 454–64. Print.

———. *Waiting for the Barbarians*. New York: Penguin, 1982. Print.

———. "What Is a Classic? A Lecture." *Stranger Shores: Literary Essays, 1986–1999*. New York: Viking, 2001. 1–16. Print.

———. *White Writing: On the Culture of Letters in South Africa*. New Haven: Yale UP, 1988. Print.

———. *Youth: Scenes from Provincial Life II*. New York: Viking, 2002. Print.

Coleridge, Samuel. "Kubla Khan." *The Complete Poetical Works of Samuel Coleridge*. *Project Gutenberg*. Project Gutenberg, n.d. Web. 26 June 2013.

Connor, Steven. "Rewriting Wrong: On the Ethics of Literary Reversion." *Limited Postmodernisms: The Postmodern, the (Post-)Colonial, and the (Post)Feminist*. Ed. Theo D'haen and Hans Bertens. Amsterdam: Rodopi, 1994. 79–97. Print.

Conrad, Joseph. *Heart of Darkness*. New York: Penguin, 1999. Print.

———. The Nigger of the *Narcissus and Other Stories*. New York: Penguin, 2007. Print.

Constable, John. *The Hay Wain*. *The National Gallery*. Natl. Gallery, n.d. Web. 5 Dec. 2013.

———. *Salisbury Cathedral from the Bishop's Ground*. *V&A: Search the Collections*. Victoria and Albert Museum, n.d. Web. 5 Dec. 2013.

Cooper, Pamela. "Metamorphosis and Sexuality: Reading the Strange Passions of *Disgrace*." *Research in African Literatures* 36.4 (2005): 22–39. Print.

Copley, Stephen, and John Whale, eds. *Beyond Romanticism: New Approaches to Texts and Contexts, 1780–1832*. London: Routledge, 1992. Print.

Crewe, Jonathan. Rev. of *Dusklands*. *Contrast* 9.2 (1974): 90–95. Print.

———. "Recalling Adamastor: Literature as Cultural Memory in 'White' South Africa." *Acts of Memory: Cultural Recall in the Present*. Ed. Mieke Bal, Jonathan Crewe, and Leo Spitzer. Hanover: UP of New England, 1999. 75–86. Print.

———. "The Specter of Adamastor: Heroic Desire and Displacement in 'White' South Africa." *Modern Fiction Studies* 43.1 (1997): 27–52. *Project Muse*. Web. 1 Oct. 2009.

Cronin, Jeremy. "Turning around Roy Campbell's 'Rounding the Cape.'" *English in Africa* 11.1 (1984): 65–78. Print.

Danner, Mark. *Torture and Truth: America, Abu Ghraib, and the War on Terror*. London: Granta, 2004. Print.

Danta, Chris, Sue Kossew, and Julian Murphet, eds. *Strong Opinions: J. M. Coetzee and the Authority of Contemporary Fiction*. New York: Continuum, 2011. Print.

Davis, G. Todd. "'Boundless Thoughts and Free Souls': Teaching Byron's *Sardanapalus*, *Lara*, and *The Corsair*." *Interrogating Orientalism: Contextual Approaches and Pedagogical Practices*. Ed. Diane Long Hoeveler and Jeffrey Cass. Columbus: Ohio State UP, 2006. 198–212. Print.

Day, Aidan. *Romanticism*. London: Routledge, 1996. Print.

Debelle, Penelope. "Citizen Coetzee." *Age*. Age, 7 Mar. 2006. Web. 20 Mar. 2013.

Defoe, Daniel. *Robinson Crusoe*. New York: Norton, 1993. Print.

de Man, Paul. *The Resistance to Theory*. Minneapolis: U of Minnesota P, 1986. Print.

Derrida, Jacques. "On Forgiveness." *On Cosmopolitanism and Forgiveness*. Trans. Mark Dooley and Michael Hughes. London: Routledge, 2001. 25–60. Print.

de Waal, Shaun. "Master in an Age of Iron." *Mail and Guardian Online*. Mail and Guardian, 29 Oct. 1999. Web. 15 Oct. 2007.

Diala, Isidore. "Nadine Gordimer, J. M. Coetzee, and Andre Brink: Guilt, Expiation, and the Reconciliation Process in Post-apartheid South Africa." *Journal of Modern Literature* 25.2 (2001–02): 50–68. Print.

Disgrace. Dir. Steven Jacobs. Perf. John Malkovich, Natalie Becker, and Jessica Haines. Screen Australia, 2008. DVD.

Donadio, Rachel. "Out of South Africa." *New York Times Sunday Book Review*. New York Times, 16 Dec. 2007. Web. 27 Feb. 2012.

Dostoevsky, Fyodor. *Demons*. New York: Penguin, 2008. Print.

———. *The Idiot*. New York: Penguin, 2004. Print.

Dovey, Teresa. "Coetzee and His Critics: The Case of *Dusklands*." *English in Africa* 14.2 (1987): 15–30. Print.

Driver, Dorothy. "Women and Nature, Women as Objects of Exchange: Towards a Feminist Analysis of South African Literature." Chapman, Gardner, and Mphahlele 454–74.

During, Simon. "Postmodernism or Post-colonialism Today." *Textual Practice* 1.1 (1987): 32–47. Print.

Durrant, Sam. "Bearing Witness to Apartheid: J. M. Coetzee's Inconsolable Works of Mourning." *Contemporary Literature* 40.3 (1999): 430–63. Print.

———. "J. M. Coetzee, Elizabeth Costello, and the Limits of the Sympathetic Imagination." Poyner, *J. M. Coetzee and the Idea* 118–34.

———. *Postcolonial Narrative and the Work of Mourning: J. M. Coetzee, Wilson Harris, and Toni Morrison.* Albany: State U of New York P, 2004. Print.

Dust. Dir. Marion Hänsel. Daska Films, 1985. DVD.

Dziob, Anne Marie. "Aristotelian Friendship." *Review of Metaphysics* 46.4 (1993): 781–801. Print.

Eagleton, Mary. "Ethical Reading: The Problem of Alice Walker's 'Advancing Luna—and Ida B. Wells' and J. M. Coetzee's *Disgrace*." *Feminist Theory* 2.2 (2001): 189–203. Print.

Easton, Kai. "J. M. Coetzee's *Disgrace*: Reading Race / Reading Scandal." *Scandalous Fictions: The Twentieth-Century Novel in the Public Sphere.* Ed. Jago Morrison and Susan Watkins. Basingstoke: Palgrave, 2006. 187–205. Print.

Eckstein, Barbara. "The Body, the Word, and the State: J. M. Coetzee's *Waiting for the Barbarians*." *Novel* 22.2 (1989): 175–98. Print.

Edelstein, Jillian. *Truth and Lies: Stories from the Truth and Reconciliation Commission in South Africa.* New York: New, 2002. Print.

Eliot, T. S. *Selected Prose of T. S. Eliot.* Ed. Frank Kermode. New York: Harcourt, 1975. Print.

———. "Tradition and the Individual Talent." 1919. Eliot, *Selected Prose* 37–44.

———. "What Is a Classic?" 1944. Eliot, *Selected Prose* 115–31.

"Empathy." *Concise Oxford Dictionary.* Oxford UP, n.d. Web. 4 Apr. 2012.

Erasmus, Desiderius. *"The Praise of Folly" and Other Writings.* New York: Norton, 1989. Print.

Esposito, Roberto. *Bíos: Biopolitics and Philosophy.* Minneapolis: U of Minnesota P, 2008. Print.

Fanon, Frantz. *Black Skin, White Masks.* 1952. Trans. Charles Lam Markmann. London: Pluto, 1986. Print.

———. *The Wretched of the Earth.* 1961. Trans. Charlotte Farrington. London: Penguin, 1990. Print.

Farred, Grant. "The Mundancity of Violence: Living in a State of Disgrace." Attridge and McDonald 352–62.

Faulkner, William. *Go Down, Moses.* New York: Random, 1942. Print.

Felman, Shoshana. "Psychoanalysis and Education: Teaching Terminable and Interminable." *Yale French Studies* 63 (1982): 21–44. Print.

Felman, Shoshana, and Dori Laub. *Testimony: Crises of Witnessing in Literature, Psychoanalysis, and History.* London: Routledge, 1992. Print.

Flanery, Patrick Denman. "Limber: The Flexibilites of Post-Nobel Coetzee." Van der Vlies, *Print* 208–24.

Ford, Ford Madox. *The Good Soldier*. 1915. *Project Gutenberg*. Project Gutenberg, n.d. Web. 2 July 2013.

Forgiveness. Dir. Ian Gabriel. Perf. Arnold Vosloo, Quanita Adams, Zane Meas, Denise Newman, and Christo Davids. Giant, 2004. DVD.

Foucault, Michel. *Abnormal: Lectures at the Collège de France, 1974–1975*. Trans. Graham Burchell. Ed. Valerio Marchetti, Antonella Salomoni, and Arnold I. Davidson. New York: Picador, 2003. Print.

———. *Discipline and Punish: The Birth of the Prison*. London: Lane, 1977. Print.

———. *The History of Sexuality: An Introduction*. Vol. 1. Trans. Robert Hurley. New York: Vintage, 1990. Print.

———. *Madness and Civilization: A History of Insanity in the Age of Reason*. 1961. Trans. Richard Howard. London: Routledge, 1989. Print.

———. *The Order of Things: An Archaeology of the Human Sciences*. London: Routledge, 1989. Print.

———. "*Society Must Be Defended*": *Lectures at the Collège de France, 1975–1976*. Trans. David Macey. Ed. Mauro Bertani, Alessandro Fontana, and Arnold I. Davidson. New York: Picador, 2003. Print.

———. "What Is Enlightenment?" *The Foucault Reader*. Ed. Paul Rabinow. Harmondsworth: Penguin, 1991. 32–50. Print.

Freud, Sigmund. "The 'Uncanny.'" *The Standard Edition of the Complete Psychological Works of Sigmund Freud*. 1919. Ed. James Strachey. Vol. 17. London: Hogarth, 1955. 217–56. Print.

Frontline. Apartheid. Parts 1–4. Prod. John Blake. PBS, 1987. VHS.

Fugard, Athol, John Kani, and Winston Ntshona. *The Island*. *Statements*. 1974. New York: Theater Communications Group, 1986. 45–78. Print.

Gallagher, Susan VanZanten. *A Story of South Africa: J. M. Coetzee's Fiction in Context*. Cambridge: Harvard UP, 1991. Print.

García Márquez, Gabriel. *The Fragrance of Guava: Conversations*. London: Faber, 1983. Print.

Gauthier, Marni. "The Intersection of the Postmodern and the Postcolonial in J. M. Coetzee's *Foe*." *English Language Notes* 34.4 (1997): 52–71. Print.

Gaylard, Gerald. "Disgraceful Metafiction: Intertextuality in the Postcolony." *Journal of Literary Studies* 21.3–4 (2005): 315–37. Print.

Geiger, Ido. "Writing the Lives of Animals." Leist and Singer, *J. M. Coetzee* 145–69.

Ghosh-Schellhorn, Martina. *Steep Stairs to Myself: Transitional Autobiography*. Trier: Wissenschaftlicher, 2008. Print.

Ghosts of Abu Ghraib. Dir. Rory Kennedy. HBO, 2007. DVD.

G. I. Jane. Dir. Ridley Scott. Perf. Demi Moore and Viggo Mortensen. Largo, 1997. DVD.

Gikandi, Simon. "Theory after Postcolonial Theory: Rethinking the Work of Mimesis." *Theory after "Theory."* Ed. Jane Elliott and Derek Attridge. London: Routledge, 2011. 163–78. Print.

Glenn, Ian. "Game Hunting in *In the Heart of the Country*." Huggan and Watson 120–37.

Goldblatt, David. *Intersections*. Munich: Prestel, 2005. Print.

Gopal, Priyamvada. "Reading Subaltern History." Lazarus, *Cambridge Companion* 139–61.

Gordimer, Nadine. *The Conservationist*. 1974. New York: Penguin, 1978. Print.

———. *The Essential Gesture: Writing, Politics, and Places*. Ed. Stephen Clingman. London: Cape, 1988. Print.

———. "The Idea of Gardening: *Life & Times of Michael K*, by J. M. Coetzee." *New York Review of Books* 31.1 (1984): 3–6. Print.

———. *July's People*. London: Cape, 1981. Print.

———. *The Late Bourgeois World*. New York: Viking, 1966. Print.

———. Preface. Huggan and Watson vii–xii.

Gorra, Michael. "After the Fall." Rev. of *Disgrace*. *New York Times* 28 Nov. 1999. Web. 12 Mar. 2012.

Graham, James. *Land and Nationalism in Fictions from Southern Africa*. New York: Routledge, 2009. Print.

Graham, Lucy. "Reading the Unspeakable: Rape in *Disgrace*." *Journal of Southern African Studies* 29.2 (2003): 433–44. Print.

———. *State of Peril: Race and Rape in South African Literature*. Oxford: Oxford UP, 2012. Print.

———. "Textual Transvestism: The Female Voices of J. M. Coetzee." Poyner, *J. M. Coetzee and the Idea* 217–35.

———. "'Yes, I Am Giving Him Up': Sacrificial Responsibility and Likeness with Dogs in J. M. Coetzee's Recent Fiction." *Scrutiny 2* 7.1 (2002): 4–15. Print.

Gray, Stephen. *Southern African Literature: An Introduction*. Cape Town: Philip, 1979. Print.

Greene, Graham. *Brighton Rock*. 1938. London: Vintage, 2010. E-book. Kindle.

Griffiths, Dominic, and Maria L. C. Prozesky. "The Politics of Dwelling: Being White / Being South African." *Africa Today* 56.4 (2010): 23–41. *EBSCO Host*. Web. 19 Oct. 2011.

Halmi, William, ed. *Wordsworth's Poetry and Prose*. New York: Norton, 2007. Print.

Hambidge, Joan. *Die Judaskus*. Halfway House: Perskor, 1998. Print.

Hamilton, Grant. "J. M. Coetzee's *Dusklands*: The Meaning of Suffering." *Journal of Literary Studies* 21.3–4 (2005): 296–314. Print.

Hardt, Michael, and Antonio Negri. *Empire*. Cambridge: Harvard UP, 2000. Print.

Harrison, Nicholas. "'A Roomy Place Full of Possibility': Said's *Orientalism* and the Literary." Ed. Ranjan Ghosh. *Edward Said and the Literary, Social, and Political World*. London: Routledge, 2009. 3–18. Print.

Harvey, Melinda. "In Australia You Start at Zero." Danta, Kossew, and Murphet 19–34.

Hašek, Jaroslav. *The Good Soldier Švejk and His Fortunes in the World War*. Trans. Cecil Parrott. New York: Penguin, 2005. Print.

Hassan, Andrew. *Sailing to Australia: Shipboard Diaries by Nineteenth-Century British Emigrants*. Manchester: Manchester UP, 1994. Print.

Head, Dominic, ed. *The Cambridge Introduction to J. M. Coetzee*. Cambridge: Cambridge UP, 2009. Print.

————. "Coetzee's Life." Head, *Cambridge Introduction* 1–21.

————. "Gardening as Resistance: *Life & Times of Michael K.*" *J. M. Coetzee*. Cambridge: Cambridge UP, 1998. 93–111. Print. Studies in African and Caribbean Lit. 6.

————. "The (Im)Possibility of Ecocriticism." *Writing the Environment: Ecocriticism and Literature*. Ed. Richard Kerridge and Neil Sammells. London: Zed, 1998. 27–39. Print.

————. *J. M. Coetzee*. Cambridge: Cambridge UP, 1997. Print.

Healy, Chris. *From the Ruins of Colonialism*. Cambridge: Cambridge UP, 1997. Print.

Heidegger, Martin. *Being and Time*. Trans. John Macquarrie and Edward Robinson. New York: Harper, 2008. Print.

Helgesson, Stefan. *Writing in Crisis: Ethics and History in Gordimer, Ndebele and Coetzee*. Pietermaritzburg: U of Kwazulu-Natal P, 2004. Print.

Hemingway, Ernest. *The Sun Also Rises*. 1926. New York: Scribner's, 2003. Print.

Hirson, Denis, ed. *The Lava of This Land: South African Poetry, 1960–1996*. Evanston: Triquarterly, 1997. Print.

Holiday, Anthony. "Forgiving and Forgetting: The Truth and Reconciliation Commission." Nuttall and Coetzee 43–56.

Holland, Michael. "'Plink-Plunk': Unforgetting the Present in Coetzee's *Disgrace*." Attridge and McDonald 395–404.

Holub, Robert. "Reception Theory: School of Constance." *The Cambridge History of Literary Criticism*. Ed. Raman Selden. Vol. 8. Cambridge: Cambridge UP, 2005. 319–46. Print.

Honwana, Luis Bernardo. *"We Killed Mangy-Dog" and Other Stories*. London: Heinemann, 1977. Print.

Huggan, Graham. *Australian Literature: Postcolonialism, Racism, Transnationalism*. Oxford: Oxford UP, 2007. Print.

————. "'Greening' Postcolonialism: Ecocritical Perspectives." *Modern Fiction Studies* 50.3 (2004): 701–33. Print.

Huggan, Graham, and Helen Tiffin. *Postcolonial Ecocriticism*. London: Routledge, 2010. Print.

Huggan, Graham, and Stephen Watson, eds. *Critical Perspectives on J. M. Coetzee*. Basingstoke: Macmillan, 1996. Print.

Hulme, Peter. *Colonial Encounters: Europe and the Caribbean, 1492–1797*. London: Methuen, 1986. Print.

Hutcheon, Linda. *The Politics of Postmodernism*. London: Routledge, 1989. Print.

Huxley, Aldous. "Wordsworth in the Tropics." *Do What You Will: Twelve Essays*. London: Chatto, 1956. 113–29. Print.

Iddiols, Katy. "Disrupting Inauthentic Readings: Coetzee's Strategies." Boehmer, Iddiols, and Eaglestone 185–97.

In My Country. Dir. John Boorman. Perf. Samuel L. Jackson and Juliet Binoche. Columbia Tristar, 2004. Film.

Invictus. Dir. Clint Eastwood. Perf. Morgan Freeman and Matt Damon. Warner Bros., 2009. DVD.

James, David, ed. *The Legacies of Modernism: Historicizing Postwar and Contemporary Fiction*. Cambridge: Cambridge UP, 2012. Print.

James, Henry. *Henry James: Novels, 1886–1890: The Princess Casamassima, The Reverberator, The Tragic Muse*. New York: Lib. of Amer., 1989. Print.

Jameson, Fredric. "Third-World Literature in the Era of Multinational Capitalism." *Social Text* 15 (1986): 65–88. Print.

Janes, Regina. "'Writing without Authority': J. M. Coetzee and His Fictions." *Salmagundi* 114–15 (1997): 103–21. Print.

JanMohamed, Abdul R. "The Economy of Manichean Allegory: The Function of Racial Difference in Colonialist Literature." *"Race," Writing, and Difference*. Ed. Henry Louis Gates, Jr. Spec issue of *Critical Inquiry* 12.1 (1985): 59–87. Print.

Jauss, Hans Robert. "Literary History as a Challenge to Literary Theory." Trans. Michael Shaw. *New Directions in Literary History*. Ed. Ralph Cohen. London: Routledge, 1974. 11–41. Print.

———. "Literaturgeschichte als Provokation in der Literaturwissenschaft." *Literaturgeschichte als Provokation der Literaturwissenschaft*. Frankfurt am Main: Suhrkamp, 1970. 144–207. Print.

J. M. Coetzee—Biographical. Nobelprize.org. Nobel Media AB, n.d. Web. 27 June 2013.

J. M. Coetzee: Passages. Dir. Henion Han. Dizzy Ink, 1997. DVD.

Jolly, Rosemary. *Colonization, Violence, and Narration in White South African Writing*. Athens: Ohio UP, 1996. Print.

———. "Going to the Dogs: Humanity in J. M. Coetzee's *Disgrace, The Lives of Animals*, and South Africa's Truth and Reconciliation Commission." Poyner, *J. M. Coetzee and the Idea* 148–71.

Kafka, Franz. "Before the Law." 1919. Kafka, *Franz Kafka* 22–23.

———. "The Burrow." 1919. Kafka, *Franz Kafka* 354–59.

———. *Franz Kafka: The Complete Stories*. Trans. Edward Muir and Willa Muir. Ed. Nahum N. Glatzer. 1946. New York: Schocken, 1983. Print. Centennial ed.

———. "A Hunger Artist." 1919. Kafka, *Franz Kafka* 300–10.

———. "The Hunger Strike." Kafka, *Parables* 187–88.

———. "An Imperial Message." Kafka, *Franz Kafka* 324–59.

———. "In the Penal Colony." Kafka, *Franz Kafka* 165–92.

———. *Kafka's Selected Stories*. Trans. Stanley Corngold. New York: Norton, 2005. Print. Norton Critical ed.

———. *Parables and Paradoxes: In German and English*. 1935. New York: Schocken, 1961. Print.

———. *The Trial*. Oxford: Oxford UP, 2009. Print.

Kannemeyer, John. *J. M. Coetzee: 'n Geskryfde Lewe*. Johannesburg: Ball, 2012. Print.

———. *J. M. Coetzee: A Life in Writing*. Trans. Michiel Heyns. Johannesburg: Ball, 2012. Print.

Kendal, Rebekah, Charis Le Riche, and Kimberly Yu. "Meet Your Meat: Animal Group Lobbies for Warnings on Factory-Farmed Products." *Big Issue* 23 Sept.–13 Oct. 2011: 27–31. Print.

Kiefer, Daniel. "Sympathy for the Devil: On the Perversity of Teaching *Disgrace*." B. McDonald 264–75.

Knox-Shaw, Peter. "*Dusklands*: A Metaphysics of Violence." *Contrast* 14.1 (1982): 26–38. Print.

Kohler, Peter. "Freeburghers, the Nama, and the Politics of the Frontier Tradition: An Analysis of Social Relations in the Second Narrative of J. M. Coetzee's *Dusklands*: Towards an Historiography of South African Literature." Wits History Workshop: The Making of Class. U of Johannesburg, 14 Feb. 1987. *WireDSpace*. Web. 9 Dec. 2013.

Kossew, Sue. "Border Crossings." Boehmer, Iddiols, and Eaglestone 60–67.

———. "Literary Migration: Shifting Borders in Coetzee's Australian Novels." Danta, Kossew, and Murphet 113–24.

———. *Pen and Power: A Post-colonial Reading of J. M. Coetzee and André Brink*. Amsterdam: Rodopi, 1994. Print.

———. "The Politics of Shame and Redemption in J. M. Coetzee's *Disgrace*." *Research in African Literatures* 34.2 (2003): 155–62. Print.

Krog, Antjie. *Country of My Skull: Guilt, Sorrow, and the Limits of Forgiveness in the New South Africa*. New York: Random, 1999. Print.

Krzychyłkiewicz, Agata. "The Reception of J. M. Coetzee in Russia." *Journal of Literary Studies / Tydskrif vir Literatuurwetenskap* 21.3–4 (2005): 338–67. Print.

Lacan, Jacques. "The Mirror Stage As Formative of the Function of the I As Revealed in Psychoanalytical Experience." *Modern Literary Theory: A Reader*. Ed. Philip Rice and Patricia Waugh. London: Arnold, 1996. 126–31. Print.

LaCapra, Dominick. *Writing History, Writing Trauma*. Baltimore: John Hopkins UP, 2001. Print.

Lawrence, D. H. *"Study of Thomas Hardy" and Other Essays*. Ed. Bruce Steele. Cambridge: Cambridge UP, 1985. Print.

Lazarus, Neil, ed. *The Cambridge Companion to Postcolonial Literary Studies*. Cambridge: Cambridge UP, 2004.

———. "Modernism and Modernity: T. W. Adorno and Contemporary White South African Literature." *Modernity and Modernism / Postmodernity and Postmodernism*. Spec. issue of *Cultural Critique* 5 (1986–87): 131–55. Print.

———. "Representations of the Intellectual in *Representations of the Intellectual*." *Research in African Literature* 36.3 (2005): 112–23. Print.

Leist, Anton, and Peter Singer. "Introduction: Coetzee and Philosophy." Leist and Singer, *J. M. Coetzee* 1–18.

———, eds. *J. M. Coetzee and Ethics: Philosophical Perspectives on Literature*. New York: Columbia UP, 2010. Print.

Lenta, Margaret. "*Autre*biography: J. M. Coetzee's *Boyhood* and *Youth*." *English in Africa* 30.1 (2003): 157–69. Print.

Lenta, Patrick. "Legal Illegality: *Waiting for the Barbarians* after September 11." *Journal of Postcolonial Writing* 42.1 (2006): 71–83. Print.

Lévinas, Emmanuel. *Difficult Freedom: Essays on Judaism*. Trans. Seán Hand. Baltimore: Johns Hopkins UP, 1990. Print.

———. *Ethics and Infinity: Conversations with Philippe Nemo*. Pittsburgh: Duquesne UP, 1985. Print.

———. *Otherwise Than Being; or, Beyond Essence*. Trans. Alphonso Lingis. Dordrecht: Kluwer, 1991. Print.

Levine, George. "Real Toads in Imaginary Gardens, or Vice Versa." *Realism, Ethics and Secularism: Essays on Victorian Literature and Science*. Cambridge: Cambridge UP, 2008. 261–69. Print.

The Lion King. Dir. Roger Allers and Rob Minkoff. Disney, 1994. DVD.

Long Night's Journey into Day. Dir. Frances Reid and Deborah Hoffmann. Iris Films, 2000. DVD.

Macaskill, Brian. "Charting J. M. Coetzee's Middle Voice." *Contemporary Literature* 35.3 (1994): 441–75. Print.

Mamdani, Mahmood. "Amnesty or Impunity? A Preliminary Critique of the Report of the Truth and Reconciliation Commission of South Africa (TRC)." *Diacritics* 32.3–4 (2002): 33–59. Print.

———. "The Truth according to the TRC." *The Politics of Memory: Truth, Healing and Social Justice*. Ed. Ifi Amadiume and Abdullah An-Na'im. London: Zed, 2000. 176–83. Print.

Mamet, David. *Oleanna*. New York: Vintage, 1992. Print.

Marais, Michael. "Death and the Space of the Response to the Other in J. M. Coetzee's *The Master of Petersburg*." Poyner, *J. M. Coetzee and the Idea* 83–99.

———. "From the Standpoint of Redemption: Aesthetic Autonomy and Social Engagement in J. M. Coetzee's Fiction of the Late Apartheid Period." *Journal of Narrative Theory* 38.2 (2008): 229–48. Print.

———. "J. M. Coetzee's *Disgrace* and the Task of the Imagination." *Journal of Modern Literature* 29.2 (2006): 75–93. Print.

———. "'Little Enough, Less Than Little: Nothing': Ethics, Engagement, and Change in the Fiction of J. M. Coetzee." *Modern Fiction Studies* 46.1 (2000): 159–82. Print.

———. *Secretary of the Invisible: The Idea of Hospitality in the Fiction of J. M. Coetzee*. Amsterdam: Rodopi, 2009. Print.

———. "Very Morbid Phenomena: 'Liberal Funk,' the 'Lucy Syndrome,' and J. M. Coetzee's *Disgrace*." *Scrutiny* 2 6.1 (2001): 32–38. Print.

Martel, Yann. *Life of Pi*. New York: Harcourt, 2001. Print.

Marx, John. "Postcolonial Literature and the Western Literary Canon." Lazarus, *Cambridge Companion* 83–96.

Mathuray, Mark. "Sublime Abjection." Boehmer, Iddiols, and Eaglestone 159–72.

May, Brian. "J. M. Coetzee and the Question of the Body." *Modern Fiction Studies* 47.2 (2001): 391–420. Print.

———. "Reading Coetzee, Eventually." *Contemporary Literature* 48.4 (2007): 629–38. Print.

McClintock, Anne. *Imperial Leather: Race, Gender, and Sexuality in the Colonial Context*. London: Routledge, 1995. Print.

McCoy, Alfred W. *A Question of Torture: CIA Interrogation, from the Cold War to the War on Terror*. New York: Metropolitan–Henry Holt, 2006. Print.

McCoy, Horace. *They Shoot Horses, Don't They?* London: Serpent's Tail, 1995. Print.

McDonald, Bill, ed. *Encountering* Disgrace: *Reading and Teaching Coetzee's Novel.* Rochester: Camden, 2009. Print.

McDonald, Peter D. "*Disgrace* Effects." Attridge and McDonald 321–30.

McKenzie, Craig. "Our Literary Disgrace." *Mail and Guardian Online.* Mail and Guardian, 21 Oct. 2011. Web. 10 Jan. 2012.

McLeod, John. *Beginning Postcolonialism.* Manchester: Manchester UP, 2000. Print.

McWilliams, Erin. "Touchy Subjects: A Risky Inquiry into Pedagogical Pleasure." *British Educational Research Journal* 22.3 (1996): 305–17. Print.

Mda, Zakes. *Ways of Dying.* New York: Picador, 1995. Print.

Melville, Herman. "Bartleby the Scrivener." 1853. *"Billy Budd, Sailor" and Selected Tales.* Oxford: Oxford UP, 1992. 3–41. Print. Oxford World's Classics.

Memmi, Albert. *The Colonizer and the Colonized.* 1963. Trans. Howard Greenfield. London: Souvenir, 1974. Print.

Mennecke, Arnim. *Koloniales Bewusstsein in den Romanen J. M. Coetzees.* Heidelberg: Carl Winter UP, 1991. Print.

Merivale, Patricia. "Audible Palimpsests: Coetzee's Kafka." Huggan and Watson 152–67.

Michaels, Walter Benn. *The Shape of the Signifier: 1967 to the End of History.* Princeton: Princeton UP, 2004. Print.

Microcosmos: Le peuple de l'herbe. Dir. Claude Nuridsany and Marie Pérennou. Miramax, 1996. Film.

Midgley, Mary. *Animals and Why They Matter.* Harmondsworth: Penguin, 1983. Print.

Miller, Arthur. *The Crucible.* 1957. Harmondsworth: Penguin, 1970. Print.

Mitchell, W. J. T., ed. *The Politics of Interpretation.* Chicago: U of Chicago P, 1983. Print.

Morphet, Tony. "Reading Coetzee in South Africa." *World Literature Today* 78.1 (2004): 14–16. Print.

Mulhall, Stephen. *Wounded Animal: J. M. Coetzee and the Difficulty of Reality in Literature and Philosophy.* Princeton: Princeton UP, 2009. Print.

Murphy, Patrick D. *Farther Afield in the Study of Nature-Orientated Literature.* Charlottesville: U of Virginia P, 2000. Print.

Murray, Sally-Anne, and Anthony E. Voss. "Roy Campbell's *Adamastor*: Reading and Rereading the South African Poems." Postscript by Marcia Leveson. Chapman, Gardener, and Mphahlele 94–112.

Murray, Senan. "The New Face of Nigerian Literature?" *BBC News.* BBC, 8 June 2007. Web. 26 Aug. 2011.

Nashef, Hania A. M. *The Politics of Humiliation in the Novels of J. M. Coetzee.* New York: Routledge, 2009. Print.

Ndebele, Njabulo. *"Fools" and Other Stories.* 1983. London: Readers Intl., 1993. Print.

———. "The Year of the Dog: A Journey of the Imagination." *Fine Lines from the Box: Further Thoughts about Our Country.* Roggebaai: Umuzi, 2007. 251–56. Print.

Ngũgĩ wa Thiong'o. *Decolonising the Mind: The Politics of Language in African Literature*. Portsmouth: Heinemann, 1986. Print.

Nietzsche, Friedrich. The Birth of Tragedy *and Other Writings*. Cambridge: Cambridge UP, 1999. Print.

"Nobel Prize in Literature 2003: John Maxwell Coetzee: Press Release." *Nobelprize .org*. Nobel Media AB, 2 Oct. 2003. Web. 31 Aug. 2011.

Nuttall, Sarah, and Carli Coetzee, eds. *Negotiating the Past: The Making of Memory in South Africa*. Oxford: Oxford UP, 1998. Print.

Nwapa, Flora. *Efuru*. Portsmouth: Heinemann, 1966. Print.

———. "The Poetics of Economic Independence for Female Empowerment: An Interview with Flora Nwapa." By Marie Umeh. *Research in African Literature* 26.2 (1995): 22–29. Print.

O'Hehir, Andrew. Rev. of *Disgrace*. *Salon*. Salon Media Group, 5 Nov. 1999. Web. 4 Jan. 2010.

Oliphant, Andries Walter. "Other Ethiopians: Sideways Glances at Fiction, History, and Myth in *The First Life of Adamastor*." Vladislavić, *T'kama-Adamastor* 59–69.

Ozick, Cynthia. "The Sister Melons of J. M. Coetzee." 1983. *Metaphor and Memory*. New York: Knopf, 1989. 28–33. Print.

Palahniuk, Chuck. *Choke*. New York: Anchor, 2008. Print.

Parry, Benita. *Postcolonial Studies: A Materialist Critique*. London: Routledge, 2004. Print.

———. "Speech and Silence in the Fictions of J. M. Coetzee." Attridge and Jolly 149–65.

Patrik, Linda E. *Existential Literature: An Introduction*. Independence: Wadsworth, 2000. Print.

Pechey, Graham. "Coetzee's Purgatorial Africa: The Case of *Disgrace*." Attridge and McDonald 374–83.

Pellegrini, Anne. *Performance Anxieties: Staging Psychoanalysis, Staging Race*. New York: Routledge, 1997. Print.

Penguin Handbook: Custom Edition for University of Massachusetts, Amherst. Boston: Pearson Custom, 2007. Print.

Penner, Dick. *Countries of the Mind: The Fiction of J. M. Coetzee*. New York: Greenwood, 1989. Print.

Plato. *Phaedrus*. Trans. Christopher Rowe. Penguin: New York, 2005. Print.

———. *The Seventh Letter*. Trans. J. Harward. *Internet Classics Archive*. MIT, n.d. Web. 27 June 2013.

Plumwood, Val. *Feminism and the Mastery of Nature*. London: Routledge, 1993. Print. Opening, Out ser.

Poirier, Richard. *The Renewal of Literature: Emersonian Reflections*. London: Faber, 1987. Print.

Pollan, Michael. "An Animal's Place." *New York Times Magazine*. New York Times, 10 Nov. 2002. Web. 10 May 2004.

———. *The Omnivore's Dilemma: A Natural History of Four Meals*. New York: Penguin, 2006. Print.

Pollard, Charles W. "Teaching Contemporary Responses to *Robinson Crusoe*: Coetzee, Walcott, and Others in a World Literature Survey." *Approaches to Teaching Defoe's* Robinson Crusoe. Ed. Maximillian E. Novak and Carl Fisher. New York: MLA, 2005. 161–68. Print.

Pollitt, Katha. "Any Relation to Biography Is Pure Fiction (in a Way)." Rev. of *Summertime*. *New York Times*. New York Times, 30 Dec. 2009. Web. 16 Mar. 2012.

Popescu, Monica. *South African Literature beyond the Cold War*. New York: Palgrave, 2010. Print.

Posel, Deborah. "The TRC Report: What Kind of History, What Kind of Truth?" *Commissioning the Past: Understanding South Africa's Truth and Reconciliation Commission*. Ed. Posel and Graeme Simpson. Johannesburg: U of Witwatersrand P, 2002. 142–72. Print.

Poyner, Jane, ed. *J. M. Coetzee and the Idea of the Public Intellectual*. Athens: Ohio UP, 2006. Print.

———. *J. M. Coetzee and the Paradox of Postcolonial Authorship*. Burlington: Ashgate, 2009. Print.

Pratt, Mary Louise. *Imperial Eyes: Travel and Transculturation*. London: Routledge, 1992. Print.

Probyn, Fiona. "J. M. Coetzee: Writing with/out Authority." *Jouvert* 7.1 (2002): n. pag. Web. 31 Jan. 2013.

Profile: Coetzee: Stranger at the Gate. Dir. Sebastian Barfield. BBC4, 2003. Television.

Quayson, Ato. *Aesthetic Nervousness: Disability and the Crisis of Representation*. New York: Columbia UP, 2007. Print.

Ransom, John Crowe. *The New Criticism*. Norfolk: New Directions, 1941. Print.

Ratcliffe, Sophie. *On Sympathy*. Oxford: Oxford UP, 2008. Print.

Report of the Truth and Reconciliation Commission. 7 vols. Cape Town: Truth and Reconciliation Commission, 1998–2003. Print.

Rhys, Jean. *Wide Sargasso Sea*. New York: Norton, 1998. Print.

Rich, Paul. "Apartheid and the Decline of the Civilization Idea: An Essay on Nadine Gordimer's *July's People* and J. M. Coetzee's *Waiting for the Barbarians*." *Research in African Literatures* 15.3 (1984): 365–93. Print.

Roberts, Sheila. "'City of Man': The Appropriation of Dante's *Inferno* in J. M. Coetzee's *Age of Iron*." *Current Writing* 8.1 (1996): 33–44. Print.

Robinson Crusoe on Mars. Dir. Byron Haskin. Perf. Paul Mantee, Victor Lundin, and Adam West. Paramount, 1964. DVD.

Rose, Jacqueline. *On Not Being Able to Sleep: Psychoanalysis in the Modern World*. Princeton: Princeton UP, 2003. Print.

Ross, Robert. *A Concise History of South Africa*. 2nd ed. Cambridge: Cambridge UP, 2008. Print.

Rousseau, Jean-Jacques. *Emile; or, On Education*. Trans. Allan Bloom. London: Penguin, 1991. Print.

Sachs, Albie. "Preparing Ourselves for Freedom." *Spring Is Rebellious*. Ed. Ingrid de Kok and Karen Press. Cape Town: Buchu, 1990. 19–29. Print.

Said, Edward. *Culture and Imperialism*. London: Vintage, 1994. Print.

———. "Opponents, Audiences, Constituencies, and Community." *"Reflections on Exile" and Other Literary and Cultural Essays*. London: Granta, 2000. 118–47. Print.

———. *Orientalism*. 1978. Harmondsworth: Peregrine-Penguin, 1985. Print.

———. *The Pen and the Sword: Conversations with David Barsamian*. Monroe: Common Courage, 1994. Print.

———. *Representations of the Intellectual: The 1993 Reith Lectures*. New York: Vintage, 1996. Print.

———. *The World, the Text, and the Critic*. Cambridge: Harvard UP, 1983. Print.

Samuelson, Meg. *Remembering the Nation, Dismembering Women? Stories of the South African Transition*. Pietermaritzburg: U of KwaZulu-Natal P, 2007. Print.

Sanders, Mark. *Ambiguities of Witnessing: Law and Literature in the Time of a Truth Commission*. Stanford: Stanford UP, 2007. Print.

———. *Complicities: The Intellectual and Apartheid*. Durham: Duke UP, 2002. Print.

Santner, Eric L. *On Creaturely Life: Rilke, Benjamin, Sebald*. Chicago: U of Chicago P, 2006. Print.

Sartre, Jean-Paul. *Being and Nothingness: A Phenomenological Essay on Ontology*. Trans. Hazel Barnes. New York: Washington Square, 1992. Print.

———. "Existentialism Is a Humanism." 1946. *Jean-Paul Sartre Archive, 1905–1980*. Marxists Internet Archive, Feb. 2005. Web. 27 June 2013.

———. *What Is Literature?* Trans. Bernard Frechtman. London: Methuen, 1987. Print. Trans. of *Qu'est-ce que la littérature?*

Scarry, Elaine. *The Body in Pain: The Making and Unmaking of the World*. Oxford: Oxford UP, 1998. Print.

Schaffer, Kay. *Women and the Bush: Forces of Desire in the Australian Cultural Tradition*. Cambridge: U of Cambridge P, 1988. Print.

Schmitt, Carl. *Political Theology: Four Chapters on the Concept of the Sovereign*. Trans. George Schwab. Chicago: U of Chicago P, 2005. Print.

Schreiner, Olive. *The Story of an African Farm*. Jeppestown: Donker, 1975. Print.

Segall, Kimberly Wedeven. "Pursuing Ghosts: The Traumatic Sublime in J. M. Coetzee's *Disgrace*." *Research in African Literatures* 36.4 (2006): 40–54. Print.

Selvadurai, Shyam. *Funny Boy*. Orlando: Harcourt, 1994. Print.

Shakespeare, William. *Macbeth*. London: Methuen, 2001. Print.

———. *The Tempest*. New York: Norton, 2003. Print.

Shapcott, Jo. "Goat." *Her Book: Poems, 1988–1998*. London: Faber, 2000. 48. Print.

Sharpe, Jenny. *Allegories of Empire: The Figure of Woman in the Colonial Text*. Minneapolis: U of Minnesota P, 1993. Print.

Shklovsky, Viktor. *Theory of Prose*. Trans. Benjamin Sher. Elmwood Park: Dalkey Archive, 1990. Print.

Sibbett, Caryl, and William Thompson. "Nettlesome Knowledge, Liminality, and the Taboo in Cancer and Art Therapy Experiences: Implications for Learning and Teaching." *Threshold Concepts within the Disciplines*. Ed. Ray Land, Jan H. F. Meyer, and Jan Smith. Rotterdam: Sense, 2008. 227–42. Print. Educational Futures: Rethinking Theory and Practice 16.

Silvani, Roman. *Political Bodies and the Body Politic in J. M. Coetzee's Novels.* Berlin: LIT, 2011. Print.

Singer, Peter. *Animal Liberation.* 3rd ed. New York: Harper, 2002. Print.

Smith, Pauline. *The Beadle.* Claremont: Pomona, 2006. Print.

Smuts, Barbara. "Reflection." Coetzee, *Lives* 107–20.

Spark, Allister Haddon. *Tomorrow Is Another Country: The Inside Story of South Africa's Road to Change.* Chicago: U of Chicago P, 1996. Print.

Spencer, Robert. *Cosmopolitan Criticism and Postcolonial Literature.* London: Palgrave, 2011. Print.

———. "J. M. Coetzee and Colonial Violence." *Interventions* 10.2 (2008): 173–87. Print.

Spiegel, Marjorie. *The Dreaded Comparison: Human and Animal Slavery.* New York: Mirror, 1988. Print.

Spivak, Gayatri Chakravorty. "Can the Subaltern Speak?" *Marxism and the Interpretation of Culture.* Ed. Cary Nelson and Lawrence Grossberg. Urbana: U of Illinois P, 1988. 271–313. Print.

———. *A Critique of Postcolonial Reason: Toward a History of the Vanishing Present.* Cambridge: Harvard UP, 1999. Print.

———. "Ethics and Politics in Tagore, Coetzee, and Certain Scenes of Teaching." *Diacritics* 32.3–4 (2002): 17–31. Print.

———. "Theory in the Margin: Coetzee's *Foe* Reading Defoe's *Crusoe/Roxana.*" *Consequences of Theory.* Ed. Jonathan Arac and Barbara Johnson. Baltimore: John Hopkins UP, 1991. 154–80. Print.

———. "Three Women's Texts and a Critique of Imperialism." *Critical Inquiry* 12.1 (1985): 243–61. Print.

Splendore, Paola. "J. M. Coetzee's *Foe*: Intersexual and Metafictional Romances." *Commonwealth Essays and Studies* 11.1 (1988): 55–60. Print.

Stone, E. Kim. "Good Housekeeping: Single Women and Global Feminism in J. M. Coetzee's *In the Heart of the Country.*" *Ariel* 34.2–3 (2003): 215–35. Web. 31 Aug. 2011.

"Sympathy." *Concise Oxford Dictionary.* Oxford UP, n.d. Web. 4 Apr. 2012.

Szymborska, Wisława. "Seen from Above." *Miracle Fair: Selected Poems.* Trans. Joanna Trzeciak. New York: Norton, 2002. 66. Print.

Thompson, Leonard. *A History of South Africa.* 3rd ed. New Haven: Yale UP, 2001. Print.

Tremaine, Louis. "The Embodied Soul: Animal Being in J. M. Coetzee." *Contemporary Literature* 44.4 (2003): 587–612. Print.

Trengrove-Jones, Timothy. "No Redemption in a Bleak Tale of Colonialism Reversed." *Sunday Times* [Johannesburg] 22 Aug. 1999: 17. Print.

Truth and Reconciliation Commission. *Truth and Reconciliation Commission Final Report.* 7 vols. *Republic of South Africa.* Dept. of Justice and Constitutional Development, Republic of South Africa, 1 Sept. 2009. Web. 5 Dec. 2013.

Tutu, Desmond. *No Future without Forgiveness.* New York: Doubleday, 1999. Print.

Tyson, Lois. *Critical Theory Today: A User-Friendly Guide*. New York: Routledge, 2006. Print.

Ungar, Stephen. "The Professor of Desire." *Yale French Studies* 63 (1982): 81–91. Print.

The Usual Suspects. Dir. Bryan Singer. PolyGram Filmed Entertainment, 1994. DVD.

van den Heever, C. M. *Somer*. N.p.: CruGuru, 2011. Print.

van der Vlies, Andrew. "*In* (or *From*) *the Heart of the Country*: Local and Global Lives of Coetzee's Anti-pastoral." Van der Vlies, *Print, Text and Book Cultures* 166–94.

———. *J. M. Coetzee's* Disgrace: *A Reader's Guide*. London: Continuum, 2010. Print.

———, ed. *Print, Text and Book Cultures in South Africa*. Johannesburg: Wits UP, 2012. Print.

van Melle, Johannes. *Dawid Booysen*. Hatfield: Van Shaik, 1933. Print.

van Onselen, Charles. "Witches of Suburbia: Domestic Service on the Witwatersrand, 1890–1914." *New Nineveh*. Johannesburg: Ravan, 1982. 1–73. Print. Vol. 2 of *Studies in the Social and Economic History of the Witwatersrand, 1886–1914*.

van Wyk Smith, Malvern. "From 'Boereplaas' to Vlakplaas: The Farm from Thomas Pringle to J. M. Coetzee." *Strangely Familiar: South African Narratives in Town and Countryside*. Ed. C. N. van der Merwe. Cape Town: Content Solutions, 2001. 17–35. Print.

———. Introduction. *Shades of Adamastor: Africa and the Portuguese Connection: An Anthology of Poetry*. Ed. Van Wyk Smith. Grahamstown: Inst. for the Study of English in Africa; Natl. English Lit. Museum, 1988. 1–37. Print.

Vaughan, Michael. "Literature and Politics: Currents in South African Writing in the Seventies." *Journal of Southern African Studies* 9.1 (1982): 118–38. Print.

Vera, Yvonne. *The Stone Virgins*. Harare: Weaver, 2002. Print.

Vermeulen, Pieter. "Wordsworth and the Recollection of South Africa." Boehmer, Iddiols, and Eaglestone 47–59.

Viswanathan, Gauri. *Masks of Conquest: Literary Study and British Rule in India*. New York: Columbia UP, 1989. Print.

Vladislavić, Ivan. *Propaganda by Monuments*. Cape Town: Philip, 1996. Print.

———, ed. *T'kama-Adamastor: Inventions of Africa in a South African Painting*. Johannesburg: Witwatersrand UP, 2000. Print.

Vonnegut, Kurt. *Slaughterhouse-Five*. New York: Dell, 1995. Print.

Wade, Michael. *White on Black in South Africa: A Study of English-Language Inscriptions of Skin Color*. New York: St. Martin's, 1993. Print.

Waiting for the Barbarians: An Opera in Two Acts from the Novel of J. M. Coetzee. Comp. Philip Glass. Libretto by Christopher Hampton. Dir. Guy Montavon. Erfurt Theater, Erfurt, Germany. 10 Sept. 2005. Orange Mountain Music, 2008. CD.

Walker, Cherryl. *Landmarked: Land Claims and Land Restitution in South Africa*. Johannesburg: Jacana Media; Athens: Ohio UP, 2008. Print.

———. "The Limits to Land Reform: Rethinking the 'Land Question.'" *Journal of Southern African Studies* 31.4 (2005): 805–24. Print.

———. "Relocating Restitution." *Transformation* 44 (2000): 1–14. Print.

Warnes, Christopher. "'Everyone Is Guilty': Complicitous Critique and the Plaasroman Tradition in Etienne van Heerden's *Toorberg (Ancestral Voices)*." *Research in African Literatures* 42.1 (2011): 120–32. *EBSCO Host*. Web. 19 Oct. 2011.

Watson, Stephen. "Colonialism and the Novels of J. M. Coetzee." *Research in African Literatures* 17.3 (1986): 370–92. Print.

———. "Colonialism and the Novels of J. M. Coetzee." Huggan and Watson 13–36.

Watt, Ian. *The Rise of the Novel: Studies in Defoe, Richardson, and Fielding.* Berkeley: U of California P, 1957. Print.

Wenzel, Jennifer. "Keys to the Labyrinth: Writing, Torture, and Coetzee's Barbarian Girl." *Tulsa Studies in Women's Literature* 15.1 (1996): 61–71. Print.

———. "Meat Country (Please Do Not Feed the Baboons and Wild Animals)." *Safundi: Journal of South African and American Studies* 11.1–2 (2010): 123–32. Print.

———. "The Pastoral Promise and the Political Imperative: The Plaasroman Tradition in an Era of Land Reform." *Modern Fiction Studies* 46.1 (2000): 90–113. Print.

White, Patrick. *Voss.* London: Vintage, 1994. Print.

White, Richard. *Inventing Australia: Images and Identity, 1688–1980.* Sydney: Allen, 1981. Print.

Wicomb, Zoë. *You Can't Get Lost in Cape Town.* 1987. New York: Feminist, 2000. Print.

Williams, Patrick, and Laura Chrisman, eds. *Colonial Discourse and Post-colonial Theory: A Reader.* New York: Columbia UP, 1994. Print.

Wilson, Monica. "The Nguni People." *South Africa to 1870.* Ed. Wilson and Leonard Thompson. Oxford: Oxford UP, 1969. 75–130. Print. Vol. 1 of *The Oxford History of South Africa.*

Wilson, Richard. *The Politics of Truth and Reconciliation.* Cambridge: Cambridge UP, 2001. Print. Cambridge Studies of Law and Society.

Winberg, Marlene, and Paul Weinberg. *Back to the Land.* Johannesburg: Porcupine, 1996. Print.

Winterson, Jeannette. *Oranges Are Not the Only Fruit.* London: Vintage, 1991. Print.

Winton, Tim. *Breath.* London: Picador, 2008. Print.

———. *Dirt Music.* London: Picador, 2004. Print.

Wittenberg, Hermann. "The Taint of the Censor: J. M. Coetzee and the Making of *In the Heart of the Country*." *English in Africa* 35.2 (2008): 133–50. *EBSCO Host.* Web. 31 Aug. 2011.

Wittgenstein, Ludwig. *Philosophical Investigations.* 3rd ed. Trans. G. E. M. Anscombe. Oxford: Blackwell, 2001. Print.

Wohlpart, James. "A (Sub)Version of the Language of Power : Narrative and Narrative Technique in J. M. Coetzee's *In the Heart of the Country*." *Critique* 35.4 (1994): 219–28. *EBSCO Host.* Web. 18 Aug. 2011.

Wood, Marcus. *Blind Memory: Visual Representations of Slavery in England and America, 1780–1865.* Manchester: Manchester UP, 2000. Print.

Woolf, Virginia. *A Room of One's Own.* New York: Harvest, 1989. Print.

Worden, Nigel. *The Making of Modern South Africa: Conquest, Segregation, and Apartheid.* 3rd ed. Oxford: Blackwell, 2000. Print.

Wordsworth, William. *The Prelude, 1799, 1805, 1850: Authoritative Texts, Contexts, and Reception, Recent Critical Essays*. Ed. Jonathan Wordsworth, M. H. Abrams, and Stephen Gill. New York: Norton, 1979. Print. Norton Critical ed.

———. *Wordsworth's Poetry and Prose*. Ed. William Halmi. New York: Norton, 2007. Print. Norton Critical ed.

"'The Worlds of J. M. Coetzee' on View in the Lobby of the Perry-Castenada Library." *Libraries*. U of Texas, 29 Oct. 2003. Web. 6 Jan. 2010.

Wright, Derek. "Black Earth, White Myth: Coetzee's *Michael K.*" *Modern Fiction Studies* 38.2 (1992): 435–44. Print.

Wright, Laura. "A Feminist-Vegetarian Defense of Elizabeth Costello: A Rant from an Ethical Academic on J. M. Coetzee's *The Lives of Animals*." Poyner, *J. M. Coetzee and the Idea* 193–216.

———. "Minor Literature and 'The Skeleton of Sense': Anorexia, Franz Kafka's 'A Hunger Artist,' and J. M. Coetzee's *Life & Times of Michael K.*" *Journal of Commonwealth and Postcolonial Studies* 8.1–2 (2001): 109–23. Print.

———. *Writing "Out of All the Camps": J. M. Coetzee's Narratives of Displacement*. New York: Routledge, 2006. Print.

Yeoh, Gilbert. "J. M. Coetzee and Samuel Beckett: Ethics, Truth-Telling, and Self-Deception." *Critique: Studies in Contemporary Fiction* 44.4 (2003): 331–48. Print.

———. "J. M. Coetzee and Samuel Beckett: Nothingness, Minimalism, and Indeterminacy." *Ariel* 31.4 (2000): 117–37. Print.

Yoshida, Kyoko. "Eating Dis(Order): From Metaphoric Cannibalism to Cannibalistic Metaphors." Boehmer, Iddiols, and Eaglestone 134–46.

Young, Iris Marion. *Responsibility for Justice*. Oxford: Oxford UP, 2011. Print.

Zembylas, Michalinos. *Five Pedagogies, A Thousand Possibilities: Struggling for Hope and Transformation in Education*. Rotterdam: Sense, 2007. Print. Educ. Futures: Rethinking Theory and Practice 6.

Z. N. "Much Ado about Nobody." Rev. of *Life & Times of Michael K. African Communist* 97 (1984): 101–03. Print.

INDEX

Modern Language Association of America

Approaches to Teaching World Literature

Achebe's Things Fall Apart. Ed. Bernth Lindfors. 1991.

Arthurian Tradition. Ed. Maureen Fries and Jeanie Watson. 1992.

Atwood's The Handmaid's Tale *and Other Works.* Ed. Sharon R. Wilson, Thomas B. Friedman, and Shannon Hengen. 1996.

Austen's Emma. Ed. Marcia McClintock Folsom. 2004.

Austen's Pride and Prejudice. Ed. Marcia McClintock Folsom. 1993.

Balzac's Old Goriot. Ed. Michal Peled Ginsburg. 2000.

Baudelaire's Flowers of Evil. Ed. Laurence M. Porter. 2000.

Beckett's Waiting for Godot. Ed. June Schlueter and Enoch Brater. 1991.

Behn's Oroonoko. Ed. Cynthia Richards and Mary Ann O'Donnell. 2014.

Beowulf. Ed. Jess B. Bessinger, Jr., and Robert F. Yeager. 1984.

Blake's Songs of Innocence and of Experience. Ed. Robert F. Gleckner and Mark L. Greenberg. 1989.

Boccaccio's Decameron. Ed. James H. McGregor. 2000.

British Women Poets of the Romantic Period. Ed. Stephen C. Behrendt and Harriet Kramer Linkin. 1997.

Charlotte Brontë's Jane Eyre. Ed. Diane Long Hoeveler and Beth Lau. 1993.

Emily Brontë's Wuthering Heights. Ed. Sue Lonoff and Terri A. Hasseler. 2006.

Byron's Poetry. Ed. Frederick W. Shilstone. 1991.

Works of Italo Calvino. Ed. Franco Ricci. 2013.

Camus's The Plague. Ed. Steven G. Kellman. 1985.

Writings of Bartolomé de Las Casas. Ed. Santa Arias and Eyda M. Merediz. 2008.

Cather's My Ántonia. Ed. Susan J. Rosowski. 1989.

Cervantes' Don Quixote. Ed. Richard Bjornson. 1984.

Chaucer's Canterbury Tales. First edition Ed. Joseph Gibaldi. 1980.

Chaucer's Canterbury Tales. Second edition. Ed. Peter W. Travis and Frank Grady. 2014.

Chaucer's Troilus and Criseyde *and the Shorter Poems.* Ed. Tison Pugh and Angela Jane Weisl. 2006.

Chopin's The Awakening. Ed. Bernard Koloski. 1988.

Coetzee's Disgrace *and Other Works.* Ed. Laura Wright, Jane Poyner, and Elleke Boehmer. 2014.

Coleridge's Poetry and Prose. Ed. Richard E. Matlak. 1991.

Collodi's Pinocchio *and Its Adaptations.* Ed. Michael Sherberg. 2006.

Conrad's "Heart of Darkness" and "The Secret Sharer." Ed. Hunt Hawkins and Brian W. Shaffer. 2002.

Dante's Divine Comedy. Ed. Carole Slade. 1982.

Defoe's Robinson Crusoe. Ed. Maximillian E. Novak and Carl Fisher. 2005.

DeLillo's White Noise. Ed. Tim Engles and John N. Duvall. 2006.

Dickens's Bleak House. Ed. John O. Jordan and Gordon Bigelow. 2009.

Dickens's David Copperfield. Ed. Richard J. Dunn. 1984.

Dickinson's Poetry. Ed. Robin Riley Fast and Christine Mack Gordon. 1989.

Narrative of the Life of Frederick Douglass. Ed. James C. Hall. 1999.

Works of John Dryden. Ed. Jayne Lewis and Lisa Zunshine. 2013.

Duras's Ourika. Ed. Mary Ellen Birkett and Christopher Rivers. 2009.

Early Modern Spanish Drama. Ed. Laura R. Bass and Margaret R. Greer. 2006.

Eliot's Middlemarch. Ed. Kathleen Blake. 1990.

Eliot's Poetry and Plays. Ed. Jewel Spears Brooker. 1988.

Shorter Elizabethan Poetry. Ed. Patrick Cheney and Anne Lake Prescott. 2000.

Ellison's Invisible Man. Ed. Susan Resneck Parr and Pancho Savery. 1989.

English Renaissance Drama. Ed. Karen Bamford and Alexander Leggatt. 2002.

Works of Louise Erdrich. Ed. Gregg Sarris, Connie A. Jacobs, and
     James R. Giles. 2004.

Dramas of Euripides. Ed. Robin Mitchell-Boyask. 2002.

Faulkner's As I Lay Dying. Ed. Patrick O'Donnell and Lynda Zwinger. 2011.

Faulkner's The Sound and the Fury. Ed. Stephen Hahn and Arthur F. Kinney. 1996.

Fitzgerald's The Great Gatsby. Ed. Jackson R. Bryer and Nancy P. VanArsdale. 2009.

Flaubert's Madame Bovary. Ed. Laurence M. Porter and Eugene F. Gray. 1995.

García Márquez's One Hundred Years of Solitude. Ed. María Elena de Valdés and
     Mario J. Valdés. 1990.

Gilman's "The Yellow Wall-Paper" and Herland. Ed. Denise D. Knight and
     Cynthia J. Davis. 2003.

Goethe's Faust. Ed. Douglas J. McMillan. 1987.

Gothic Fiction: The British and American Traditions. Ed. Diane Long Hoeveler
     and Tamar Heller. 2003.

Poetry of John Gower. Ed. R. F. Yeager and Brian W. Gastle. 2011.

Grass's The Tin Drum. Ed. Monika Shafi. 2008.

H.D.'s Poetry and Prose. Ed. Annette Debo and Lara Vetter. 2011.

Hebrew Bible as Literature in Translation. Ed. Barry N. Olshen and
     Yael S. Feldman. 1989.

Homer's Iliad *and* Odyssey. Ed. Kostas Myrsiades. 1987.

Hurston's Their Eyes Were Watching God *and Other Works*. Ed. John Lowe. 2009.

Ibsen's A Doll House. Ed. Yvonne Shafer. 1985.

Henry James's Daisy Miller *and* The Turn of the Screw. Ed. Kimberly C. Reed and
     Peter G. Beidler. 2005.

Works of Samuel Johnson. Ed. David R. Anderson and Gwin J. Kolb. 1993.

Joyce's Ulysses. Ed. Kathleen McCormick and Erwin R. Steinberg. 1993.

Works of Sor Juana Inés de la Cruz. Ed. Emilie L. Bergmann and Stacey Schlau. 2007.

Kafka's Short Fiction. Ed. Richard T. Gray. 1995.

Keats's Poetry. Ed. Walter H. Evert and Jack W. Rhodes. 1991.

Kingston's The Woman Warrior. Ed. Shirley Geok-lin Lim. 1991.

Lafayette's The Princess of Clèves. Ed. Faith E. Beasley and
    Katharine Ann Jensen. 1998.

Works of D. H. Lawrence. Ed. M. Elizabeth Sargent and Garry Watson. 2001.

Lazarillo de Tormes *and the Picaresque Tradition.* Ed. Anne J. Cruz. 2009.

Lessing's The Golden Notebook. Ed. Carey Kaplan and Ellen Cronan Rose. 1989.

Works of Naguib Mahfouz. Ed. Waïl S. Hassan and Susan Muaddi Darraj. 2011.

Mann's Death in Venice *and Other Short Fiction.* Ed. Jeffrey B. Berlin. 1992.

Marguerite de Navarre's Heptameron. Ed. Colette H. Winn. 2007.

Works of Carmen Martín Gaite. Ed. Joan L. Brown. 2013.

Medieval English Drama. Ed. Richard K. Emmerson. 1990.

Melville's Moby-Dick. Ed. Martin Bickman. 1985.

Metaphysical Poets. Ed. Sidney Gottlieb. 1990.

Miller's Death of a Salesman. Ed. Matthew C. Roudané. 1995.

Milton's Paradise Lost. First edition. Ed. Galbraith M. Crump. 1986.

Milton's Paradise Lost. Second edition. Ed. Peter C. Herman. 2012.

Milton's Shorter Poetry and Prose. Ed. Peter C. Herman. 2007.

Molière's Tartuffe *and Other Plays.* Ed. James F. Gaines and
    Michael S. Koppisch. 1995.

Momaday's The Way to Rainy Mountain. Ed. Kenneth M. Roemer. 1988.

Montaigne's Essays. Ed. Patrick Henry. 1994.

Novels of Toni Morrison. Ed. Nellie Y. McKay and Kathryn Earle. 1997.

Murasaki Shikibu's The Tale of Genji. Ed. Edward Kamens. 1993.

Nabokov's Lolita. Ed. Zoran Kuzmanovich and Galya Diment. 2008.

Works of Ngũgĩ wa Thiong'o. Ed. Oliver Lovesey. 2012.

Works of Tim O'Brien. Ed. Alex Vernon and Catherine Calloway. 2010.

Works of Ovid and the Ovidian Tradition. Ed. Barbara Weiden Boyd and
    Cora Fox. 2010.

Poe's Prose and Poetry. Ed. Jeffrey Andrew Weinstock and Tony Magistrale. 2008.

Pope's Poetry. Ed. Wallace Jackson and R. Paul Yoder. 1993.

Proust's Fiction and Criticism. Ed. Elyane Dezon-Jones and
    Inge Crosman Wimmers. 2003.

Puig's Kiss of the Spider Woman. Ed. Daniel Balderston and Francine Masiello. 2007.

Pynchon's The Crying of Lot 49 *and Other Works.* Ed. Thomas H. Schaub. 2008.

Works of François Rabelais. Ed. Todd W. Reeser and Floyd Gray. 2011.

Novels of Samuel Richardson. Ed. Lisa Zunshine and Jocelyn Harris. 2006.

Rousseau's Confessions *and* Reveries of the Solitary Walker. Ed. John C. O'Neal
    and Ourida Mostefai. 2003.

Scott's Waverley Novels. Ed. Evan Gottlieb and Ian Duncan. 2009.

Shakespeare's Hamlet. Ed. Bernice W. Kliman. 2001.

Shakespeare's King Lear. Ed. Robert H. Ray. 1986.

Shakespeare's Othello. Ed. Peter Erickson and Maurice Hunt. 2005.

Shakespeare's Romeo and Juliet. Ed. Maurice Hunt. 2000.

Shakespeare's The Taming of the Shrew. Ed. Margaret Dupuis and Grace Tiffany. 2013.

Shakespeare's The Tempest *and Other Late Romances*. Ed. Maurice Hunt. 1992.

Shelley's Frankenstein. Ed. Stephen C. Behrendt. 1990.

Shelley's Poetry. Ed. Spencer Hall. 1990.

Sir Gawain and the Green Knight. Ed. Miriam Youngerman Miller and Jane Chance. 1986.

Song of Roland. Ed. William W. Kibler and Leslie Zarker Morgan. 2006.

Spenser's Faerie Queene. Ed. David Lee Miller and Alexander Dunlop. 1994.

Stendhal's The Red and the Black. Ed. Dean de la Motte and Stirling Haig. 1999.

Sterne's Tristram Shandy. Ed. Melvyn New. 1989.

Works of Robert Louis Stevenson. Ed. Caroline McCracken-Flesher. 2013.

The Story of the Stone (Dream of the Red Chamber). Ed. Andrew Schonebaum and Tina Lu. 2012.

Stowe's Uncle Tom's Cabin. Ed. Elizabeth Ammons and Susan Belasco. 2000.

Swift's Gulliver's Travels. Ed. Edward J. Rielly. 1988.

Teresa of Ávila and the Spanish Mystics. Ed. Alison Weber. 2009.

Thoreau's Walden *and Other Works*. Ed. Richard J. Schneider. 1996.

Tolstoy's Anna Karenina. Ed. Liza Knapp and Amy Mandelker. 2003.

Vergil's Aeneid. Ed. William S. Anderson and Lorina N. Quartarone. 2002.

Voltaire's Candide. Ed. Renée Waldinger. 1987.

Whitman's Leaves of Grass. Ed. Donald D. Kummings. 1990.

Wiesel's Night. Ed. Alan Rosen. 2007.

Works of Oscar Wilde. Ed. Philip E. Smith II. 2008.

Woolf's Mrs. Dalloway. Ed. Eileen Barrett and Ruth O. Saxton. 2009.

Woolf's To the Lighthouse. Ed. Beth Rigel Daugherty and Mary Beth Pringle. 2001.

Wordsworth's Poetry. Ed. Spencer Hall, with Jonathan Ramsey. 1986.

Wright's Native Son. Ed. James A. Miller. 1997.